TORONTO
REMEMBERED

TORONTO
REMEMBERED
A CELEBRATION OF THE CITY

William Kilbourn

Stoddart

TORONTO

To the memory of Eric Arthur

First published in 1984 by
Stoddart Publishing
a division of General Publishing Co. Limited
30 Lesmill Road
Don Mills, Ontario M3B 2T6

Produced for Stoddart by
Newcastle Publishing Limited, Toronto

Canadian Cataloguing in Publication Data

Kilbourn, William, 1926–
    Toronto Remembered

Includes index.
ISBN 0-7737-2029-4

1. Toronto (Ont.) – Addresses, essays, lectures.
I. Title.

FC3097.35.K54 1984   971.3′541   C84-099021-9
F1059.5.T6845K5 1984

Printed and bound in Canada

 *This book was published with the assistance of a grant from the Toronto
Sesquicentennial Board in honour of the 150th anniversary of the City of Toronto.*

CONTENTS

INTRODUCTION

This book is very parochial. It's about one city, the older parts mainly, and one person's city, the Toronto I have known for half a century and through my friends and forebears for somewhat longer. Except for five years away in Oxford, England, and Cambridge, Massachusetts, to learn my craft, and nine in a small Ontario town and nearby city where I more or less practised it, I have always lived in Toronto.

Most of the important things that ever happened to me happened within a few hundred yards of Yonge Street. I was born in the Wellesley Hospital when it was a couple of converted mansions, grew up in Moore Park when there were still farms on its northeast border, went to Dr. Blatz's School in a big old house on the edge of the Mount Pleasant Cemetery ravine, and three other schools not too far from there.

I met my wife at the University of Toronto, where we were doing Canadian history with Frank Underhill, Harold Innis and Donald Creighton; wrote my first book about William Lyon Mackenzie and his friends marching down Yonge Street to capture Montgomery's Tavern; helped start York University when it was all still contained on its little campus in the Don Valley; and became part of Holy Trinity Church downtown—to be healed, and to work eventually on a dozen urban projects. One of these turned out to be a seven-year term full-time at city hall. My aldermanic ward ran from Bloor Street up Yonge to the city limits. On the south it had been part of the old Ward 2, for which my great uncle, Professor Morley Wickett, and my great-grandfather Wickett the tanner, were aldermen; Mayors Lamport, Dennison, Sewell and William Lyon Mackenzie also represented that area as aldermen.

As I write this I am perched high above the corner of Yonge and Bloor, with the Yorkville firehall and the Metropolitan Reference Library out one window, and the trees and roofs of Rosedale (including the one our five children grew up under) out the other, and in front, the shining glass and steel of Insurance Alley, the dispiriting concrete grids of the Bay and Plaza II towers, with several prospects, through the gaps, of the downtown towers and the lake and the Niagara Escarpment beyond.

Every summer in my childhood we took off from the ferry docks near the foot of Bay Street for Centre Island. In our cottage at 9 St. Andrew's Avenue I lived with two parents, two uncles, two aunts, four cousins, two grandparents and one great-grandfather, our tribal chieftain. When the next batch of young cousins bid fair to burst the place at its seams, half the tribe pulled our stuff in big hand carts up the sidewalk street to 1 St. Andrew's.

My father and my Uncle Roy went to work by bicycle to the Centre Island ferry dock, or else in an outboard motorboat down the lagoon and across the bay, to the little tannery they ran at the mouth of the Don River. My cousins and I worked there occasionally on Saturday mornings and school holidays, unloading tanbark, hauling hides in the beam house or feeding the leather-measuring machine upstairs. The old tannery was eventually absorbed by a big modern Winnipeg firm, mainly I think to acquire my cousin Peter's managerial talents as its new chief. But throughout its first century it only had two presidents, my great-grandfather and my father. The smell of leather on clothing is pungent and it is one of my earliest and strongest household memories.

But this book is not just for indulging in memories of my childhood Toronto. I want to evoke the postwar city of many peoples and cultures, the explosion of wealth and population in the metropolis of the '50s and '60s, the withdrawal of the '70s and '80s into conservation and reform. I want too to tell about the city my ancestors knew, western Ontario farmers all of them, the earliest crossing the Niagara River from New York state in 1794, the year Governor Simcoe was busy establishing his new capital at York. Timothy and Benjamin and Joseph Kilbourn, like most of the Americans who came to the Toronto region and beyond, were not United Empire Loyalists, they were just moving west in search of land, scarcely aware that they had left one country for another.

I also celebrate the town of our two spiritual founders, John Strachan and William Lyon Mackenzie; and the paradisal little forest settlement described by Elizabeth Simcoe, our Eve new-naming things in the Garden. Beyond that again, these images of a city range back, through the quarter millenium of French and British settlement on this spot, to the brief visitations in the 1600s of British and Dutch fur traders from New York and of *coureurs de bois* and missionary-explorers from Quebec, to the Indians whose occasional encampments on the banks of the Humber are but dimly known even to the most learned students of our prehistory.

Toronto used to be the sort of place you could define easily enough. It was an Indian village once; then a trading post; a fort on the edge of Empire; a sleepy colonial town; a bustling Victorian city; and, only yesterday, a modern metropolis that aspired to be another London or New York and managed, just, to rank with Belfast and Buffalo.

It did not please visitors. "The vilest blue-devil haunt on the face of the earth," was what one English novelist called it. "A sanctimonious icebox," wrote another a century later. In between, the habit of hating Toronto has helped, in its own small way, to bind a far-flung, unlikely lot of Maritimers and Westerners and French Canadians into one Confederation. Even though you loved Toronto and knew such detractors missed its subtler virtues, you also knew just what they meant and why they felt that way. You knew, that is, if you had ever lived any place else.

Then, quite suddenly, things changed. In the 1960s and '70s Toronto was something unique and glorious under the sun. It became a place to praise, extravagantly, but much harder to define.

"In the world's endless nightmare of malfunctioning cities," wrote a visiting journalist, Toronto was "a model of the alternative future—a city that works." Political scientists visited Toronto to study patterns of metropolitan government or of popular pressure groups. The United States Committee on Economic Development urged American cities to be guided by "the Toronto experience." Urbanists made pilgrimage to consult one of their peers, Jane Jacobs, who had herself become a Torontonian, or to hear Toronto's own global villager, Marshall McLuhan, tell them that cities should avoid wearing cement kimonos. And Toronto connoisseurs wistfully hoped that the city might remain (or just become) half as good a place as the visiting writers and television producers said it was.

But how shall we define Toronto now?

A forest of neighbourhoods—situated between the world's widest expressway and the world's tallest tower—all dedicated to keeping cars out and buildings low.

A vista of suburbs—split-levels and apartment towers stretching to the horizon—crisscrossed by lovely ravines and garish festivals of free enterprise.

A collection of communities—Chinese, Italian, Ukrainian, Greek, Polish, Pakistani and more—bountifully provided with the benefits of French schools and television and vaguely presided over by the same WASP family compact that has dominated business and society in Toronto ever since Governor Simcoe laid down Yonge Street.

A settlement of refugees—from poverty and unemployment and dead ends back home, from American draft boards or Soviet tanks or the pogroms and prejudices of an older Europe; an encampment of island peoples from Trinidad, Taiwan and Malta, from the Azores and the Philippines and Newfoundland.

Lakeport and oceanport, Hogtown the Good, city of sin and churches; head office to a nation; mining exchange to the world; cultural capital of English Canada; seat of government for an Empire province stretching from the icebergs of James Bay to the cherry orchards of Niagara, from the edge of the western prairie to the exurbs of Montreal.

But the litany must stop. Such tags and labels do not tell us much about the life and character of Toronto as it really is. In the end some of them are not even accurate. Perhaps a couple of paradoxes come closer to the truth: that the core of the city has changed drastically without driving residents or the street life out of it; and that in the midst of galloping progress Toronto has not yet been cut off from its historic roots—both tory and radical, conservative and rebel.

No single doctrine or plan has ever quite succeeded in totally taking over the city. The tension between competing ideologies and interests is as much a creative as a destructive one. Problems of class and race, poverty and urban ecology, are many and serious, but ones that can still be faced without despair.

If any one person is patron saint and saviour of mid-twentieth-century Toronto, it is Professor Eric Arthur from New Zealand, who rescued old buildings and spaces, helped make new ones like city hall and Nathan Phillips Square, and among his many Toronto books wrote the classic *No Mean City*. "We are citizens of no mean city," this Eric of Dunedin and Toronto told us, recalling the boast of Paul of Tarsus and Rome.

I will not much try for generalities and definitions in what follows. This is mainly a book of particulars. All art, including that of the collector and arranger of memories, seeks to give to "aery nothing a local habitation and a name." To generalize, as Blake put it, is to be an idiot. Certainly for the storyteller it is, both the child who listens and the child who speaks.

A word about selection. In assembling some of my writings on Toronto and preparing new ones, I soon decided that the way I could best celebrate the life and times of the city would be to get help from many hands. Like the barn-raisings of my ancestors, it would be a communal project—my plans and my barn, and my work mostly, but taking help where I needed it, especially from those whose skills and experiences were ones I could never acquire or only absorb after years of practice. So I am assisted in this quilting bee by gratefully received contributions from nine poets, several essayists and visual artists, and though they have not all been here to give consent, dozens of Toronto residents and visitors from Elizabeth Simcoe and Henry Scadding to Thoreau and Trollope, Enrico Caruso and Emma Goldman, Andrei Voznezhensky and Viljo Revell.

I am especially grateful to Josef Škvorecký, Pier Giorgio di Cicco, Walter Bauer, George Faludy, George Jonas, Waclaw Iwaniuk and Robert Zend, writers nourished in another tongue than English, who have responded so generously to my appeal for a bit of work that reflects their experience of being a citizen of Toronto.

1

A SENSE OF THE PLACE

Structures, Streets and Urban Landscapes

ON THE
WATERFRONT

My earliest memories of Toronto are of the Island summers, lying awake in the late evening light listening to the sound of the lake waves roaring and the bell buoy crying, lonely and human; and dark, quiet mornings waking to the terrible *harrumph-umph* of the fog horn, a crouched monster.

Later, when I was old enough to roam free among the lagoons and the rushes, there was the sudden amazement of the Toronto skyline appearing through the willows over the water; the sidewheeler *Trillium* (or one of her three flower-named sisters) churning the bay with huge paddles, a thousand people cramming her decks; the big lake boats with red, white and black funnels at the back, their bows high, and hundreds of feet of deck between; and the little ocean tramp steamers, sturdy, with superstructures at the centre and flags from all over the world.

Toronto was born of the water. Governor Simcoe planted his naval base and capital here because the enclosed bay and harbour offered shelter from the violence of both the lake and the American navy. The peninsula, as the Island was called until cut off from the shore by a violent storm, pleased Mrs. Simcoe too, for her own reasons. "It breaks the horizon of the lake," she wrote, "which greatly improves the view." She loved riding there, galloping over the sands or quietly examining the ponds and meadows, the ground creepers and the wild flowers, and "the water of the bay so beautifully clear

*The town of York from Gibraltar
Point. Drawn by J. Gray, aquatinted
by J. Gleadah, London, 1828.
The point (later renamed Hanlan's
after the great oarsman) was fortified by
Simcoe because it is near the Western
gap into the Bay and from there an
invading fleet could be fired upon.*

and transparent."

Toronto has treated its watery heritage recklessly over the years and many times appeared to turn its back on the shores of the bay. Railway tracks and expressways, land fill and buildings, storage elevators and parking lots have blocked the view here, the best access there. But Torontonians have made nearly 100 million ferryboat trips across the bay to the Island since Simcoe's time. The mainland waterfront has stretched to 20 miles of boardwalk and parkland and beaches, hotels and clubs and houses, docks and sheds and marinas, floating restaurants and maritime museums. The port has thrived and kept Toronto growing.

The shoreline has been moving continually, the sands shifting both above and below the waters—at first impelled by geological forces alone and then with human assistance. Following the last northward retreat of the great ice pack, the currents of Lake Ontario, pushed by the powerful thrust of the Niagara River, began cutting away at the high white promontory of the Scarborough bluffs and piling the eroded land into a long sandbar to the west. About the time the first civilizations appeared in the valleys of the Tigris and the Nile, the sketchy outline of what was to be the Island and Toronto Bay had formed.

When the great storms of the 1850s cut through the narrowest part of the sandbar near the mouth of the Don River, they created an island of over 300 acres. Since then its area has been more than doubled, and Torontonians have used it in a multitude of ways. It is not only the city's most extensive park, but also a haven for yacht clubs and house-boats, for beer gardens and tea houses. It is a place for tennis and cycling, fishing and kite-flying, an amusement park with flume rides and merry-go-rounds and aerial cable cars. In winter you can skate for miles on the lagoons and in summer go swimming and canoeing. The filtration plant funnels the city's water supply in from the lake and the busy Island airport brings light planes to the heart of downtown. There is a residential science school where every city child can experience a week away from home to look first-hand at the biology of a pond or a bird sanctuary. For those who have never seen a cow or a barnyard except on television, there is a farm complete with all the domestic animals.

If you want to have a party for 50,000 or 100,000 people, as Toronto's International Picnic does every year, the Island is the place. If you want solitude and tranquillity there are still paths and copses and sand dunes, and even bits of dense wilderness where most times of day or year you will never meet another soul.

Much of the Island's rich past has vanished without a trace. Toronto's first race track ran along the Lake Ontario shore; our earliest baseball stadium was on Hanlan's Point, and for years after the ball club had moved across the harbour to the mainland shore, the old stadium stood like an abandoned Roman coliseum, wonderful to explore, and only restored to roaring life for a day in August by the gladiators of the Police Games' tug-of-war and the circus of the Miss Toronto beauty contest.

There was a time when the Island produced Toronto's most celebrated local heroes—generations of world-champion oarsmen from Ned Hanlan to Jack Guest, Junior, of Ward's Island—and the Toronto rowing clubs from Parkdale to the Beaches teemed with scullers and their admirers.

Until about 1915, the bay always froze solid in winter and was crowded with horse-drawn sleighs, citizens with skates buckled to their boots ("donning the magic irons," as the Victorians put it) and a variety of iceboats from the 15-passenger giants to the pint-size shirtsail sledges used by Island children crossing the bay to school. The police boats with their huge sails reached dizzying speeds of 70 miles per hour, as fast as the crack trains. By 1920, however, the bay was dotted with fir trees marking thin ice; one of the great winter sports and sights of Toronto had all but vanished.

Gone too, from the Island, are the summer hotels and the lively ragtime world of Manitou Avenue, the convalescent homes and children's hospitals, and the summer residences of the rich with their tea and parasols and croquet lawns, the land now transformed into acres of flower-bed geometry and trim greensward.

But there are still bits of history to be discovered: lovely old bridges, beer-stein street lamps, a frame church that still holds summer services, a few ruins and foundations that have escaped the prophylactic hand of the parks department. Row upon row of huge willow trees on Centre Island mark the sidewalk streets where a thousand pleasant cottages once sheltered. The nineteenth-century life-saving paraphernalia, on their tall wooden crosses, still stand sentinel by the beaches and lagoons like prehistoric birds or marine sculptures. They are more efficient and modern than the antique warning signs beside them suggest, since they are regularly repaired in the Villiers Street blacksmith shop of the Harbour Commissioners, who also find it more efficient to make their own replacement bollards and other old but useful harbour equipment than have them custom-made by a modern foundry.

Eighteenth-century tourists used to watch Governor Simcoe's garrison in the blockhouse at the west end of Gibraltar Point do parade drill, practise musketry and milk their goats. Nearby is the oldest still-standing structure in Toronto, the stone lighthouse of 1808. It was faithfully kept for a century, but is now empty except for its ghosts—a keeper or a soldier or both, depending on which version of the haunting you believe, or have experienced.

Island old-timers will tell you the tale of the last famous shipwreck, that of the freight schooner, *Reuben Dowd*, which went aground in a terrible storm near the eastern gap. The Island rescue crew manned their lifeboat and saved all hands before the ship broke up. Lumps of coal could be found on the beaches for years afterward, but the most lasting effect was the invasion by the schooner's rats, which escaped to infest the Island. Fortunately they are long since gone and the Island's most noticeable and dominant wildlife are the great squadrons of mallard ducks and noble Canada geese, which march ceremoniously and swim proudly about the place as if they were its sole owners.

Some of the human population has been on the Island a lifetime. At least one family, the Wards, who settled back in 1830, have been there for a century and a half, in spite of the drowning of five daughters in a single boating accident, and the perennial threat that the Metropolitan government would obliterate their homestead and complete the removal of all residents from the Island.

This points to the most important of all the historical facts about the Island: the existence of its year-round residential community. In a city committed to the preservation of old-fashioned neighbourhoods, this has been the ultimate example. It is a community that lives without motor traffic and shopping plazas, without liquor outlets and cigar stores, without crime and locked doors. Most of its 700 members must commute to stores and their work on the mainland by boat, and they live in the communal interdependency of a pioneer village. There is much borrowing from neighbours, and a standing invitation to all visitors from the mainland to join their homemade festivals and entertainments in the community halls or on the village green.

The Islanders are of all ages, all vocations and income levels, but their style is reminiscent of an earlier time and place. A few are of a more recent bygone era: former flower children who are into organic vegetables and who carry children of their own in backpacks, with names like Willow and Cricket, Bree and Sky. The older children are a hardy breed; they always have the smallest, youngest and most short-handed hockey team in the city's public-school tournament, but this does not stop them from beating all comers and winning the championship. For the mainland children, at the residential science school next door, sharing in the way of life of the Island kids is perhaps the ultimate benefit of being there.

The Island community and its alternate lifestyle are also the ultimate threat to the Metropolitan officials and councilors who run the Island park, and who have been committed, with the encouragement of all three Toronto daily newspapers, to the community's elimination for more than a quarter-century. For years now the most passionate political debates at city hall have revolved around the use of Toronto's waterfront lands, although the killing of the Island community has been postponed once again, perhaps until the next century.

The original peninsula and islands have recently been joined by others. To the east, a narrow manmade spit juts three miles out into the lake and is already occupied by thousands of birds of at least 90 different species. And anchored off the Exhibition grounds to the west is Ontario Place, Eberhard Zeidler's dazzling fantasy playground of new islands, magic, soaring bridges, decks, pods, tents, shelters and grassy knolls, and a vast, glittering sphere that seems to float like a bubble on the water but actually houses a seven-storey movie screen.

If you want to see what the central waterfront might have been these past 100 years you must visit Chicago's magnificent Lake Michigan shore. It embodies the scheme drawn up for Toronto by our greatest nineteenth-century architect, F.W. Cumberland, and his young assistant, Sandford Fleming (later renowned as surveyor of the CPR and father of standard time). When it went unheeded here it was taken to a more receptive client. But there are projects that begin to restore the waterfront to the people: Harbourfront, a 40-acre recreation and arts complex amid the old docks and warehouses, and the St. Lawrence Community, a group of cooperatives built on land reclaimed from the bay, immediately adjacent to the old town of York.

By the 1920s the largest steam dredge in North America and the muscle power of an army of immigrant labourers had filled in the acreage of the bay between Front Street and the present docks along Queen's Quay. The remnants of the original town—perched at water's edge on the little cliff that ran from Fort York at the harbour entrance to the windmill of the Gooderham and Worts distillery near the mouth of the Don River—were left landlocked.

Before World War II, the Island airport was built by narrowing the western gap. Near the landing field settled the pilots of Little Norway and their families—Liv Ullmann and her parents among them—until they could return to their homeland.

With the coming of the St. Lawrence Seaway in 1959, the Port of Toronto increased in size and scope, and more than 50,000 Torontonians now hold jobs related to its activities. Near the wharves where three generations of immigrants once landed by schooner, ships from the Baltic and the Caribbean now dock to trade West Indian sugar cane or East European wines for Holland Marsh vegetables and Canadian manufactured goods.

The white fleet of passenger steamers has gone from the bay: the *Cayuga* took her last boatload of picnickers to Niagara in 1957. The *Chicora*, built in England just too late for her intended purpose as a Civil War blockade runner, plied the Great Lakes for half a century, and finally ended her life as a Toronto waterfront barge about the same time as the giant, black-hulled *Noronic* burned at her mooring, the waterfront's most disastrous fire. Gone too are such strange apparitions as the rolling-pin boat whose paddle revolved completely round its hold and the passengers inside; the *Peninsula Packet*, whose paddles were propelled by horses marching round its deck; the dinosaurlike forms of the little lagoon weed-cutter and the huge steam dredges and the old whale-back freighters.

But on a bright weekend afternoon, the bay is as alive with sails as it ever was in the days when most of Toronto's traffic came and went by boat. The Island ferries plough back and forth, mingling with the powerful speedboats of the police, the glass-topped sightseeing launches and the little excursion boats, the cabin cruisers from the canals and rivers of North America, and the elegant nineteenth-century refitted steamer *Hiawatha* of the Royal Canadian Yacht Club, the oldest ship on Lloyd's register.

Against the green and golden twilight sky, the forest of downtown skyscrapers, and the CN Tower's quarter-mile span of red lights, flashing as if it were about to take off into space, there emerges the ancient lady of the harbour herself, the *Trillium*, restored to life and walking on the water again after almost two decades of neglect in an Island lagoon, with a summer evening's excursion-load of passengers outward bound for the lake.

Toronto Bay and the city skyline glimpsed through the Island willows still are sights to catch the heart: all that energy and power filtered by distance into a dream of cloud-capped towers, with the water lapping close by against the low and distant music of the roaring city.

LAKE

In all my wishes I pray for words.
Here in this sober, dreamless city
perched on a vast Lake,
beneath the Northern Lights,
rich and flat,
prominent and butchered,
I pray for words.

Loud waves, bare and lovely, move to the shore
to meet their lovers,
interrupted by noisy seagulls
claiming in loud voices
the ownership of the Lake.

Yet my wish goes by unnoticed.
For years I have been waiting here,
facing the Lake and facing myself,
with my past as dead as the Dead Sea
and my future new.
Nothing to fear now.
Nothing to regret.

This Lake lives for me.
Tied to the earth since the Ice Age,
it does not rush around.
The fat sun moves over the lazy waves
hiding its helpful hands.

Sometimes the Lake may trespass its border
and flood the shore, destroying
roads and the basements of summer cottages.
Perhaps it satisfies Nature,
but most of the time
it is full of unconventional majesty.
It looks like a human being

who has suddenly awakened.
Then it is real.
It is a Lake full of sunlight
resting near Toronto.
It is also one inside me,
which is always dark.
WACLAW IWANIUK

THE LONGEST
STREET
IN THE WORLD

Toronto grew up alongside Yonge Street, and Yonge Street is a reflection of the city itself. Even its most ardent admirers would hardly call the picture grand or beautiful. A patchwork of preoccupations and uses, a pawnshop of our several urban dreams, a cacophony of unfinished business ripe for bankruptcy or the quick profit of wallet or soul, a string of little shopping districts and big stores, a street-vendors' haven, a sin strip, a strollers' alley, a mix of ritzy and rubby and rube, it rambles on and on like a picaresque novel, one shining or sorry or tawdry or funny adventure after another. After leaving the city it becomes the main street of several dozen Ontario towns and villages, ending up west of Lake Superior more than 1,200 miles from Toronto Bay.

Yonge Street has cast a shadow over many of Toronto's nobler aspirations. It is an affront to planners, engineers, efficiency experts, moralists, aesthetes, epicureans and history buffs. It is even a nuisance to anybody who wants to buy a drink in the small hours of the morning when other entertainments are still open. To dedicated boosters of Toronto, Yonge Street is an outright offence. A few years ago the director of the National Gallery of Canada described it as "400 outhouses leaning up against Eaton's." Nathan Phillips, whose career on city council spanned five decades, called it "a disgrace to a city of the size and importance of Toronto," but he never managed to change it.

For years, roads officials and traffic movers have been trying to widen it or one-way it, to make more of a race track and less of a traffic jam; but the one-block, one-acre bulge below College Street and the six lanes north of the old city limits are as far as they have got. Lower Yonge Street has remained stubbornly narrow, and promises to stay that way. From one sidewalk you can even see what is in the shop windows on the other side, as well as who is walking there. At times cars travel at the pace of delivery vans—which is frequently zero miles per hour—or of the sporting folk who roll their windows or convertible tops down in order to be part of the general street theatre. Drivers in a hurry don't bother with Yonge Street any more. Toronto's sweeping boulevard, University Avenue, is close by to the west and Jarvis Street does its best to serve as traffic workhorse to the east, but neither of them is a very healthy place for street life that isn't wrapped up in two tons of metal.

For three sunny summers Yonge Street was actually a full-dress pedestrian mall, complete with café tables, draft beer and shrubbery, guitars and pot and panhandlers. Lower Yonge may well be a mall again, but in the meantime the parade of people wanders out and across and back and forth among the trucks and taxis and bicycles and roasted-chestnut vendors. The rest of Yonge is much like the rest of Toronto: a series of neighbourhoods at the pedestrian pace and scale, not quite ruined by through traffic or by a single dominant special function that drives everything else away.

Yonge Street has also resisted, for most of its urban length, the ministrations of the lighting engineers who, in the name of saving kilowatts or of safe driving or of catching purse-snatchers, would have it permanently bathed in the bright orange-yellow sodium vapour glow that floods modern American cities and even some stretches of Toronto's thoroughfares.

Yonge Street is still mostly low-rise with only a few canyons here and there, and the occasional architectural monument. Which is fine if what you want is one or other side of the street sunny all day, and none of the manmade wind storms that swirl down at you from skyscrapers. But not so fine if you like to think Toronto's chief thoroughfare should look different from midwest Main Street, somewhere in AmCan country.

Almost all of its original buildings within the old city limits have been torn down. To find a really exquisite piece of early nineteenth-century history on Yonge Street, you must go all the way to the Gibson House in North York, whose original

Yonge Street near Asquith Avenue, the
first car running north of Bloor,
photographed in the 1860s.
The big building is the village of
Yorkville's town hall.

owner helped lead the 1837 Rebellion, or even further north to the occasional superb farm building between Thornhill and Holland Landing.

Yonge Street is not consistently anything. Though it is designated commercial, it is also home for thousands who live in the second-storey flats. For miles and miles, mixed in with the shops, there are little old apartment buildings, churches, cinemas, parkland, cemeteries, even a subway rail yard. Though the fragrant aroma of Jesse Ketchum's tannery has long since gone from the corner of Yonge and Adelaide, and the fires of Good's Foundry have gone out at Queen, bits of cottage industry still flourish on Yonge Street beyond the downtown core.

And as for commerce, there are instant goods and services in plenty: piña colada, pinball, pregnancy tests, pop records, body building, formals for rent, fast foods, faster prints, fastest pant pressing, nonstop topless dancing, atomic cleaners, army surplus stores, nude services, Canadian antiques and Scandinavian modern, meetings with Jesus, encounters with Krishna or a rendezvous with your own inner self. Whether it is in big stores that sell everything or at little stores that sell utterly and only one thing—nuts, jeans, sex aids, stereo sets or coffee—on Yonge Street you can get almost anything you want.

The number of major institutions scattered along the street, although they do not dominate or deaden it, seems formidable when you start to count them: the Toronto Star building at 1 Yonge, OECA's television studios, the boardrooms of the MacLaren advertising agency, the richly restored elegance of the six-cinema Imperial and the five-cinema Uptown theatres, the vast but dramatic red brick bulk of the new Metropolitan Toronto Reference Library, and three of Canada's largest radio stations—CKEY, CFRB and CHUM.

Just a few yards off Yonge are the three great downtown cathedrals, Roman Catholic, Anglican and United, along with temples to two of Canada's many cults and cultures, Maple Leaf Gardens and Massey Hall.

The buildings of Toronto's four levels of government are also nearby: the dull, green-glass bulk of Ottawa's contribution, incongruously named after Toronto's rebel mayor, William Lyon Mackenzie; and the creeping elephantiasis of the Queen's Park provincial bureaucracy, which stops just short of destroying the rich cultural life of Yonge Street's backyards (a lovely lane like St. Nicholas Street, for example). For the first time ever, Toronto's city and metropolitan hall is directly and pleasantly accessible to Yonge Street, through Trinity Way, which crosses the galleria of the Eaton Centre into the intimate space of Trinity Square with its historic church and Victorian houses.

One crucial centre of political power is located right on Yonge Street. At 5000 Yonge are the borough offices and council chambers of North York, in its own right Canada's fourth-largest municipality, and the political focus and hope of those Torontonians who would like to see Yonge Street's throat widened from the top of Metro right down to the lake.

The map of Toronto—the city itself, not the metropolitan area—looks a bit like a Christmas tree. Yonge Street is its tall trunk, the east-west roads its tapering top and long horizontal branches. The north-south arteries on either side of the trunk—Church, Jarvis, Sherbourne and Parliament, and Bay, University, Beverly-St. George and Spadina—extend northward only a couple of miles from the waterfront and end at or near Bloor Street, originally the first concession road north of the old town. It was north from Bloor that Yonge Street was first planned.

Yonge Street was surveyed by Governor Simcoe and his red-coated York Rangers in 1794. The route was designed to run parallel to and replace the old Indian and French portage from the Toronto Carrying-Place on the Humber River, up and over the divide to the streams and lakes that flowed north, thus making a shortcut from Lake Ontario to the Upper Lakes. The great Canadian fur-trading enterprise, the Northwest Company of Montreal, was interested in the prospect of a better way of hauling their boats and goods between the St. Lawrence River and the Canadian west, and they offered cash contributions toward the clearing of Yonge Street.

But Simcoe's immediate purpose was strategic and military. Yonge Street was part of his grand design for resisting the Americans, and he named it after his friend and superior, the British war secretary, Sir George Yonge. Building Yonge Street was thus an early Canadian war measures act, both anti-American and counterrevolutionary in intent. The Duc de la Rochefoucauld-Liancourt, an early Toronto visitor and refugee from the world's other revolution, which was busy sending his relatives in tumbrels to the guillotine, observed how Governor Simcoe looked at every hill and valley carefully and critically as if he were assessing them for the site of a fort or battle.

The first section of Yonge Street was hacked out of the woods by Pennsylvania Dutch axemen hired for Simcoe by Toronto's first major colonizer and builder, Wilhelm von Moll Berczy. The mire was so deep, and in some spots deepened further still by rivulets and quicksand, that only the patient oxen these German colonists had brought with them from the United States could get through with the road building equipment and the supplies needed for their new farm settlements in Markham Township, east of Yonge Street.

The muddiness of Toronto's first streets inspired prodigious story-telling: there was this fellow, you know, who saw a fine, new hat in the middle of the road. When he managed to reach it and pick it up, he discovered the head of a living man underneath it, who made a special appeal for rescue of his horse, which was underneath him. "The usual mode of extrication by shovels and oxen was soon applied and the man and horse were excavated."

Most serious travel had to be reserved for wintertime, when the ground was frozen, but Yonge Street quickly became the principal highway for all the settlers north of Toronto bringing their wagons of produce and squadrons of hissing geese and lowing cattle down to the St. Lawrence Market and hauling the supplies of salt and seed and rope, axes and ploughs and stoves back to the farm.

Next to the streams and mires that had to be forded, the most formidable obstacle for travellers on early Yonge Street was the steep rise just below the present St. Clair Avenue. It was originally called Gallows Hill and it commanded a sweeping view of the gently forested rolling plain to the south, the distant spires of Toronto rising out of the treetops, and the blue horizon of Lake Ontario. Toronto's earliest historian, Dr. Henry Scadding, recalls that the hill had to be climbed by means of a narrow excavated notch or trench, over which a giant tree had fallen. "Teams on their way to town had to pass underneath it like captured armies of old under the yoke, and to some among the country folk it suggested the beam of the gallows tree," the latter a familiar enough sight to the cheerful holiday crowds that gathered from all over the county to view public hangings near the market.

The ships and the supplies of the North West Company were hauled up Yonge Street by oxen or horses, but at Gallows Hill they were windlassed up by means of a large capstan. Other early ships to sail Yonge Street—at least in pieces—were the big Lake Simcoe steamer engines, manufactured in Toronto, which Mr. Charles Thompson of Summerhill had moved to his docks at Holland Landing on rollers made of tree trunks.

In the seasons when they could get through at all, three regular stagecoach lines connected Toronto with the boat service at Holland Landing. But, in 1853, the stages' days were numbered by the strange and wonderful sight of the *Toronto*, the "first railway locomotive ever manufactured in a British colony," being dragged down Yonge from the corner of Queen. A decade later there was a railway station on Yonge Street, located on the present site of the O'Keefe Centre at Front. After being replaced by a large structure west of Yonge, the station lasted on as a fruit market until its destruction in 1952.

On Yonge Street itself it was not the steam engine but the electric railway that eventually took over from the stagecoach. After a short interval when horse-drawn omnibuses ran on rails or sleigh runners, the electric streetcar came to Yonge Street in the 1890s, following its world premiere in the grounds of the Canadian National Exhibition. One stagecoach still carried mail to the postal villages dotted along Yonge Street until it was replaced by electric radial cars in 1893. These ran from the foot of Gallows Hill, where they connected with the Yonge Street car, all the way to Lake Simcoe and were part of the hydro knight Sir Adam Beck's marvellous system of electric public transport throughout southern Ontario. These modern wonders swayed and rocketed down the slopes of Hoggs Hollow and up to Thornhill at five or 10 times the speed of the old stage; and although they occasionally jumped the tracks, they were still doing yeoman service on Yonge Street during the gasoline shortages of World War II. They were finally removed in the 1950s, just before the opening of Canada's first subway line—under Yonge Street.

Public transport history on lower Yonge Street has come full circle in recent years. While Torontonians by the millions speed up and down Yonge Street by train 20 feet below, a slow and old-fashioned surface omnibus service has returned, albeit a horseless one this time. The Yonge Street bus, known as the Happy Times Geriatric Special, provides slow but friendly curbside service for those who will not or cannot contend with stairways and escalators, and who wish to hop on or off at midblock.

Just about everything under the sun has passed up or down or across Yonge Street: Santa Claus and his reindeer, department-store floats and clowns; King Billy on his white horse with the fife and drum corps of every Orange Lodge from Aurora to Cabbagetown; peace marchers, grape boycotters, and Premier Kosygin; Wendell Wilkie, the Salvation Army, and the Gurkha Rifles with their bagpipes and murderous knives; the Knights of Labour, and every kind of leftist from Wobblies to J.S. Woodsworth. Yonge Street has seen church parades, temperance marchers, suffragettes and sports heroes; the roaming mobs of VE Day, the state funerals of John Strachan and of the soldiers killed at Ridgeway during the Fenian invasions. The parades are almost endless: the Forty-Eighth Highlanders of Canada in feather bonnets and regimental scarlet; the gay community in drag every Hallowe'en; the Shriners making whoopee with squealers and water bags, paunchy good ole boys from Texarkana and Hamtramck, dressed Mouseketeer-style and driving toy buggies in weaving precision formation. As Raymond Souster recalls, we've even had elephants on Yonge Street:

> Ten gray eminences moving
> with the daintiest of steps
> and the greatest unconcern
> up the canyon.
> Too bored to yawn
> or toss the fools riding them,
> they slowly twist their trunks
> and empty their bowels
> at a pace which keeps
> the two men following
> with shovels and hand cart
> almost swearingly busy.

But the wildest parades were for cheering on Toronto's recruits who marched to the railway station to become soldiers of the Queen and put down rebellions by Louis Riel and the Métis in the Northwest Territories, or Oom Paul Kruger and his Boers in South Africa. The crowds were so thick, the Toronto *Leader* reported, you could have walked on their heads.

But of all the processions on Yonge Street, the most remarkable occurred in the 1830s, the decade in which Toronto became a city and turned back an armed rebellion. Both involved William Lyon Mackenzie, Upper Canada's most inflammatory newspaper editor and Toronto's first mayor.

Of the scores of inns and taverns that lined Yonge Street for the rest and refreshment of farmers and draymen travelling into Toronto, the Red Lion at the Bloor Street tollgate in

Snowing up the Toronto Street Car Company. Engraving from the Canadian Illustrated News, *Feb. 12, 1881. After heavy snow the storekeepers battled with tramway crews. The plough on each horse-drawn tram made the street impassable for pedestrians and other vehicles, so the merchants' armies shovelled the snow back on to the tracks every time a tram passed.*

Yorkville was the most spacious. From the hustings in the inn yard of the rambling old building with its low roofs and mullioned windows, Mackenzie was elected member for the Assembly for the County of York on January 2, 1832. A square dance and celebration were held in the ballroom of the Red Lion Inn and when the speeches were finished, an exuberant and noisy procession of sleighs moved south on Yonge Street. The biggest of them, two storeys high, carried Mackenzie and his committee on the top deck, with pipers piping and streamers and banners illuminated by torch light. Another covered sleigh carried a small printing press, heated by a stove to keep the ink from freezing, and Mackenzie's New Year's message was cranked out by hand and distributed to little knots of cheering spectators, gathered all the way down to King Street and west to the doors of the assembly itself.

A few years later there was another memorable procession occasioned by the great fancy-dress midsummer's ball given by William Botsford Jarvis—sheriff of the Home District and scion of a Toronto first family—at his Rosedale estate. Dr. Scadding recalled that "in the dusk of the evening and again in the grey dawn of morning an irregular procession thronged the highway and toiled up and down the steep approaches . . . the simulated shapes and forms that revisit the glimpses of the moon at masquerades—knights, crusaders, Plantagenet and Tudor and Stuart princes, queens and heroines, all mixed up with an incongruous ancient and modern canaille, a Tom of Bedlam, a Nicholas Bottom with amiable cheeks and fair large ears, an Ariel, a Paul Pry, a Pickwick. . . ."

William Lyon Mackenzie had mocked many a social or state occasion in his newspaper—he once described a formal viceregal procession as "the move from the blue bed to the brown." On this midsummer's eve at the Jarvises, however, he was not present to comment, but was a refugee from Canada with a £1,000 price on his head. For he and the good sheriff had met at the corner of Yonge and Carlton in the twilight of Tuesday, December 5, 1837. When the Upper Canadian farmers and artisans marched down Yonge Street, led by Mackenzie on a little white mare, the city's only armed defence was Jarvis and his 27-man picket. But one volley was enough to put the invaders to flight. Three days later, with the militia assembled, bands playing and flags flying, the gentlemen of Upper Canada marched north on Yonge Street, set fire to Montgomery's Tavern, the rebel headquarters, and scattered the Queen's enemies to the four winds.

Montgomery swore that when his Family Compact enemies were "all frizzling in hell," he would still be a taverner on Yonge Street. He kept his promise about the tavern, returning from a rebel's exile to a very different Canada. So did Mackenzie, and enjoyed another triumphant election to Parliament. Sheriff William Jarvis ended his days on his Rosedale estate.

I suppose, for what it's worth, all this makes William Lyon Mackenzie and Sheriff Jarvis the patron saints of Yonge Street. But it is the lively presence of Timothy Eaton more than any other man who made the biggest difference in bringing the flow of people onto Yonge Street. Perhaps the Reverend Doctor Scadding and his successors at Trinity Square should also be mentioned in dispatches, not just for keeping track of the people who have travelled or settled on Yonge Street this past century or two, but also for seeing that a bit of history and peace were preserved for them in the heart of the city next to Timothy's store when they got there.

If I had to name a presence for modern Yonge Street, I would be torn between two: Sam Sniderman, alias Sam the Record Man, who besides making his block the liveliest part of Yonge Street has purveyed more music than anyone else to the people of Toronto; and Rompin' Ronnie Hawkins, the expatriate singer and impresario from Arkansas who put together Bob Dylan's The Band, a bunch of Canadian musicians who played in Hawkins' Yonge Street tavern gloriously named The Le Coq d'Or (Toronto's second language is *not* French). Hawkins used to say respectfully to customers who looked like lawyers or PhDs or at least wore ties, in that wise cornpone drawl of his, "Yo're uptown, ah'm downtown." And he was. And so is Yonge Street.

PHARAOH'S MYSTERY

I suddenly realized, walking up that hideous bit of Bay Street from Wellesley Street to Bloor which has mostly showrooms for cars and automobile parts—I suddenly realized these signs were beautiful, all those gorgeous blues, and I realized that if an Egyptian from the time of one of the great Pharaohs were to walk down the street he would have found them a mystery, an overwhelming mystery. There's everything here.
        HAROLD TOWN, "Harold Town Talks," Waterloo Review *(1960)*

THE
OLDEST SUBURB

Every morning and afternoon, sharp at 11 and three, the tour buses leave the roar of downtown traffic and cross the bridge among the treetops into the ravine-bound peace of Rosedale, Toronto's oldest surviving residential suburb. Slowly, respectfully they wind through the narrow streets among the great maples, the little parks and the stately homes. The tourists will be told that this is a community of old wealth and new media stars, of the movers and shakers of the various professional worlds of English-Canadian culture: lawyers, doctors, architects, editors, brokers, bankers and board chairmen. Down that street, a former governor general resides; down this one, Gordon Lightfoot, and the Roman Catholic archbishop; on another, a retired prime minister used to live, not far from Harold Town, Morley Callaghan and the Anglican primate of all Canada.

The streets are a jumble of crescents, lanes, ways, places and paths. Sometimes five of them meet at odd angles, and as if that were not inhibiting enough to cars, they are thoroughly sprinkled with stop signs and speed limits, lest anyone try to negotiate them in a hurry. One road, Chestnut Park, with its red brick sidewalks, ample grass boulevards and globe lamps on ornamental iron posts wired from underground, consists of three attached semicircles.

Visitors to Rosedale may glimpse among the trees almost any mansion from the realm of fancy: Bleak House, Seven

*A photograph of Sheriff Jarvis' original
Rosedale house (long since demolished)
after which Toronto's oldest suburb was
named. Guests at garden parties such
as this one often included veterans of the
War of 1812 and the Rebellion of
1837. The site was near the corner of
what is now Rosedale Road
and Cluny Avenue.*

Gables, Jalna, even the pillars of Tara or the decks of Falling Waters. Some command knolls and hillocks; others are perched on the edges of the valleys that surround and cut through Rosedale and make it a cluster of islands. Embrasures, cornices, groins and turrets abound—almost everything but flying buttresses. Richly glowing bits of pre-Raphaelite or art nouveau stained glass can be glimpsed at night. The dominant mood is still set by the great fanciful red brick piles built in the last years of Victoria. The American novelist John Updike described them as ''lovingly erected brick valentines to a distant dowager queen, with their intimations of lost time and present innocence across the lake from grimy, grubby America.'' For Victoria's birthday—still a public holiday, to the astonishment of visiting Englishmen—Rosedale puts out its Union Jacks and Red Ensigns.

The majority of Rosedale residences actually date from the first half of the twentieth century. Elegant William Morris and Charles Mackintosh derivations jostle with pseudish and Moorish and Tudorbethan fakery, occasionally mixed with a low, drab yellow brick apartment house of the 1940s or a row of salmon pink semidetached decorator Georgian from the 1960s. Inspiration from colonial Boston is neighbour to a sprawling prairie split-level, or a contemporary architect's latest, all stilts and exposed ducts.

The thing that any stereotype of Rosedale is apt to miss is the variety of people who live there, and the unlikely mixture of lifestyles and income levels. On one short street are four of the city's largest and least-expensive rooming houses, three crowded apartment buildings, a community of Jesuits, a girls' private school, mansions converted to high-priced flats, and the homes of a senator, a film mogul, a poet, a sculptress, Lord Thomson of Fleet and a former cabinet minister.

Half of the people in south Rosedale are not homeowners at all, but tenants—from remnants of old Toronto families in reduced circumstances to young secretaries and filing clerks just off the plane from London or Vancouver. Rosedale has attics full of college students and great-aunts, smart young couples in narrow town houses, interior decorators in exquisite old coach houses. Near the CPR freight line to Vancouver there are pockets of bungalows housing mums and dads on pensions, welfare recipients and working people, and scattered throughout there are blocks that for the first time in many years swarm with children.

Rosedale was originally the estate of Sheriff William Jarvis, rebel-fighter and member of early York's Family Compact. All of the buildings except a coach house are gone now. But every June the wild roses, for which Mrs. Jarvis named the estate, still burst out here and there like little waterfalls, following the spring fountains of forsythia and lilac and orange blossoms. And Mrs. Jarvis' dale is there too, to be glimpsed by every Yonge Street subway passenger who looks up long enough to glance out the window as the train bursts into the open between the downtown tunnel and the tunnel under the escarpment to the north. Through this space of greenery and light, the train also passes within 90 feet of the famous Studio Building, built for Tom Thomson and members-to-be of the Group of Seven back in 1913. Four storeys tall and flooded with northern light, it is still used by Toronto artists. When Harold Town needs a razor blade to work with, he can always pick out one of A.Y. Jackson's through the hole in the floor where it was dropped.

The most renowned of Rosedale's historic sites is the park where the cup donated by His Excellency the Governor General Earl Grey for supremacy in the new game of rugby football was first fought over by two teams of rather unpadded and bony young men back in 1909. The park was called the Lacrosse Grounds in those days and was reached by electric streetcars which rattled into South Drive and over the rickety wooden trestle of the northerly Glen Road Bridge. (The southerly one was for lighter traffic: buggies and bicycles, ladies' electric cars and the horseless carriages driven by goggled and dustered adventurous spirits.) The park had a grandstand and was part of the St. Andrew's College grounds. The college, like the Rosedale golf course beside it, has long since moved miles up Yonge Street. But the old sports grounds are still there, the site of tennis and hockey and skating. On the field where Dr. Smirle Lawson's Varsity Squad won the first Grey Cup there are now teams of Torontonians from the West Indies playing cricket, from the antipodes playing rugger, and from all parts of the world playing soccer. And yes, there are even squads of very small boys in very large helmets playing an Americanized but recognizable version of the Grey Cup football game of 1909.

Two of Rosedale's grandest estates have become parkland. To open the Ontario Legislature or attend church, the lieutenant-governor used to sally forth from his 57-room mansion, Chorley Park, in grey topper and morning coat, his landau drawn by two teams of high-stepping chestnut horses. Used as a wartime hospital for convalescing soldiers, the old place was later torn down, but its memory lives on in one of the entries to the ravine-bound islands of Rosedale: the Governor's Bridge.

Sir Edmund Osler, MP, financial tycoon and brother of the great physician, helped found the Rosedale Association in 1905, to protect homes like his from progress and city hall. The association still does so, but Sir Edmund bequeathed his own Craigleigh, with its great oaks, gardens and valley, its noble iron and masonry gates, to the city, and for a half a century now it has been one of Toronto's loveliest parks.

The site of Rosedale's earliest industry, Joseph Bloor's brewery, just below Sherbourne where the street named after him used to end, has now reverted to wilderness; its crystal stream is a ravine drive. But the kilns in the Don Valley are still baking red brick, and high above the valley, Drumsnab, the oldest house in Rosedale, sits settled and comfortable, still a residence after 150 years. Armies of fat raccoons scurry about the streets at night, and you can still watch for the migratory warblers in spring or hear an owl in the morning dusk.

WHEN I WENT UP TO ROSEDALE

When I went up to Rosedale
I thought of kingdom come,
Persistent in the city
Like a totem in a slum.

The ladies off across the lawns
Revolved like haughty birds.
They made an antique metaphor.
I didn't know the words.

Patrician diocese: the streets
Beguiled me as I went
Until the tory founders seemed
Immortal government.

For how could mediocrities
Have fashioned such repose?
And yet those men were pygmies,
As any schoolboy knows.

For Head reduced the rule of law
To frippery and push.
Tradition-conscious Pellatt built
A drawbridge in the bush.

67 Glen Road: a 1962 wood
engraving by Rosemary Kilbourn,
R.C.A. The house, at the corner of
Elm, was built by Ford Howland in
1905 for his uncle Peleg, one of the
former mayor's brothers; it was later
occupied by the Huycke family, and
from 1961 to 1982 by seven Kilbourns
and several boarders from
the University of Toronto.

And Bishop Strachan gave witness, by
The death behind his eyes,
That all he knew of Eden
Was the property franchise.

And those were our conservatives!
A claque of little men
Who took the worst from history
And made it worse again.

The dream of tory origins
Is full of lies and blanks,
Though what remains when it is gone,
To prove that we're not Yanks?

Nothing but the elegant
For Sale signs on the lawn,
And roads that wind their stately way
To dead ends, and are gone.

When I came down from Rosedale
I could not school my mind
To the manic streets before me
Nor the courtly ones behind.

DENNIS LEE

VIEW
FROM THE
VIADUCT

A place I like to stand in the evening if I want to assemble the disparate elements of Toronto's past and present in my mind is in one of the ponderous and rarely used viewing embrasures near the eastern end of the great viaduct over the Don Valley, which connects Bloor Street with the once-isolated communities of east Toronto. Their main street, the Danforth, has always been Canada's ultimate used-car lot and general festival of free enterprise, but in recent years it has been given its liveliest colour and street life by the Greek merchants who have settled there, much as they colonized the Aegean Islands and the coast of Asia Minor more than 2,500 years ago.

I am tempted to go on over the bridge and buy things for a moussaka and kefaloteri supper, but instead turn my back to the Danforth and look south and west over one of the most spectacular views of downtown Toronto. The great towers, lit up against the darkening sky, rise magically out of a solid green mass of trees in the middle foreground. The Don Valley at its amplest breadth spreads out below. The motor traffic hums and grinds continually on two expressways, the big one hugging the left bank of the valley, the smaller one, the right. The main lines of both national railways run closer to the water in the centre, and the river itself, too polluted for swimming or to freeze for skating in the winter, meanders peacefully down the middle, still refusing the funeral that a team of ecologists gave it a few years back. Who knows, the

Don may be preparing for the return of the great schools of fish that used to glide through its waters for so many millennia—they are running again in the rivers to the west of Toronto.

From that knoll on the west bank of the valley, the site of Castle Frank, Elizabeth Simcoe observed a flight of eagles, and in the deepening shadows below saw the Don River illuminated by the flares of Indians in their canoes spearing salmon as they swam to their spring spawning grounds in the little creeks and pools that are now dried up or driven underground beneath the built-up city.

For many years the local deity of the river was a white-bearded hermit named Tyler who lived in a cave cut out of the western slope just north of Queen Street. He cultivated Indian corn and tobacco, made tar and resin in a dug-out kiln, and split pine knots to be used for fishermen's lights. He poled his produce in to town, and sometimes barrels of farm-made beer from upriver, in a long boat carved from two 40-foot pine trunks. He would also ferry travellers across the river in it, when they could find him.

In winter the frozen river made a smooth highway for the sleighs loaded with firewood and hay to fuel the stoves and horses of Toronto. The snow was printed with the footmarks of deer, wolf, lynx and thousands of smaller creatures.

That forest in the middle distance to the south between the valley and the downtown towers shelters much of Toronto's history: the old Riverdale Zoo; Wellesley Park, where a row of houses have a sidewalk for their main street and the cars are kept back in the alley with the garbage cans; the exquisite little church of St. James the Less, surrounded by generations of the Family Compact sleeping beneath the marble and the grass and the trees; the Necropolis where the rebels Mackenzie, Lount and Matthews are buried, as is Toronto's own Father of Confederation, George Brown of the *Globe*.

There, too, in the forest are the thousand lovely Victorian homes of Don Vale, east of Parliament, once a district of working people but now largely white-painted and sandblasted into high fashion and higher prices. Further south is what is left of Cabbagetown, once described by its native bard, Hugh Garner, as "North America's only Anglo-Saxon slum," a place where respect for the royal family, the Conservative party and such members of the local elite as a policeman or a streetcar conductor ran high, and all heathen religions, higher education, foreigners and social workers were suspect. Two of Toronto's old working-class neighbourhoods were destroyed entirely, one to make way for the public housing blocks of Regent's Park, and another for the vast private development of St. James Town, with its 20- and 30-storey apartment towers and acres of grass and asphalt.

One of the most recent revivals of old Toronto lies in the area from Yonge Street east to the Don River and from Queen south to what was once the water's edge at Front. Here was located the original 10-block townsite of eighteenth-century York, and while much of it has been rebuilt again and again, it has not been wiped out by the canyons of commerce and finance like its counterpart to the west of Yonge Street.

Here are warehouses and firehalls and factories now transformed into theatres and artists' studios and a downtown campus for George Brown College. Here is the lovely St. Lawrence Hall where Jenny Lind sang in the 1850s and crinolined ladies and their officers danced the schottische, where the National Ballet of Canada found a home, and where in its revived splendour after 1968 citizens rallied and banquets were consumed. Here are the shops of ship chandler and harness salesman and furrier, Toronto's oldest pub and the handsome south wall of Front Street's old commercial buildings. In the midst of the St. Lawrence Market is Toronto's early city hall, beneath which dungeons and wharf-pilings were found during its recent restoration.

The town well and pump, the little weigh-house for wagons, the stocks and pillory where public offenders were branded or flogged or exhibited on market day are long since gone; but farmers still sell their produce at the market as they did even before Governor Hunter officially established the Saturday market in 1803.

Just north of the market stands St. James' Cathedral and the tomb of John Strachan, chief spokesman for the town when the Americans landed, and moving spirit for six decades in the affairs of church and state, education and society. The little Greek Revival temple on nearby Toronto Street was once our main post office and is now the headquarters of Argus Corporation, the many-headed holding conglomerate assembled by E.P. Taylor. The elegant York County courthouse on Adelaide Street has been made over into a theatre and restaurant.

In the vicinity, too, are Toronto's saucy new adventurers in the media gang: CITY television, which will try anything from blue movies to five straight hours of live political programming to the spontaneous chaos of *Free for All*; the offices of the *Toronto Sun*, one of the rare successful new North American dailies; and of *Toronto Life* magazine, which will tell you what is smart to eat and wear and see and think, and where to get expensive things cheap—more or less.

Further to the east, beyond Parliament Street, named for the buildings the American invaders burned in 1813, are Toronto's two loveliest churches, St. Paul's Roman Catholic and Little Trinity Anglican, and the first free school for the city's poor, Enoch Turner Schoolhouse. Just south again on Trinity Street are the dozens of grey stone buildings of the Gooderham and Worts distillery—a whole mid-Victorian industrial complex surviving intact.

Jarvis Street, the western boundary of the original town of York, runs from the waterfront to Bloor. In the twentieth century it has been famous for gentlemen of the road and ladies of the night. It is the address of small, once-genteel apartment hotels, the Sally Ann's Harbour Light and several choice flophouses; Toronto's first collegiate descends from the old grammar school of 1807, and the CBC's English-language broadcasting transmits from the old red brick building that used to be a girl's school. The Family Court, the Metropolitan Toronto Police headquarters and the new fortress of the Royal Canadian Mounted Police coexist with the traditional haunts of Toronto's gangsters, although the Warwick Hotel, which once graced the corner of Dundas, no longer remains. It was the Warwick, long renowned for the performances of Brandee, prizefighter turned female impersonator, that first got the word that "Mickey's out" scrawled on its washroom wall, when the great Mickey MacDonald was released from Kingston Penitentiary.

The flowering chestnuts and the clatter of hooves on paving stones are gone from Jarvis Street. But the mansions of the Victorian plutocracy, behind their modern facade of gas stations and restaurants and signs and offices, still impose something of their ponderous magnificence. My great-grandfather, a considerable tanner but no merchant prince or captain of industry, lived close by. His place on Isabella Street, with its antlered, arras-hung, bearskin-spread rooms and corridors echoing to the hymns he played on flute or cornet, loomed large and terrible in my infant nightmares. But I think of him as I look from the viaduct downriver toward the old tannery on the Don where my cousins and I were occasionally employed. Forty years before I knew him, he was alderman for this ward on city council, as was his son after him, a great-uncle who died before I was born.

I suspect great-grandfather's main concern at city hall was to defend the right of enterprise to use the Don River for dumping. My great-uncle's was to build an east-west subway, but he and his allies on council lost and the most they could salvage at the time the viaduct was built were the underpinnings for a future subway beneath it. I think of him, too, as the ground beneath me shudders slightly; 60 years late, the Bloor train rumbles eastward across the Don and out along the Danforth.

SHERBOURNE MORNING

I begin to understand the old men, parked on benches
smoking a bit of July, waiting for the early
bottle; the large tears of the passers-by, wrapped
in white cotton, the world bandaged at 7 a.m.;
when the day goes old, they lean over
and nod into their arms, lovers, one-time carriers
of their separate hearts; their wives, their children
are glass partitions through which they see themselves
crying. Love them, or better yet, imagine a world
without a footstool for the creased and lame; imagine how that
sun above them spins halos for angels gone berserk.
                    PIER GIORGIO DI CICCO

WEST
OF SPADINA

BY JACK LUDWIG

My Toronto starts with silence, not any old silence but a particular one, a Sunday morning silence quite early in spring.

Silence is deserted space, or space too early to be anything but grey of sky and sidewalk and road. A light wind picks up a tough old survivor of autumn, one torn, unsymmetric oak leaf, and slides it in a whisper along the gutter. A door creaks open, footsteps scuff out a little hesitation, a little sleepiness. An empty crate keeps the door ajar. The aroma of bread baking escapes through the newly opened door like a signal. Windows shoot up. Doors swing wide. Feet move and men and woman come out.

The grey backdrop is quickly flushed with a crate of oranges, a basket of pale red greenhouse tomatoes, a table of yellow and black bananas, mangoes of green touched by sunrise, yams with insides white as snow, machete-hacked coconuts, sugar canes neatly stacked like cordwood. An old truck-garden truck unevens it over the lumpy street. Tailgates bang down, great greens fill in more expanses of grey. A CHUM car-radio hysterias the street, one Portuguese song takes its stand from a second-floor window, the first burst of children throws blue and yellow sweaters against the losing grey.

Reddish-brown root clumps sit in a box outside the West Indian window now, leaned over by a gorgeous girl of an even better colour. The birdcages are hooked into the awn-

A small corner of Toronto's lively and colourful Kensington Market, painted by Hans Zander in 1981.

ings, the dresses, coats, sweaters pushed up on long poles like the paintbrushes Dufy used when arthritis and bad eyes forced him to retreat from his work. Serendipity swings into the act with a miniskirt the colour of the cheeseman's Edam, an Irish sweater pallid as his cottage cheese. A Polish lady seems unconcerned though her duster's in secret league with the Hungarian butcher's shrivelled sausage.

You will nothing, nor does anyone else, but in an instant Bruegel's working the planes, the roofs, the walls, the signs, the poles, the headgear, the backs, the shoes, the hands, that dead grey dead quiet street jumping with sound and colour and motion, Babel unified because food is a unifying theme. A Bruegel-stooped old man in a long midnight blue coat has just come from mass (or was it the early morning service at the old synagogue?). He shouts a hello at the man and wife of equal size planted in front of their junk shop like two very alert cigar-store Indians. The man's hands are thrust deep in his mackinaw pockets, the woman's equally deep in a rough red wool cardigan. It's hard to know what they're thinking. A ragged old woman passes a pile of discarded fruits and vegetables, sniffs her disdain, passes on.

That's the key to my Toronto. I borrow Bruegel's eye. Steal one more peek, okay? And hope it comes out "Children's Games" and not "The Massacre of the Innocents." Bruegel doesn't go much for the inhuman unanimal purity of white, so we'll put the billowed goose wings down as an unearned bonus. The man unloading geese from a packed station wagon holds three in each hand, between his fingers, as if their necks were just cigars. Six violently fluttering backsides vibrate to the gabble of the doomed. Their betrayer wears a pencil behind his ear and carries an invoice to atone for his treachery. A white-coated, blood-daubed butcher, equally at home with crime, shoulders a wine-red, fat-rimmed carcass nobody seems to connect with a slaughtered cow. Bruegel, no, Soutine, catch the floundering flounder patting their fins against the cold comfort of a window's shaved ice. Or that fowl man oblivious of the larger canvas, pushing a shopping cart full of stoned ducks, patting their heads as if they were babies.

All the street's a screen, and all these fabulous players on it—girls in maxicoats and miniskirts and boots and, spring's harbinger, barefoot. The long, flowing scarves of last night's Yorkville are here now (most likely on their trip home); the kid with the mouth organ, three or four with guitars. Widows black and Greek as Zorba's add dignity to the unSunday primary chips.

Okay, so that's the street, but who among you knows Toronto and doesn't know my Mrs. Daiter? Drunk on sound and colour, I steal into her store for the respite of sour cream and fabulous yogurt. I'm in love with Mrs. Daiter, it must be obvious even to her husband, though good taste precludes vaulting the counter that separates us. Mrs. Daiter is not excessively tall, I should tell you, nor is she extreme in other ways, like Twiggy. Which is why when Mrs. Daiter weighs a bicycle-saddle shape of cheesecloth-wrapped cottage cheese curds she stands tiptoe, and reads the scale with a magnifying glass, and talks in a child's voice.

I've never heard a note of Muzak in Mrs. Daiter's store (thought I must confess I didn't try that much). Hard as I've looked, I've yet to find the supermarket aisle. Someone is always leaning over the halvah and the trayed eggs, shouting into the Daiter pay phone. Conwomen conjure imaginary bad buys but they do not sway my Mrs. Daiter. She has trouble with her feet, it seems; in a properly tuned society, shoemen from all corners of Toronto would come willingly, like Cinderella's prince, to do a high courtesy for Mrs. Daiter. She suffers on her feet for passing strangers. She, I will confess it here and now, is the queenpin of my Toronto.

Say a bad Merlin claps his hands. Say I emerge from Mrs. Daiter's to find the children gone, the music stopped, the crates pounded into splinters, a long gouge taken out of Bruegel's painting. A bad-dream bulldozer skidded that junk shop into kingdom come. A parking lot greets me like a nightmare, a sudden bleep-up of wall and window uglies the sky with a rise just high enough to tell me I'm in Chicago—or is it Detroit? Some other part of Toronto already razed for the sky? "Alice, Alice, I know what it was like now, Alice." Back through the looking glass, right? Back into Mrs. Daiter's.

But where's Mrs. Daiter's now? Where, now, is my Toronto? Concrete encroaches, like a fungus. Concrete turns my town abstract. Boxes of bricks, so-much-a-foot, so-much-a-room, creep like lava from the underground volcanoes where Turn-the-paper lives next to In-my-pocket. Which of these guys, I ask myself in the nightmare, could ever make a tree? The Developer grins, the Alderman hangs his head (in proud solemnity, not shame), the Zoners give another victory sign. "What good is uniqueness?" says Bully Boy Fast-Buck, and slips a board its weekly take of envelopes. "Did uniqueness ever have to meet a payroll?"

"You need a shopping bag?" Mrs. Daiter says to me.

"Excuse me, Mrs. Daiter, I was thinking of something."

"You shouldn't think of something when I'm trying to serve you."

"You are right, Mrs. Daiter."

Chastened, I back out of the store. It's still there, to my relief. Bruegel's "Children's Games," I mean (and not his "Massacre of the Innocents"). I don't know why I'm telling you all this. It's the advent of spring, maybe. And anyway, who can tell somebody else about his Toronto?

LANDMARKS

After sixteen years I remember you
Ossington bus, O'Leary Avenue.

Perhaps gravity makes them loom so large
West Lodge, St. George Street, York garage.

Northcliffe backyard, where cops used to appear
after midnight to confiscate my beer

or Glenholm boarding house, five bucks a room,
whose dome languidly crumpled into doom

and bursting water pipes had drowned in steam
the ex-mate of a German submarine.

The beanery on Queen Street where a lame
girl first sat in my booth and asked my name.

Or long before, a metal winter night,
a funeral home's sign casting a light

flickering blue on grey December slush:
with cardboard trunks, torn clothes, needing a wash,

an evil-smelling strange boy, tall and thin,
had asked to spend the night. And god knows why

they took me in.

GEORGE JONAS

A PRIDE
OF MONUMENTS

A FEELING, AN ECHO...
THE LIFE OF
UNION STATION

A railway station, especially a large one, is something like a home: it acquires a certain aura after it has been used. I do not believe in ghosts or haunted mansions but I am always conscious when I enter any old building of the unseen presence of those who came before. It does not matter if the furniture and bric-a-brac have been stripped away; a sense of presence remains—a feeling, an echo perhaps, that tells you lives were lived here, tragedies enacted, triumphs rewarded, loves consummated, and that this building knew the cycle of birth, life and death, of hope and despair, of sadness and joy. You cannot experience any of this when you enter a brand-new structure. Freshly completed edifices lack a soul. It is the older ones, the ones that have served their purpose over the years, that rejoice in this kind of psychic patina. The sense of history, the feeling of nostalgia, the echoes of the past can never be worked into an architect's blueprint.

Union Station is such a building. For more than 50 years it has been the soul and heartbeat of Toronto. There was a time when almost everybody who arrived in the city and almost everybody who left it passed between those familiar columns of Bedford limestone. Tears, not so idle, have washed those marble floors and cries of joy and despair have echoed up to that vaulted ceiling of Italian tile. How many kisses have been exchanged in that vast concourse? Ten million? Twenty million? More than we know, for there was a time when impecunious young Torontonians, lacking a front parlour or a secluded doorstep, mingled with the swirling crowds of well-wishers and, quite unremarked, smooched shamelessly in public, moving from platform to platform to make their spurious goodbyes.

It is no accident that the great station resembles a temple, for there was a time when we worshipped railways as ardently as the ancients worshipped Zeus or Apollo. At the start of World War II, when men in uniform began to crowd through in almost unbelievable numbers, a Toronto newspaper called Union Station a "cathedral of travel and traffic." The comparison is apt, for the building's basic plan was conceived 20 years before it opened—in 1907, when the railway era was at its apogee. Two more transcontinental lines were being planned and every new town that was promised a spur line was enjoying a real estate boom. No wonder, then, that the facade was conceived as monumental and that each of the 22 pillars, 40 feet in height, should weigh 75 tons and be rooted in solid rock. The building was made to last: some years ago the concealed wiring in one of the offices was laid bare and it was discovered that every wire was in a conduit, a clear example of the thoroughness of the construction policy.

The care that went into the planning of the station is reminiscent of the love lavished on medieval churches. Examine, for instance, the hall that was originally referred to as the "ticket lobby." (Ticket lobby! That pedestrian phrase scarcely does justice to a 260-foot concourse whose ceiling soars 88 feet above the customers.) The Missouri Zumbro stone in the walls was selected for its natural fossilized structure and for its high reflective qualities, so that the effect is at once mellow and light. The floor and stairways that lead to the exits are of Tennessee marble, chosen both for its beauty and its hard-wearing qualities. The arched ceiling (again the temple analogy comes to mind) is faced with vitrified Guastavino tile, whose colour harmonizes with that of the walls. Long shafts of light flood in through the arched windows, each four storeys high, at both ends of the hall; here, too, the ecclesiastical motif is undeniable. And if you look up to the cornice above you will see engraved in the stone not the names of the blessed saints, but those of all the cities and towns of Canada served by the two railways whose home this station has been since 1927.

Cathedrals usually took centuries to complete, but Union Station was built over a period of about 13 years and would have been finished sooner had the tragedy of the Great War

*The old Armouries on University
Avenue, with the Boer War Memorial
in the foreground. The Armouries
served three generations of Toronto's
military until they were torn down to
make way for the court houses north of
Osgoode Hall during the 1960s.
Colour aquatint by Nicholas
Hornyansky.*

not intervened. The young Prince of Wales, dapper and elegant then (it would be another decade before that Tyrone Power smile was replaced by the sad-hound look of an exiled duke), presided at the official opening on August 6, 1927. The happenstance of a royal tour had brought him through Toronto at a point when the station was close enough to being completed to allow it to open. The opportunity was too good to pass up. The ceremony took exactly 13 minutes—as one reporter dryly noted, a minute of pomp for each year of construction. There is no record that His Royal Highness, who had by that time seen almost everything in his endless world tours, was visibly awed by the magnificence of the structure, but a lesser ministerial member of his entourage exclaimed that "you build stations like palaces out here." After the grimy, barnlike atmosphere of Waterloo and Victoria, the marble temple on Front Street must have seemed palatial indeed.

The palace, alas, was not quite in working order. "New Union Station Hums with Life To-day," the *Star*'s headline read on August 11 when the building was thrown open to the public. The glow quickly wore off when the passengers and well-wishers discovered that the changeover from the old station to the new was by no means complete. The former, which had served the city since 1873, was some distance away, and that was where most of the tracks seemed to end. Passengers were dropped at the old station but were required to walk to the exits of the new, sometimes dodging between shunting locomotives and stumbling over a labyrinth of rails. An energetic newspaperman actually paced off the distance: 103 paces from Bay and Front to the ticket lobby, another 61 to the ticket booth, 110 from the booth to the gate, 149 from the gate to the platform and another 192 to the train itself still in the original sheds. The distance, he reported, was about a quarter of a mile. This was an extreme calculation—not everybody had to walk that far—but it was not until the end of January, 1930, when the new year's rush was done, that the completion of the viaduct allowed trains to enter the new station and the inconvenience was ended.

By that time the new station was in the process of spawning a whole series of structures and pulling the business centre of Toronto south toward the lake. The Royal York Hotel, a legitimate child of the station, had been completed and tied to its mother by the umbilical cord of a tunnel below Front Street. The largest central-heating plant in Canada had been built to heat not only the station and the hotel, but everything on the south side of the street between Yonge and Simcoe. The post office occupied the east wing of the station and the complementary Dominion Public Building completed the graceful curve reminiscent of Regent Street in London.

But the Depression had already struck and train travel was sharply reduced in the decade that followed. The Travellers' Aid Society, whose bright beacon had hung over the corner near the passenger exit ever since the station opened, was forced to cut its staff in half. Hungry families boarded trains headed for the west and what they hoped was a new life. One mother with four children, including a baby in arms, left Toronto for Alberta with just three loaves of bread, a few apples and very little else. Fortunately the Travellers' Aid spotted her, as they spotted thousands, and alerted their branches along the way to help the family at each stop.

The saga of these dedicated women, who met every train that steamed into the depot and who had an uncanny knack for finding passengers in need of succour, parallels the story of Union Station itself. Indeed, the varied work of the Travellers' Aid mirrors the change in Canadian mores from 1927 to the present. One is struck, when reading the old feature stories in the newspaper supplements, by the change of attitudes since the station first opened. In its early days, for instance, the good ladies seemed to spend a great deal of time protecting single women from the attentions of middle-aged mashers.

This concern for moral safety reflects both the makeup of the organization, which sprang out of the YWCA and the Women's Christian Temperance Union, and also conditions in Union Station at the time it opened. Runners from local bordellos haunted those marble halls, hiding in washrooms until the trains arrived and then dancing attendance on runaway farm girls, mental defectives and bewildered new-comers. Conductors were trained to spot strangers who introduced themselves to unattached women and when these men followed their new-found friends into the station, the Travellers' Aid pounced and so did the police. Those days are indeed gone forever.

When the war struck in 1939, the role of the Travellers' Aid changed and so did that of the station. For six years it was in a very real sense the hub of the city. Some of the small incidents reported in the minutes of the society underline the spirit of those times: there was a woman whose nerves gave way after she bade goodbye to her sailor son. There were the two boys from northern Ontario who arrived destitute in a city where rooms were at a premium and who were put up at the Fred Victor Mission. There was the soldier's wife who turned up en route to Stratford to show her husband the seven-week-old baby he had never seen. And there were the two newlyweds, still covered in confetti, who found the hotels were jammed but who were finally put up on a chesterfield in a house on Huron Street.

In 1941, the women's auxiliary of the Canadian Legion, 1,000 strong, dedicated a suite of reception rooms and an information bureau for the use of thousands of soldiers, sailors and airmen who haunted the station between trains. No veteran of that war who passed through Toronto—I was one—will ever forget that bright oasis in the middle of an overcrowded and often callous city.

Nor will the war brides who began to pour in through the station in the mid-'40s, awed, baffled, often frightened by the raw land their husbands had tried to tell them about. "Often they're lonely and some of them cry a little when they talk to me," Mrs. L.M. Curtis, a Travellers' Aid worker remarked at the time, "but they're very sweet...although they may dress and speak a little differently."

But the great emotional moments were reserved for the uniformed men who clambered aboard the trains puffing eastward, many of them never to return. It is no accident that the most poignant of the home front news photographs were invariably made in railroad stations. Mingling with the departing troops were stranger transients: child evacuees from London sent across the water to new foster parents; German prisoners of war, well guarded, heading for the camps of northern Ontario; and later, men on crutches, in wheelchairs and on stretchers being helped off the ambulance trains.

By this time all eyes were turned toward the station. Torontonians treated it in the same way that Muscovites treated their subway stations, and for similar reasons. A gallery of mural art was planned on a grand scale. Organ recitals on a giant Hammond were instituted from three to four every afternoon and from seven to 10 each evening with the church's Dr. Charles Peaker and the entertainment world's Quentin Maclean alternating at the console. The organ was still playing when the troops began to arrive home and the crowds, gay to the point of hysteria, surged back to the station to weep new tears of joy.

Then, for the best part of a generation, Union Station became the focal point for the greatest immigration boom the country had known since the palmy days before World War I when Clifford Sifton's "men in sheepskin coats" helped to fill up the empty plains. The difference was that most of these immigrants were settling in eastern Canada—half of them in Ontario. In the days before the big jets, the greater part swarmed through Union Station—in such numbers that the CNR's lunch counter menu was rendered in nine languages. How many came through? Nobody really knows, but there must have been at least half a million. By 1960 the CNR's colonization department was finding farm jobs for some of them at the rate of 150 a month.

The *Times* of London took note of the scene in 1961: "A particularly moving sight in this century is the arrival, generally late at night or early in the morning, of European immigrants at Toronto railway station after a tiring journey from the ports of Halifax, Quebec City, or Montreal.

"Laden with bulging suitcases and holding small fretful children, they wait bewildered and apprehensive as a large crowd of friends and relatives on the other side of the barrier in the station concourse scan the faces of the new arrivals for someone they may not have seen for many years.

"Of all the cities, it is now to Toronto, rather than to Winnipeg that the immigrant goes in large numbers, be he German, Italian, Dutch, English, Polish, Ukrainian or Hungarian. It is here that work is to be found. . . It is here that 'streets are paved with gold.'"

This was perhaps, the station's greatest hour. Within a few years the traffic declined, and again the Travellers' Aid figures tell the story. In 1945 the Society assisted 100,000 travellers. By 1957 that figure had dropped to 10,550. By 1971 it was down to 4,610. Again the station was reflecting the changing lifestyles of the nation: a large portion of those who tumble off the trains into the echoing vastness of the great hall are transient youths. Much of the work the earnest ladies performed so well has been taken over by new organizations oriented to a different generation—one that scarcely requires its morals policed.

As these words are written, the fate of Union Station remains in doubt. It seems insane that a building constructed so solidly—designed to last for generations—should be demolished after less than half a century. Europe preserved its medieval cathedrals (those that were not destroyed by war) and European cities have profited in a variety of ways from this good fortune. In Canada, alas, we refuse to allow our cities to retain the texture of the past; that may be one reason why they seem so dull to seasoned travellers. It is quite clear that there will never again be a railway station like Toronto's built on a palatial scale as a kind of monument to a time when the world ran on steel rails. The Union Station, after all, is more than a piece of architecture; it is part of our history as a transcontinental nation.

Just as St. Peter's seems to echo with the footsteps of those who went before—peasant, pope, artisan and genius—so the great station has its own echoes. There is the runaway girl of 17 from the Quebec farm, searching for a friend among the pillars of marble; there is the lost four-year-old who answers only to the name of "Dearie" and says his parents are named "Dearie" also; there are the mail robbers trundling a bundle of $25,000 in cash across the tracks and losing it all in a wild scramble for escape; and there is a young man snoring away on a stone bench early on a Sunday morning waiting for a train to come in, as so many waited before him, and so many waited after. The young man was wearing a Stetson for he was not long out of the West and so knew a great deal about railway waiting rooms—but not enough to prevent someone stealing the Stetson from his head while he slept. I have long since forgiven the unknown criminal who took my best hat, but I cannot forgive those who would steal our history from us in the name of "progress."

PIERRE BERTON in The Open Gate: Toronto Union Station *(1972)*

THE MONUMENTAL URGE

Union Station wasn't the only time. From the elegant minor glory of St. Lawrence Hall to the rich blatant vulgarity of Casa Loma and the splendid antiphony of the buildings that surround and define Civic Square, Torontonians have repeatedly been seized with the urge for the grand gesture.

The old Bank of Commerce skyscraper and the Royal York Hotel gave us a distinctive skyline for two generations. It also pleased us that they were the biggest things of their kind in the British Empire.

When the new, dominant Toronto-Dominion dwarfed them, it was satisfying to know that it was the largest work of the world's best living architect, Mies van der Rohe. A century earlier, the top of Toronto was the spire of St. James' Cathedral—not just the finest but the tallest in North America.

Obviously the beaux-arts magnificence of Union Station and the noble curving Regent Street sweep of public architecture to the east of it are right at home in Toronto. We launch

*The main hall of Union Station at the
time of its opening. Pen and ink
drawing by Owen Staples, 1927.*

these new marvels with a fanfare befitting their grandeur. We enthuse and enjoy for a time. But oh, how casually we have let them go.

When they are no longer big and fine and fashionable, when they are merely part of our urban character, we declare them unprofitable. Aided and abetted by the stupidity of our tax laws, we literally write them off and destroy them.

What happened to the once noblest of them all—that ornate Victorian skyscraper, the Temple Building, which resisted the most awesome battery from the wrecker's ball before succumbing in 1970—is but one of many examples of our casual willingness to destroy the personality of Toronto. By far the worst barbarity, only stopped by city council in 1974, was the sustained assault on the most important of our man-made assets: the thousands of fine Toronto houses built during the Victorian and Edwardian eras. More than anything else, these are what has preserved for us a safe and pleasant and civilized central city, and by their juxtaposition and proximity to public buildings and places have made the whole core a living place rather than a necropolitan museum.

Certainly there have been some encouraging individual triumphs in the saving of public buildings. Old city hall, Holy Trinity Church, Scadding House have each in turn been declared absolutely essential for the siting of a new Eaton's department store. Each in turn, after a long struggle, was saved. The Royal Alexandra is still with us, saved by the Russian-Jewish Canadian discount king Honest Ed, when the establishment was willing to let it go for a parking lot. There has been a Toronto firehall revival—one remodelled as a theatre, one as a restaurant, one a community centre and one, in spite of being gutted by fire during the process, is rebuilt as—of all things—a firehall.

But we are only just beginning to move away from the precious-relic approach. "Surely *one* nice bank is enough," said the alderman. "We don't need it: there's a better example of *that* architecture in Pittsburgh," said the history buff. "The taxpayer can only afford a few gems," said the budget chief.

These attitudes, which reflect a willingness to lose the character of our city while maintaining a few costly keepsakes of what used to be, are slowly being replaced by something like long-term self-interest, if not actual wisdom. As they see how creative (and profitable) it can be to save whole environments and to restore older buildings for new uses, at least some businessmen and politicians are moving to a new understanding of the city as a living organism. And the city, at last, has given them incentives to do so.

But in the meantime—just to cover all the options—please let me know if you'd like to join my militant little group to save the Toronto-Dominion Centre.

WILLIAM KILBOURN

CASA LOMA: A COLLAGE

I could tell you the nutty story of Sir Henry Pellatt, the coal baron, who built himself Casa Loma, complete with gold bathtubs, all still on view for the tourists.

PIERRE BERTON

All my life I have been a student of architecture and I have travelled extensively, particularly in England, Scotland, Ireland, Germany, Austria and Italy. I had an opportunity to observe and carefully examine many ancient fortresses and castles. Casa Loma is a result of my observations and travels.

SIR HENRY PELLATT

This huge and fantastic castle was built in 1914 as a private residence regardless of cost—the sum has been put at $2,000,000. With its stables and greenhouses, this sumptuous palace covers seven acres. It was fitted out inside with the utmost luxury; the bronze doors cost $10,000 each. The building is now owned by the city and operated as a show place by the Kiwanis Club for charitable purposes.

Nagel's Encyclopaedia-Guide: Canada (1955)

Sir Henry did, in truth, make some of the most generous gestures in Toronto's history. I think he was snubbed as an upstart by some of the old families, and these took told-you-so joy in his eventual financial downfall, but many a time Dad would come home from working on the panelling of the great halls while carrying a chicken, a sack of oranges, or a box of chocolates for Bessie—all the personal presentation of Sir Henry.

GORDON SINCLAIR, Will the Real Gordon Sinclair Please Stand Up?
(1966)

Still another outstanding feature of the gracious library in the castle is the ceiling. It is very elaborate, as you can see, and moulded into the plaster is the Pellatt coat of arms, with the family motto printed below the scroll in French: *Devant si je puis*, which, translated, means "Foremost if I can."

TOUR GUIDE

Sheer elaboration, as an aesthetic form of conspicuous consumption, still exists, or did until recently. My own city of Toronto possesses an extraordinary example: a palace of an exuberant millionaire known as Casa Loma, one wing of which is bastard French Renaissance and the other wing bastard Spanish Renaissance, like Siamese twins born out of wedlock. But the rise of democracy (in contrast to the oligarchy of which Casa Loma is an expression) gives a functional cast to public art, and thereby to public taste generally, and the industrial revolution has transferred the "curiously wrought" arts from craftsmanship to mechanism.

NORTHROP FRYE, The Stubborn Structure *(1970)*

It's almost sacrilegious to think of destroying Casa Loma.

NATHAN PHILLIPS

Sir Henry was looking tired and drawn. The clobbering he had suffered in the world of money was showing, and I think at the time he was living in a rather obscure apartment, denied even the ornate stables of the castle which had been seized for taxes for some other debts.

GORDON SINCLAIR, Will the Real Gordon Sinclair Please Stand Up? *(1966)*

On March 11, 1939, a raw Saturday afternoon, a military pageant wound in slow time through the snowy streets of downtown Toronto. It was the funeral, at once reverent and martial, of Major-General Sir Henry Pellett. Two months earlier he had celebrated his eightieth birthday at a banquet given by old comrades and friends.

Now he was dead, this man who was older than the Dominion of Canada. His colourful life had spanned its birth and growth.... His mortal remains were borne on a horse-drawn gun carriage, his general's cocked hat and his gold and ivory presentation sword atop the Union Jack which draped the casket. His decorations rested on a purple cushion carried by the Regimental Sergeant-Major who followed afoot immediately behind.

It was a very great funeral, a picturesque and unusual funeral, as big a funeral as Toronto ever saw. The highest dignitaries, ranking citizens and a host of common folk braved the harsh weather to pay their last respects to the departing knight.

FREDERICK GRIFFIN, A Gentleman of Toronto: 1859 – 1939 *(1939)*

If you feel energetic and are wearing warm clothing, climb to the top of the Norman Tower. On clear day you can see Oshawa in one direction, Hamilton in another, and parts of the U.S. across Lake Ontario.

As a climax to your tour, walk down to the basement and go through the underground tunnel that leads to the stables. The tunnel is 800 feet long and passes 18 feet beneath a roadway.

Star Week (1971)

Not one single quality of good architecture does it display; not one possible architectural fault has been overlooked. It is unfunctional, inconvenient, unoriginal and ill-proportioned; its detail naive and gauche, its plan chaotic, its use of materials dishonest (everything you see is a shell masking a steel and concrete frame). Architecturally it is 100 percent hopeless.

And for that very reason we should be thankful that the West Toronto Kiwanis Club was public-spirited enough to preserve it. For its like (we may hope) will never be built again. It is unique and irreplaceable, a significant cultural document of the first order.

ALAN GOWANS, Looking at Architecture in Canada (1958)

NEW CITY HALL

The construction of a monumental building like Toronto's new City Hall is an elevating and exhilarating experience for the community that watches its growth. It must have been so for London and Rome where old men could boast that they saw St. Paul's or St. Peter's rise in all its solemn majesty from the seething human tide at its base to the serenity of the loftiest cross. Such an event is rare in the life of a city or a nation and the whole populace rejoices in its presence.

Out of the 520 architects from 44 countries who submitted designs for City Hall, the Finnish architect, Viljo Revell, was the successful competitor. In the conditions of competition, there was a statement which must have given all competitors much thought, and doubtless influenced Mr. Revell even before he put pencil to paper. It was this:

"In the eighteenth-century city, the cathedral and the town hall frequently dominated the urban scene both physically and spiritually. Our present City Hall is largely overshadowed by commercial and financial buildings, but it still dominates by its presence. It differs in that respect from those centres of civic administration in North America where the 'hall' is just another office building. One of the reasons for this competition is to find a building that will proudly express its function as the centre of civic government. How to achieve an atmosphere about a building that suggests government, continuity of democratic traditions and service to the community is a problem for the designer of the modern city hall. These were qualities that the architects of other ages endeavoured to embody in the town halls of their times."

They were qualities, too, that Mr. Revell was able to embody to a remarkable degree in his design.

Where the Toronto city hall of 1844 lay just outside the shadow of St. James', the present one will dominate the whole city—not that it "vaunteth" itself unnecessarily, but that the ramification of services and the multiplicity of departments of the modern city hall demand a building of truly monumental dimensions. Far-reaching in its influence on architecture and momentous in the future history of Toronto, the new City Hall, like a spring in the desert, will give life and beauty to wide areas about it. For over a century no city anywhere has devoted so generous an amount of urban land for its public square, and the international competition for the building itself focused the attention of the entire world on the corner of Queen and Bay streets in Toronto.

Taller buildings will be built, but there will be no comparable, or no more renowned, city hall. Two centuries are as nothing in the life of a city, but, in that brief span, we have seen Toronto grow from the small military establishment which mounted guard on the lives of the Lieutenant-Governor, his family and Council, whose only protection for two summers and a hard winter was the flimsy coverings of a canvas tent. From that tiny hamlet set precariously on the edge of the wilderness to the proud metropolis of today is a record of achievement hardly to be equalled in history. The new City Hall is the very embodiment of the achievement, and is, at the same time, a portent of greatness to come.

ERIC ARTHUR, adapted 1984 from No Mean City *(1965)*

And the City Hall skyscraper in Toronto. Its two vertical planes soar like the two halves of a partly opened shell; it seems that at any moment the roar of the sea will be heard between them.

ANDREI VOZNEZHENSKY, "North Country Passing," Maclean's (1971)

Every graveyard in Canada, if it could speak, would say "amen" to the slab [Toronto's new city hall]. Well, that's what this buildings says for Toronto. You've got a head-marker for a grave and future generations will look at it and say: "This marks the spot where Toronto fell."

FRANK LLOYD WRIGHT, *quoted by Pierre Berton,* The Toronto Star

(1958)

THE ARCHER

For my office lunch
I have Henry Moore's sculpture, "The Archer,"
in front of the New City Hall,
just across the street from the majestic Old City Hall.
"The Archer" aims directly at the window
of Judge Elmore's office.
Alas, the Judge is dead.
He passed away, lynched by a mob of unfair sentences,
drowned in barrels of alcohol.
He was a friend of both.
I trust "The Archer" and have faith
in his watchdog-like silence.
When he hits the target
justice will be done
and I may abandon my post
and disappear amid the Victorian darkness
of the Old City Hall,
otherwise called by many
The Black Hole of Calcutta.

WACLAW IWANIUK

MAPLE LEAF GARDENS
AND OTHER CATHEDRALS

If I were asked by some stranger to North American culture to show him the most important religious building in Canada, I would take him to Toronto's Maple Leaf Gardens. Unlike most religious buildings, it is not dedicated to the worship of one sect or church, but with marvellous, open-jawed gluttony and Hindu profusion it engulfs the myriad rites and servants of many gods. It has, of course, been an official religious gathering-place since it was built. There, the leaders of the United Church of Canada gathered in solemn assembly to give thanks for their founding and preservation on the occasion of their tenth and twenty-fifth anniversaries. There during the 1930s Denton Massey rallied his vast Sunday school classes and the Jehovah's Witnesses of Canada, plastering town and country ahead of time with thousands of "Religion Is a Racket" signs, assembled their own faithful and anyone else who wanted a more dread-filled apocalyptic religion than the bourgeois churches could offer in those days of desperate depression and impending Armageddon. In the 1950s there was the great Billy Graham revival meeting. And I shall never forget the sight of 300 bishops at the Anglican World Congress of 1963 proceeding in medieval splendour down the main aisle of the Gardens, followed by their flocks from every land and island on earth.

But the Gardens has been used to serve other, older tribal mysteries and passions. There was the mass rally of 17,000 that gave Tim Buck a hero's welcome on his release from the Kingston Penitentiary in 1935. Mike Pearson, in 1962, almost managed to work a well-prepared crowd of partisans into a burst of dutiful frenzy at the climax of his campaign for "Sixty Days of Decision" and an end to the five-year rule of John Diefenbaker. There have been occasions to celebrate the gods of culture: the Metropolitan Opera, the ballet on ice, and the Bolshoi from Moscow. Remember the mild way the Beach Boys, oozing easy sex appeal, did with a crowd of young people what the harried priests of the ad agencies and party headquarters could not manage for the political rallies; and all those other teenage rites, as strange to most adults as high mass at St. Peter's in Rome would be to a Baptist Bible-Belter. There were the swirling, blazing lights and blasting noise of the Beatles' concerts—and screamings and faintings worthy of a mass revival run by John Wesley himself.

Above all, there was the religious cult that celebrated the Gardens' reason for being: Hockey Night in Canada. It was unlike all the other cults in that it united Canadians of all ages and classes from coast to coast: the tribal howl in the hollow of the ear drum in the darkened rooms of Depression and wartime, as Foster Hewitt's nasal radio voice winged above the roar of the crowd. Then there was the Saturday night ritual of the '50s and after, in millions of homes across seven time zones, as two or three gathered together before the household altar's moving screen to watch their gods and heroes locked in mortal combat, about the only gods and heroes left whose actions can actually be seen (or, as Marshall McLuhan would say, "touched"), rather than taken on faith or by secondhand report.

My own first recollections of Maple Leaf Gardens somehow combine the cult of the hockey hero and other, more terrible rites of death and memory. As if it was not enough excitement for an eight-year-old boy to see his first period of

NHL hockey, the vast cavern was darkened at intermission, and a small black box (with ashes in it? or bones? or was it a shrunken head?) was set out under a spotlight on a little stand at centre ice. A trumpeter sounded the last post, and after a minute's silence, the reveille. It was a memorial service for Charlie Gardiner, the great Black Hawk goalie who had died the summer before. For months after, the unnamable ghosts and solemn mysteries from somewhere high among those shadowy heights, with their flags and rafters and catwalks, haunted my dreams.

Many years later, when I moved back to Toronto, I was surprised to discover that the architect of the house we bought had had a hand in designing Maple Leaf Gardens. Ford Howland built our Rosedale house for his uncle, Peleg Howland, the mayor's brother. It was not only "a mighty house," as our four-year-old told the local rector on being asked where he lived, but it held comfortably and happily our family of seven and the two or three boarders we took in from the University Housing Service every year.

I then found that Ford Howland was responsible for other interesting buildings in Toronto. My favourite is still St. Anne's, Canada's only Byzantine church, with its vast curving apse, its gorgeous mosaics and its murals by the Group of Seven. The stunning Virgin Mary being adored by shepherds—foremost of them a self-portrait of the young Varley, red hair, craggy nose and chin, kneeling reverently before her—is in itself, as the Michelin guide would say, worth the journey.

But my subject is *secular* cathedrals. The most popular now is undoubtedly Eberhard Zeidler's magnificent 1,500-foot glass-and-steel vault for the Eaton Centre, reminiscent of the Crystal Palace and of the Galeria in Milan. It is now visited by more tourists than any other place in Canada. And for the local inhabitants, there is in the narthex, at the north of the Eaton store, the bronze effigy of St. Timothy himself, with his well-worn shoe to rub for a blessing, like St. Peter's toe in Rome, receding under the assault of a millenium of kisses.

In the southern extremity of the nave is Michael Snow's magnificent flight of Canada geese, and between and below the constant milling, murmuring crowds of pilgrims. All the place lacks is a St. Theresa in ecstasy, though perhaps I have not been looking sharp enough to see her yet.

The ultimate holy places of Toronto, however, are the headquarters of the great chartered banks. There is the elaborate green-glowing vaulted ceiling of the main hall of the old Bank of Commerce tower, and on the walls around the icons of past presidents, each with his separate lamp aglow.

And there is that fourth member of the quaternity of the Toronto-Dominion complex, the banking hall at King and Bay, black and elegant as its three companion towers, but with its low, stark, solid mass producing an effect that I have always thought must be like that of the Kaaba in Mecca.

The bank towers themselves form a giant cluster of urban sculpture: the three black ones standing among the sheen of the blue-green silver one and the splendour of the white marble one, and, just a little lower, the Royal's pair of golden polygons refracting dazzling sun showers of illumination upon even the drabbest of grey concrete structures around them.

As urban space, the bank complexes are brutally dominant, hostile to ordinary street life and the human scale. "Assyrian modern," says one of their critics. "Fit for the slaves of Tiglath-pileser." The Winnipeg writer, Heather Robertson, now a Torontonian herself, used to think of the bank towers as "malevolent tombs built out of the bled corpses of western Canadians." But she has changed: "Now when I see their tops lost in the clouds, on a silent, foggy morning, my throat catches. Just like the Rockies, I say. I love them."

WILLIAM KILBOURN

IN THE HANGING GARDENS

These are the seven wonders of West Toronto
Campbell's and Christie's and the Goodyear Co.
and the Lakeshore Lions and two I can't remember
and the Hanging Gardens of Etobicoke

Like a dark willow dying by a darker stream
or a barn broken under snow
they loom like waking on the edge of dream
the Hanging Gardens of Etobicoke

Block piled on cinder block assaults the smogbank
from every crevice the delicate ragweeds blow
where Mimico maidens await their dusty lovers
in the Hanging Gardens of Etobicoke

O come to me soon in the night and in the morning
go from me darling let me watch you go
stretching your stretch pants down the asphalt walkways
of the Hanging Gardens of Etobicoke

FRANCIS SPARSHOTT

THE ULTIMATE HEIGHTS

Why not break with the custom of most Torontonians and climb the CN Tower—if only because it is there. It looms at you everywhere, leaning out of clusters of downtown buildings, poking its spire among the treetops of outermost suburbia, sticking out the top of a fat cumulus cloud as you approach Toronto from a distant expressway, glowing at you at night from the United States or Niagara like some carnival Cape Canaveral-on-the-Lake. If you are paranoid, you can believe it is trying to get you; if apocalyptic, that it is mankind's latest repetition of the building of Babel; if tory-radical, that it is the final thrust of desexed, mechanistic liberalism's destruction of all that was Good and Christian and British. The islanders, who see it steadier and wholer than most of us, have nicknamed it God's Zipper.

Toronto is stuck with the thing, and sometime in the next century it will no doubt be the object of a citizens' campaign to clean it, restore it and make it into something useful (a firehall? a park shelter?). So I suggest you emulate the gentleman who always lunched in the restaurant in the Eiffel Tower, because it was the only place from which he could look at Paris without seeing the Eiffel Tower. I confess to being hooked on the CN Tower simply for the chance to spend a couple of hours revolving Toronto and environs around me while the sun sets and the lights come on. Ride to the top of the CN Tower on a clear day and enjoy the view.

Beneath your feet, a quarter-mile down, toy planes are banking over the bay, into the prevailing westerlies to land at the Island airport. At eye level to the east, the brilliant spotlights of the big jets appear, lining up 10 miles apart to move across the city and down to Malton on Metro's western border. From up here you can share the visitor's or the immigrant's first glimpse of Toronto.

But I'll leave the last word on our tallest landmark—and our city's unofficial logo and trademark—to an artist, the late William Kurelek:

"Torontonians seem to be preening themselves on this achievement. I myself find it fascinating and have been watching its growth with interest as I drive down the Gardiner to the west end or downtown. But it seems to me we are making the mistake of the builders of the Tower of Babel.

"In fact, some two months ago I wrote to the CN Tower company asking for permission for a small brass plate engraved with a short three-sentence prayer for humility to be attached to the top-most steel beam. They replied it wasn't feasible engineering-wise, although in the very next sentence they admitted they were attaching several plates honoring the builders.

"I'm not against Toronto's growth either sideways or upward. After all, God's first commandment to man was to multiply and fill the earth and subdue it. And it wouldn't be so important for Toronto to acknowledge its dependence on the Creator if in fact the CN Tower wasn't the tallest free-standing structure in the world. But it is, and therefore it's all the more incumbent on us to guard against coming to a bad end because of vanity."

WILLIAM KILBOURN

SONNET 89

More and more shadow fills our rooms;
high-rises, towers, office blocks
loom newly up, year upon year,
shutting out the pale blue sky, all loathsome

These bird cages of hard blue steel
are to become our death's memorials
when winds alone are the sirens of Toronto
and her streets. No matter. Wave your hand

in greeting now, for in our pots the flowers
bud and blossom still in their many colors
each one of them aware how much they mean

and how much they are loved as pigeons wander
tiptoed on our window sills each morning
tapping upon the glass to be let in.
  GEORGE FALUDY, translated by Robin Skelton

*"Streetcar Elegy", a 1972 lithograph
by Toronto artist Charles Pachter
evoking one of the street cars that have
served the city since 1937. They are
being phased out in favour of a new
model during the 1980s.*

2

THE PAST

Moments in Toronto's History

TORONTO
DURING THE
FRENCH RÉGIME

In the first half of the twentieth century, until his death in 1953, the foremost student of early Toronto was Percy J. Robinson. His book *Toronto during the French Régime 1615 – 1793* remains a thorough and fascinating piece of scholarship. Among other things, he discusses the conjecture by Toronto's first historian, Dr. Henry Scadding, that the city's name means "place of meeting." Robinson establishes instead that "Toronto," which was applied to several places on early maps of the region between western Lake Ontario and Georgian Bay, means "much or many"—appropriate words for the Hurons' land of plenty, abundant in corn, fish, game and wild fruit when it was first visited by French explorers. So when anyone asks what "Toronto" means, I would suggest that the best reply is "abundance."

What follows here is an abridged version of Robinson's romantic evocation of our earliest history.

The east bank of the Humber, where it flows into Lake Ontario, is formed by a ridge whose steep sides are still clothed by vestiges of the original forest. Along the crest of this ridge Riverside Drive winds among the trees with scarcely room here and there for the houses.

There is no monument to recall the past, but this is one of the most historic spots in the lake region, and here we may go back three centuries to the beginning of Canadian history.

*A watercolour (circa 1793) of Toronto
Bay by Elizabeth Simcoe, who made
many sketches of the town of York
during the first three years of its
existence, and with her husband
Lieutenant Governor John Simcoe, the
founder of Upper Canada's capital,
named some of its streets and such
outlying districts as Scarborough.*

This is the foot of the Toronto Carrying-Place with memories of Simcoe and Joliet, Brûlé and St. Jean de Brébeuf.

In the centuries when all travel was by canoe and trail, the Carrying-Place was the link between Lake Ontario and the upper lakes. Running from the mouth of the Humber to the west branch of the Holland, the portage was always traversed on foot. It was a long hike, but the road was good and it saved the traveller a detour of hundreds of miles over the exposed waters of the Great Lakes. The oldest maps indicate that the course was always the same. This was no ordinary trail; it was a main thoroughfare, a trunk line of communication with distant regions determined by the contours of the country traversed. The Carrying-Place possessed a permanence very different from casual paths through the forest. It was as old as human life in America.

May we for a moment anticipate research and weave the shadows of this modern street into a brief pageant of forgotten traffic along the old trail? A midsummer night and moonlight would be the best setting for this reunion of the ghosts of bygone days, but the trail was trodden for so many centuries by human feet on so many errands that if anything of outworn humanity clings to our material surroundings, here at least at any time imagination may evoke the past.

Along this street, when it was only a narrow footpath in the woods, how many grotesque and terrible figures passed in the long years before and after the coming of the white man: war parties of painted braves; lugubrious trains of miserable prisoners destined to the stake; embassies from tribe to tribe on more peaceful errands; hunters wandering into the distant north in quest of furs; Hurons and Iroquois, Ottawas and Menominees, Shawanoes and Sacs and Foxes and, last of all, the debauched Missisaugas, spectators of the white man's progress and participating with him in cruel and dramatic events: raids into New York, the defeat of Braddock, the tragedy of Fort William Henry, the fall of Quebec, the massacre of Wyoming!

Traders, too, of every description knew the mouth of the Humber and bargained here for the precious peltries. Dutchmen from the Hudson before the French themselves had gained access to Lake Ontario; French traders from Fort Frontenac; English freebooters from Albany—they all knew the Carrying-Place, and with or without licence robbed the poor Indian. How various and picturesque they were, these rascals from the Hudson and these lawless *coureurs de bois* from the St. Lawrence, wild hearts and children of the wilderness as truly as the aborigines whom they beguiled. Today there is a dance hall on the bank of the Humber on a knoll overlooking the lake; it stands at the foot of the Carrying-Place; below it is a cove where hundreds of these gentry landed for their nefarious trade. Time has shifted the scene.

Here, too, in sombre contrast with the war paint of the savages and the gay garments of the *coureurs de bois* were seen the black robes of the Jesuits and the less gloomy garb of the Récollets and Sulpicians. Hennepin was here, and Raffeix mapped the shore and traced the course of the Don as early as 1688; and Fénelon and d'Urfé came from the mouth of the Rouge to preach.

Dulhut and Frobisher and many of the other pioneers of the west passed this way. None of them stands out so vividly as the great explorer of the Mississippi with his crowd of Shawanoes and his great canoes, three feet wide, to be carried over the long portage and the "high mountains" north of Toronto. Great days, those, for the old trail when the dream of empire was maturing in the brain of La Salle, a dream that in the end was to expel the French from America!

And there are memories of Pouchot exploring the shore of Lake Ontario and perhaps already dimly conscious that he would be the last to defend the flag of France at Niagara; of de Léry carefully mapping a region so soon to slip into the hands of the English; and of all who came and went to the fort to the east, the soldier-abbé Picquet, and that Captain Douville whose wife was a niece of Madeleine de Verchères. How many of these sojourners idled a summer afternoon on the Toronto river or wandered up the enticing trail into the unbroken woods!

How the Missisauga chiefs from their village nearby must have wondered at the fallen fortunes of the French when they saw the smoke of the burning fort rising above the trees, and what tales of a new order did they bring back to the river after they had sworn allegiance to the British and to Sir William Johnson at Niagara! Strange subjects, these, of the Crown, these first citizens of a British Toronto!

Here, too, at the foot of the old trail, Surveyor Aitkin and Colonel Butler debated with the Missisaugas the limits of the land purchased the year before at Quinte. The Indians had sold more than they intended or they had forgotten the limits of the sale. Here they are, the white men strong in the destinies of their race, and the red men fated to disappear and relinquishing with reluctance the lands of their fathers. Herodotus loved local history and he would have made a striking picture of so dramatic an incident.

Yonder is Jean Baptiste Rousseau, the last citizen of the old French Toronto and the first of the new York, putting out in the early dawn of a midsummer morning from his house at the foot of the trail to pilot HMS *Mississaga* into the bay. The vessel carries Governor Simcoe and his lady and numerous officials. They have crossed the lake in state to found the new town. The band of the Rangers is on board, and for the first time British martial music is heard in these savage wilds.

A few weeks later, the Governor's gentle wife is to be seen taking her rides along the ridge where the trail ran; and in the autumn of the same year the governor himself setting out with a well-equipped party on horseback to explore the communications to the north. And then the trail vanishes from history. The story of the Carrying-Place comes to an end, for a great highway called Yonge Street presently takes its place.

FLOOD-TIME, HUMBER RIVER

Well, our dirt must go somewhere
so why not down this river
so far fallen in grace
that even the loud smell
of our excretion
will not trouble her:

these shallows which once knew
the ships of France gliding over
these cliffs which faced the stern
eye of Brûlé and threw back at him
proud silence, crash of waterfalls.
RAYMOND SOUSTER

EVENTS: 1615–1793

1615, September 9: Etienne Brûlé, one of Champlain's men, becomes the first European to visit Toronto, probably the first explorer to see each of the Great Lakes. Wild, illiterate, irreligious and unpatriotic, he was eventually persona non grata in New France. After some years among the Indians of Toronto, he was murdered and likely eaten by them.

1640 – 90: The Toronto Carrying-Place visited by Dutch and British traders from New York, as well as by French explorers and missionaries.

1720: First French trading post established at Toronto, lasting about a decade.

1750 – 51: A small royal fort, 180 feet square, established on the lakeshore near what is now the foot of Dufferin Street. Fort Toronto (also called Rouillé) is manned by one officer and seven men. It has a store, a bakery and a blacksmith's shop. French labourers and boatmen live nearby. Trading with the Indians is substantial.

1759: When Fort Niagara falls to the British, Commandant Douville of Toronto (related by marriage both to the officer who captured Captain George Washington in 1753 and to the heroine Madeleine de Verchères) burns his fort as instructed and withdraws to Montreal.

1760: Major Rogers and his Rangers take possession in the name of King George.

1763: By the Treaty of Paris the Toronto region, along with the rest of New France, becomes British.

1770: Jean Baptiste Rousseau of Montreal receives a British trading licence and builds a house on the east bank of the Humber.

1774: The Quebec Act preserves the old Province of Quebec (including Toronto) as a British fur-trading enclave. This is one immediate cause of the American Revolution (after which the British abandon the area south of the Great Lakes to the new American republic).

1787, September 23: At a meeting in the Bay of Quinte, the Toronto region is purchased by the British from three Missisauga chiefs for the price of £1,700 in cash and goods.

1788, August 1: HMS *Seneca* arrives in Toronto Bay with 149 barrels of goods for the Indians, including 24 brass kettles, 10 dozen looking glasses, 2,000 gun flints, 24 laced hats, a bale of flowered flannel and 96 gallons of rum.

1791: A separate British colony of Upper Canada is created.

1792: Colonel John Simcoe, a Revolutionary War veteran, is appointed Upper Canada's governor. Certain that war with the Americans will be renewed, Simcoe picks Toronto, with its sheltered bay and peninsula (now Toronto Island), as the natural site for his naval arsenal and dockyard. The capital is also to be moved here from Niagara until a permanent one can be established at an inland site to be called London.

1793, July 30: Simcoe and his party land at Toronto and establish a small townsite and fort, and a blockhouse on Gibraltar (now Hanlan's) Point. Elizabeth Simcoe and her three youngest children set up house in a tent purchased in England from the effects of the Pacific explorer Captain Cook. Her sketches and diary record many pictures and events of the settlement's first two years, but not the sad loss of her baby, born the year before in Niagara.

ELIZABETH SIMCOE'S DIARY: A SAMPLER

Monday, July 29, 1793: We were prepared to sail for Toronto [from Niagara-on-the-Lake] this morning but the wind changed suddenly. We dined with the Chief Justice & were recalled from a walk at 9 o'clock this Evening as the wind had become fair. We embarked on board the *Mississaga* the band playing in the Ship. It was dark so I went to bed & slept until 8 o'clock the next Morning when I found myself in the Harbour of Toronto. We had gone under an easy sail all night for as no person on board had ever been at Toronto Mr. Bouchette was afraid to enter the Harbour till day light when St. John Rosseau an Indian trader who lives near came in a boat to Pilot us.

Tuesday, July 30: The Queens Rangers are Encamped opposite to the Ship. After dinner we went on Shore to fix on a spot whereon to place the Canvas Houses & we chose a rising ground divided by a Creek from the Camp which is ordered to be cleared immediately. The Soldiers have cut down a great deal of wood to enable them to pitch their Tents. We went in a Boat 2 miles to the bottom of the Bay & walked through a grove of fine Oaks where the Town is intended to be built. A low spit of Land covered with wood forms the Bay & breaks the Horizon of the Lake which greatly improves the view which indeed is very pleasing. The water in the Bay is beautifully clear & transparent.

Sunday, August 4: We rode on the Peninsula so I called the spit of land for it is united to the mainland by a very narrow neck

Oil portrait of Lieutenant-Colonel John Graves Simcoe, first Lieutenant Governor of Upper Canada and founder of Toronto (which he renamed York), painted by Jean Laurent Mosnier in 1798.

of ground. We crossed the Bay opposite the Camp, & rode by the Lake side to the end of the Peninsula.

We met with some good natural meadows & several Ponds. The trees are mostly of the Poplar kind, covered with wild Vines & there are some fir. On the ground were everlasting Peas creeping in abundance of a purple colour. I was told they are good to eat when boiled & some pretty white flowers, like lillies of the Valley. We continued our Ride beyond the Peninsula on the sands of the North Shore of Lake Ontario till we were impeded by Large fallen Trees on the Beach. We then walked some distance till we met with Mr. Grant's (the surveyor's) Boat. It was not much larger than a Canoe but we ventured into it & after rowing a mile we came within sight of what is named in the map the high lands of Toronto. The Shore is extremely bold & has the appearance of Chalk Cliffs but I believe they are only white Sand. They appeared so well that we talked of building a summer Residence there & calling it Scarborough.

Wednesday, August 7: I rode on the peninsula from 1 till four. I saw Loons swimming on the Lake they make a noise like a Man hollowing in a tone of distress. One of these Birds was sent me dead at Niagara, it was as large as a Swan, black with a few white marks on it. At a distance they appear like small fishing boats. The air on these Sands is peculiarly clear & fine. The Indians esteem this place so healthy that they come & stay here when they are ill.

Friday, August 9: Some Indians of the Gibbeway [Ojibway] tribe came from near Lake Huron. They are extremely handsome & have a superior air to any I have seen, they have been little among Europeans therefore less accustomed to drink Rum. Some wore Black Silk handkerchiefs covered with silver Brooches tied right round the head, others silver bands, silver arm bands & their shirts ornamented with broaches, scarlet leggings or pantaloons, & black, blue and scarlet broadcloth Blankets.

These Indians brought the Gov. a Beaver blanket to make his bed as they expressed themselves, apologized for not having done it sooner & invited him to visit their Country.

Saturday, August 10: I went to my favourite sands, the Bay is a mile across. The Gov. thinks from the Manner in which the sandbanks are formed, they are capable of being fortified so as to be impregnable, he therefore calls it Gibraltar Point, though the Land is low.

Sunday, August 11: Lt. Smith of the 5th Regiment (who is here as Acting Deputy Surveyor General) read Prayers to the

Queens Rangers assembled under some trees near the Parade. This Evening we went to see a Creek which is to be called the River Don. It falls in to the Bay near the Peninsula. After we entered we rowed some distance among Low Lands covered with Rushes, abounding with wild ducks & swamp black birds with red wings. About a mile beyond the Bay the banks become high & wooded, as the River contracts its width.

Tuesday, August 13: I brought a favourite white Cat with grey spots with me from Niagara. He is a native of Kingston. His sense & attachment are such that those who believe in transmigration would think his soul once animated a reasoning being. He was undaunted on board the Ship, sits composedly as Sentinel at my door amid the beat of drums & the crash of falling Trees & visits the Tents with as little fear as a dog would do.

Saturday, August 24: The Gov. has received an official account of the Duke of York having distinguished himself in an action at Famars by which the French were dislodged & driven out of Holland. The Gov. ordered a Royal Salute to be fired in commemoration of this event & took the same opportunity of naming this station York.

Wednesday, September 11: We rowed 6 miles up the Donn to Coons, a farm under a hill covered with Pine. I saw very fine Butternut Trees. The nuts are better than Walnuts, gathered berries of Cockspur Thorns. I landed to see shingles made which is done by splitting large blocks of Pine into equal divisions. We found the River very shallow in many parts & obstructed by fallen Trees. One of them lay so high above the water that the boat passed under the Rowers stooping their heads. It looked picturesque & a bald eagle sat on a blasted Pine on a very bold Pt. just above the fallen Tree. The Gov. talks of placing a Canvas House on this Point for a summer residence. Vencal the Swede rowed the Boat, a very intelligent man born at Unterburgh.

Saturday, September 14: We walked to the spot intended for the scite of the Town. Mr. Aitkin's Canoe was there we went into it & himself & his man paddled. We went at the rate of 4 notts an hour. I liked it very much being without the noise of Oars is a great gratification. I gathered purple berries from a Creeping plant, seeds of Lillies & spikenard. To see a Birch Canoe managed with that inexpressible ease & composure which is the characteristic of an Indian is the prettiest sight imaginable. A man usually paddles at one end of it & a woman at the other but in smoothe water little exertion is wanting & they sit quietly as if to take the air. The Canoe appears to move as if by clockwork. I always wish to conduct a Canoe myself when I see them manage it with such dexterity & grace. A European usually looks awkward & in a bustle compared with the Indian's quiet skill in a Canoe.

Monday, September 23: I rode on the Peninsula. My horse has spirit enough to wish to get before others. I rode a race with Mr. Talbot to keep myself warm. I gathered wild grapes, they are pleasant, but not sweet.

Capt. Smith is gone to open a Road to be called Dundas Street. . . .

Sunday, October 25: A road for walking is now opened up three miles on each side of the Camp. I can therefore now take some exercise without going to the Peninsula. Mr. McDonell arrived with the Soldiers from Holland's River. He brought some Wild Ducks from Lake Simcoe which were better than any I have ever tasted, these Birds are so much better than any in England from their feeding on wild Rice. . . . Capt. Smith is returned from cutting the Road named Dundas Street. It is opened for 20 miles.

They met with quantities of wild Grapes & put some of the Juice in Barrels to make vinegar & Capt. Smith told me it turned out very tolerable Wine. They killed numbers of rattle snakes every day but nobody was bitten by them. Capt. Smith brought two in a barrel to show me, as I had never seen any alive.

Tuesday, October 29: The Gov. having determined to take a Lot of 200 acres upon the River Don for Francis [their son], & the law obliges persons having Lots of land to build a house upon them within a year, we went today to fix upon the spot for building his House. We went 6 miles by water & landed, climbed up an exceedingly steep hill or rather a series of sugar-loafed hills & approved of the highest spot from whence we looked down on the tops of Large Trees & seeing Eagles near I suppose they build there. There are large Pine plains around it which being without underwood I can ride and walk on, & we hope the height of the situation will secure us from Musquitos. We dined by a large fire on wild ducks & chowder on the side of a hill opposite to that spot.

Friday, November 1: I walked this Morning. At 8 this dark Evening we went in a Boat to see Salmon speared. Large torches of white birch bark being carried in the boat the blaze of light attracts the fish which the Men are dexterous in spearing. The manner of destroying the fish is disagreeable, but seeing them swimming in Shoals around the boat is a very pretty sight.

The flights of wild Pidgeons in the Spring & Autumn is a surprizing sight. They fly against the wind & so low that at Niagara the Men threw sticks at them from the Fort & killed numbers, the air is sometimes darkened by them. I think those we have met with here have been particularly good. Sometimes they fix a bullet to a string tied to a Pole & knock them down.

Tuesday, November 19: At this season of the year there is usually a fortnight of foggy weather, the air is perfectly dry & hot & smells & feels like smoke, it is called Indian summer. I have never heard these smoky foggs well accounted for.

Wednesday, November 20: We dined in the Woods & ate part of a Raccoon, it was very fat & tasted like lamb if eaten with Mint sauce.

Thursday, November 21: An Owl was sent to me shot at Niagara, it measured 5 feet from wing to wing when they were extended.

Monday, December 2: The Great Sail, his wife & 10 children came here, they grouped themselves like Van Dyke's family pictures. They brought us Deer. Francis handed plates of Apples to them. He shakes hands with the Indians in a very friendly manner, tho he is very shy & ungracious to all his own Countrymen.

Monday, January 6, 1794: I sketched a Connewaghna [Caughnawaga] Indian today whose figure was quite antique. I have often observed (but never had more reason to do so than today) that when the Indians speak their air & action is more like that of Greek or Roman orators than of Modern nations. They have a great deal of impressive action, & look like the figures painted by the Old Masters.

Thursday, January 14: There is a great deal of Snow on the River Don, which is so well frozen that we walked some miles upon it today, but in returning I found it so cold near the Lake that I was benumbed & almost despaired of ever reaching my own house & when I came near it the Hill was frightfully slippery. Near the river we saw the track of Wolves & the head & Hoofs of a Deer. The workmen who reside in a small hut near the Place, heard the Wolves during the night & in the Morning saw the remains of the Deer.

Saturday, January 18: The Queen's birthday. The weather is so mild we breakfasted with the Window open. An experiment was made of firing Pebbles from Cannon. A salute of 21 guns & a Dance in the evening in honour of the day. The Ladies much dressed.

Saturday, March 1: The News received of the death of the Queen of France [Marie Antoinette]. Orders given out for Mourning in which everybody appeared this Evening & the dance was postponed.

Tuesday, March 4: Though I wore 3 fur tippets I was so cold I could hardly hold My cards this Evening. This is the first time we have felt the want of a Ceiling which we have not had made in our drawing Room because the Room was rather low.

Wednesday, March 5: There have been apprehensions that the french Republicans at New York would attack Lower Canada from Albany this winter, but a mutiny on board some of their Ships carried them to France. If the Americans were to attack this Province I should go to Quebec.

Wednesday, March 19: This is the Month for making Maple Sugar, a hot sun and frosty nights cause the Sap to flow most. Slits are cut in the bark of the Trees & wooden troughs set under the Tree into which the Sap—a clear sweet water— runs. It is collected from a number of trees & boiled in large Kettles till it becomes of a hard consistence.

Monday, September 8: Mr. McKenzie [Alexander Mackenzie] who has made his way from the Grand Portage to the Pacific Ocean is just returned from thence & brought the Gov. a Sea Otter skin as a proof of his having reached that Coast.

EVENTS: 1793 – 1813

1793, August 27: Simcoe, as part of his efforts to expunge the savage influence and bring British civilization to the wilderness, renames his capital York, in honour of the Duke of York's victory against the French revolutionary armies.

1794: William Berczy, a German American, settles in Markham Township with 60 German families. Berczy constructs a number of York's early homes but fails financially in his colonization, and leaves for Montreal in 1797 to become one of Canada's finest early portrait painters.

1797: For the first time Parliament meets at York instead of Niagara, summoned by Peter Russell, the colony's administrator in the governor's absence. Russell extends the Town of York westward from near Jarvis Street to near Spadina.

1812: John Strachan becomes rector of York and master of the Grammar School (now Jarvis Collegiate).

1813: Invading American forces capture York, occupy the town and fort, and burn the Parliament buildings.

A dramatic aerial evocation of the invading American fleet bombarding Fort York from Toronto Bay, 1813; done in watercolour and pen-and-ink by Owen Staples a century after the event.

THE
TOWN OF YORK

York was the capital of the British colony of Upper Canada and one of its chief military posts. It was the biggest market centre for the farmers and merchants of the colony. It had as many schools and churches as Kingston, its only serious rival. Such was progress, indeed, that by 1825 the population of York had attained the grand total of 2,000 souls and in 1834, its last year as a town, more than four times that many.

York was best reached by boat. In rainy seasons, when stretches of the road disappeared into impassable bog, this was the only way. Coming in from Lake Ontario, the pilots made for the tall lighthouse on the peninsula and steered through the western gap into Toronto Bay.

The bay was always busy: barges, bateaux, York boats, Durham boats with their big hulls and fat single sail, and the timber rafts, each an acre or two of floating camp with crew's shacks and sails stuck on at random like posters in a parade. Smokestack-topped, the immense new black hull of the side-wheeler *Frontenac*, one of the earliest steamers ever built, often lay anchored there. But the schooner was still queen of the lakes, and the two tall masts and graceful expanse of white sail were the more familiar sight.

Across the bay stood the town, a few lines of severely elegant frame buildings perched above the swampy shore on the little cliff that ran between Garrison Creek at the foot of Bathurst Street and the Don River mouth. The flag of Fort

Sleighing and skating on Toronto Bay
in the 1830s, as portrayed by John
Howard, the drawing master of Upper
Canada College, architect of many fine
Toronto buildings and donor of his
High Park property to the city.

York marked one end, the four huge arms of Gooderham's windmill and the desolate shell of the Parliament Buildings, burned in the American invasion, marked the other. Behind the town rose the solemn green-black of the endless forest, still the most inescapable fact that imposed itself upon existence in Upper Canada. A thin gap in the trees at the centre of the long ridge (familiar now as the slope below St. Clair Avenue) showed where Yonge Street climbed Gallows Hill and picked its way northward to the scattered farms and villages in the wilderness.

In front of the town, a jauntier forest met the eye: masts, rigging, sails, warehouses and the bell-towers on the docks. The waterfront was noisy. The fishwives in the market at the foot of Church Street cried their wares. The hammers and saws of the shipwrights were busy on the hulls of new ships. Captains of small ships, the truckers and taxi men of their day, loudly offered to carry freight or cattle or passengers to any of the hundred tiny ports and creeks on the lake. A steamer signalled her arrival by cannon; there was no steam to spare for a whistle. The docking ship was boarded by a swarm of porters, each seeking to snatch a traveller's belongings and carry them ashore. Hotel runners competed to carry off the travellers themselves to their employers' hostelries. It was quieter a few hundred yards west along the shore, where Fisty Masterson, lake captain and smuggler, maintained his cottage and rented punts to admiring schoolboys. Farther west again, just below the well-designed Georgian length of new building that was to provide a permanent home for Parliament, the sentry post was kept, a reminder that the Americans had landed here and captured the town.

In 1834, the town of York scarcely covered the small rectangle from Queen to Front and Simcoe to Parliament streets, today the heart of downtown Toronto. The spot where the big department stores now stand was on the far northwestern edge of town, and a traveller once lost his way in a swamp for hours while hunting for an isolated dwelling in that neighbourhood. Scattered among the woods beyond were the country homes and estates of the well-to-do members of the community. Before the traveller reached the corner of Yonge and Bloor, where the village of Yorkville clustered around a tollgate, he was well into the country of the first pioneer farms.

The countryside abounded in game and wildlife that spilled over into the town. Waterfowl by the thousands inhabited York's bogs and marshes. Deer were a common sight on the streets, and in the nearby fields they were sometimes so numerous that they pastured among the cattle. Mink and beaver, trout and salmon could be taken in the creeks that flowed through and about the town. At least one farmer, driving "a load of pork" before him to market, was chased, pigs and all, down Bay Street to the docks by a bear whose path had been crossed. Early settlers remembered swamps that were the haunt of wildcat and rattlesnake.

In appearance, the shops and houses and public buildings of colonial York were humble enough and, seen in a cluster, faintly suggestive of a barracks. Even so, they were constructed with a certain knack for that civilized clarity of proportion, that superb symmetry in windows and doors that is the mark of eighteenth-century design. Most of the important buildings were on King Street. Near the west end was the famous corner known as "Education, Legislation, Salvation, Damnation." It was occupied by Upper Canada College, Government House, a church and a tavern. On the site of the modern city's giant Commerce Court stood York's first Methodist meetinghouse, two storeys high and constructed of logs. Just north of King and Yonge was the home and tannery of Jesse Ketchum, whose leather made many of the shoes in Upper Canada and whose profits built the first Protestant churches and schools for the benefit of those who were not among the town's leading families. In spring Ketchum covered the swampy road beside his property with tanbark—Muddy York's first real sidewalk.

King Street East was adorned with several fine mansions, perhaps the best of them that of the Canada Company, dealers in land and owners of a vast stretch of territory between Lake Erie and Lake Huron. Also on King East, the square in front of the courthouse afforded space for the assembling of the Orangemen's parades, for the country throngs in town to watch a public hanging, for the promenade of people of fashion on a spring day, or for the small, informal gatherings for gossip and talk and argument that are necessary if a collection of individuals is to become a community.

Across the square stood St. James' Church of England. Although it was small, the classic simplicity of its proportions gave it an air of importance and proclaimed a God of Reason, Aristocracy and Good Taste.

Inside, the Sunday morning sunlight is captured and enlivened by the brilliant white of the pews and the wall panelling.

The elaborate, colourful dresses of the ladies and the men's frilled shirt bosoms and white cravats—"not apologies for cravats but real envelopes for the neck"—are worn as if in defiance of the surrounding forest and the difficulties of life in a pioneer community.

Round the edges of the church are benches for the poor and for the red-coated soldiers who, on certain festival Sundays, parade across town from the Fort York garrison with band blazing and colours flying. In the centre, boxlike pews are ranged in rank for persons of quality: one for members of the legislature, another for the judges and a third for other officers and gentlemen and their families.

At the far end is the pew of state surmounted by a canopy on four square white pillars and emblazoned with the lion and the unicorn, the crown and the shield, of the royal coat of arms. Here sits the lieutenant-governor of Upper Canada, chosen representative of His Majesty King William IV.

The real, the awful presence in that assemblage is not to be found in the pew of state. Look instead to the pulpit, where the formidable robed figure of John Strachan, archdeacon of York, looms like some visible antiphon to the lectern's great eagle of St. John. If York society has a leader, it is this man. The whole bent of his powerful will and considerable intellect is turned to the achievement of his vision. He sees another England in the wilderness of Upper Canada, with the Church as its heart and soul. The Church is to be provided by law with valuable lands, with political privileges, and with the sole right of solemnizing marriages and as many of the other sacraments and ceremonies of society as she deems fit; her schools and universities are to provide an educated clergy for the churches and an aristocracy fit to rule the colony. That he believes it all possible is some indication of how bold and tough a man he is.

John Strachan was once a schoolmaster to the sons of the better families back in the 1800s. Now he and many of his former pupils sit in the councils or the courts of the colony to advise and assist the lieutenant-governor. Now, too, many of the same men sit listening to their old master's sermon. Perhaps it will be enough to mention only the most distinguished of them. This proves to be the tall young man whom any observer must have already singled out as much the handsomest person in the congregation. John Beverley Robinson is the present head of the town's leading family. A militia officer in Brock's campaign of 1812, acting attorney general at the age of 22, for 10 years government leader in the

House of Assembly, he was in 1830 appointed Speaker of the Upper House, president of the executive council and chief justice of Upper Canada.

Archdeacon Strachan's aristocratic pupils are not the only Tories in church. There are possibly more merchants and bank directors and land agents than anything else, bound to the government by the financial privileges and social distinction they receive. In the case of the Family Compact, money is even thicker than blood.

But look at that splendid old Irish gentleman in the corner. He is Dr. Baldwin, the squire of "Spadina," who has recently finished constructing Spadina Avenue to reach his estate on the rise above town. He was once a schoolmaster himself, as well as a medical man, but of late he has been practising law. He recently excused himself from pleading for a client in court, hastened out to deliver a baby, and returned to sum up his case. It is generally believed that he holds some dangerously radical ideas about politics. His notion of responsible government will one day be the foundation stone of the British Commonwealth and will make his son Robert the first popularly chosen premier of Canada. If it were not for Dr. Baldwin and his family, and perhaps a few opposition members from the legislature, one might apply the old saying, to this congregation at least, that the Church of England is the Tory party at prayer.

When William Lyon Mackenzie was in church on an early 1830s Sunday, he would most likely be found not here but at St. Andrew's Presbyterian, taking notes on the sermon for publication in his newspaper *The Colonial Advocate*. His own editorials on the subject of Strachan and Robinson occasionally sound like a Presbyterian sermon on sin, and there are times when his bookstore window is decorated with unflattering portraits of the lieutenant-governor and several prominent members of St. James' Church being roasted by a red gentleman with a pitchfork.

But better not try to picture Mackenzie listening to a sermon. For one thing, it is hard to imagine him sitting still. You had best see him at work, at which, in one way or another, he spends almost every hour of the day and night. In a small, plain structure built a generation earlier for Dr. Baldwin's family, and situated on the bay at what is now the corner of Front and Frederick streets, Mackenzie kept house, newspaper office, editorial room, printing press and bookstore all together. Over the door a small sign announces "The Colonial Advocate, Wm. Lyon Mackenzie Editor &

Prop." Inside it is dim and smells of printer's ink. Long after his apprentices have finished their work and departed, Mackenzie can still be found there, proofreading perhaps, writing out an editorial or, if he is rushed, cramming the words right into the type case as they come to mind.

He is only five foot six and looks smaller because of a slight, wiry build and a large head and high brow. The prominence of chin and the lips pressed together like a vise suggest a will that cannot be broken. One observer particularly remembered the "keen, restless, piercing blue eyes which, when they met your gaze at all, seemed to read your innermost thoughts." His features announce plainly that he is honest through and through, and uncomfortably suggest that if you do not agree with their owner, you must be *dis*honest or something worse. He has lost his hair from a fever and covers his baldness with a loose, flame-red wig that in moments of jubilation he tosses at a friend or hurls to the floor. It would be understating the matter to say that Mackenzie is excitable.

His restless spirit and his popular advocacy of the cause of the neglected farmers who live beyond the town limits have already made him the most controversial member of the legislature. They will lead soon, after a brief detour into the office of mayor of Toronto, to his generalship of an armed uprising and a march down Yonge Street against the government of Strachan and Robinson and everything they stand for.

Adapted 1984 from The Firebrand *(1956)*

EVENTS: 1824 – 1838

1824: William Lyon Mackenzie's *Colonial Advocate* begins publication and soon becomes Upper Canada's most popular newspaper.

1829 – 34: Within five years, British and Irish immigration increases York's population to 9,000.

1832: A cholera epidemic catches York without adequate hospitals, drains and other municipal services.

1834, March 6: Town of York becomes the City of Toronto. Mackenzie attacks the move as a Tory plot to raise taxes:

> *Come hither, come hither, my little dog Ponto*
> *Let's trot down and see where Little York's gone to*
> *Forty big Tories assembled in junta*
> *Have murdered poor York in the city of Toronto.*

1834, April 3: Alderman-elect William Lyon Mackenzie is chosen first mayor of Toronto by city council.

1837, December: Family Compact government, hard times

and political agitation lead to open rebellion. Ex-mayor Mackenzie marches his rebel army down Yonge Street to attack the city. Repulsed, the rebels retreat to Montgomery's Tavern, where they are routed by the militia on December 7. Mackenzie, sheltered by friendly farmers along his route, escapes across the Niagara River to the United States.

1838: Captured rebel leaders Lount and Matthews are hanged.

THE REBELLION
AND AFTER

MACKENZIE'S CALL
TO ARMS, NOVEMBER, 1837

C*anadians! Do you love freedom?*
I know you do.
Do you hate oppression?
Who dare deny it?
Do you wish perpetual peace, and a government
   founded upon the eternal heaven-born principle
   of the Lord Jesus Christ—
a government bound to enforce the law to do to
   each other as you would be done by?
Then buckle on your armour,
and put down the villains who oppress and enslave
   our country—
   a wicked and tyrannical government has
   trampled upon the law—
robbed the exchequer—
divided the plunder—
and declared that, regardless of justice
they will continue to roll their splendid carriages,
and riot in their palaces, at our expense—
that we are poor spiritless ignorant peasants,
who were born to toil for our betters.
But the peasants are beginning to open their eyes
and to feel their strength—
too long have they been hoodwinked by Baal's
   priests—
by hired and tampered with preachers,

*Members of William Lyon
Mackenzie's army marching down
Yonge Street in their attempt to capture
Toronto, December, 1837. Wood
engraving by Rosemary Kilbourn,
R.C.A., 1956, from the original
Clarke Irwin edition of* The
Firebrand *by William Kilbourn.*

wolves in sheep's clothing.
You give a bounty for wolves' scalps.
Why? because wolves harass you.
The bounty you must pay for freedom
(blessed word)
is to give the strength of your arms
to put down tyranny at Toronto.
One short hour will deliver our country
from the oppressor.
We cannot be reconciled to Britain.
We have humbled ourselves to the Pharaoh of England.
They will neither rule us justly nor let us go.
Up then, brave Canadians!
Get ready your rifles and make short work of it.

MACKENZIE'S ARMY MARCHES ON TORONTO

In the last of the December twilight, at 10 minutes past six, the insurgent army set out south down Yonge Street from the Bloor tollgate. The riflemen made up the van, marching three abreast, with a grim determination in their stride, the stovepipe hats of the more prosperous of them stuck dead on the vertical and transforming the first platoon into a silhouette of moving chimneypots against the last crack of the western sky. Behind them the 200 pikemen marched, trailing the 20-foot staves tipped with new-smithied iron, a gesture of respect to the formidable weapon that once had made the Spanish infantry the terror of Europe. The pikes were followed by an oddly assorted crew of musketeers and persons equipped for duck hunting or a turkey shoot. Lastly, by the hundreds, came the shades of the Jacquerie—the great bulk of the army, with their pitchforks and beech-root clubs. Around the whole company, shouting orders or breathing out hoarse Gaelic encouragements, a tiny, bundled figure on a little white mare darted and hustled and circled, like a sheepdog herding its flock to the fold.

The front ranks had covered over half the distance between Bloor and the city limits at Queen when they hove into view of Sheriff Jarvis and his advance picket. These had spent the better part of the afternoon crouching, against the governor's orders and without his knowledge, in the summer vegetable garden of one William Sharpe, Esquire, the back of whose farm figures in twentieth-century Canadian history as the site of Maple Leaf Gardens. In the last of the twilight, all the sheriff could see was a group of dark figures led by a horseman, with a little ghost of a pony coming up beside them. But he knew well enough who they were. He had been waiting a long time for this moment. It was 11 years since the day his oldest Jarvis cousin had inspired the fashionable young men of York to give the *Advocate*'s type cases a ducking the bay, and failed to catch Mackenzie, its editor.

Sheriff Jarvis sent a whispered order along the snake-rail fence. Twenty-seven muskets poked out, aimed toward the van of the advancing column. In another minute the rebels would be on top of them. They could see, indistinctly, the whole rifle company now, and hear the tramp of more men coming behind. Jarvis stood up, glancing along the row of raised muskets. The ground set up a slight, increasing shudder. He gripped his long pistol and peered out into the dusk at the rebels. A hundred yards off still, but they looked closer. Another long second's wait. Then Jarvis roared out the command.

There was a great flash and blast as the muskets discharged. The rebels were abruptly aware of a thunder and lightening leaping up at them from the roadside ahead.

A scene of dark confusion followed. The sheriff's 27 musketeers had no sooner fired than they dropped their weapons and began to scatter, forcefully propelled by a sudden certitude of the rebels' keen marksmanship by owl-light.

The sheriff bugled out curses and commands at his pickets, who were making off every which way into the night at what was really a dangerous clip, considering the risk of a broken leg from the roughness of terrain and dimness of visibility. But this was clearly no time for considerations of safety or obedience, and the sheriff failed to hold a single man to the ground.

Captain Sam Lount, the blacksmith, ordered his front ranks to return the fire, which they did. Then they dropped to the ground to let those behind have a clear shot. But this action was mistaken for the dreadful effects of the enemy's fire. To the riflemen in the rear it appeared that they had lost their bravest comrades at a single blow. For all they could tell, Yonge Street was lined with Tories clear down to Toronto, and another volley would follow directly. Several of the riflemen wheeled and broke the ranks of the pikemen and duck hunters behind. As for the hosts to the rear, it needed nothing more than a few bodies hurtling into their midst, posthaste upon the awful blast, to turn hesitation into panic and a halt into a rout. Mackenzie chased and screamed at one headlong group after another. He might as well have whistled at a stampede. The general *sauve qui peut* had soon put a mile between the opposing forces.

Lount and a few riflemen held their ground, firing sporadically, until they saw that they had the battlefield to themselves. They could not take Toronto alone, so there was nothing for it but to retire up Yonge Street in search of their army. They discovered most of it, halted at last behind the safety of the Bloor tollgate, stoutly refusing to be persuaded by Mackenzie and the other leaders to re-form for another attack. The men said they would willingly advance again into the valley of death, but only by daylight, when they could get a good clear squint at who and what might choose to attack them.

Sheriff Jarvis picked himself up off the frozen ground of Mrs. Sharpe's garden and walked back to Toronto under the total silence of the winter stars. He was not yet aware that he had broken the back of the rebellion.

Through the night Mrs. Sharpe kept watch from her window over the corpse of a cooper from Sharon, a former British soldier, who was the only immediate victim of the picketers' volley. But she saw no more traffic on Yonge Street that evening, and no one returned to break the peace of her garden.

The Firebrand (1956)

W.L.M./1838

The Compact sat in parliament
To legalize their fun.
And now they're hanging Sammy Lount
And Captain Anderson.
And if they catch Mackenzie
They will string him in the rain.
And England will erase us if
Mackenzie comes again.

The Bishop has a paper
That says he owns our land.
The Bishop has a Bible too
That says our souls are damned.
Mackenzie had a printing press.
It's soaking in the bay.
And who will spike the Bishop till
Mackenzie comes again?

The British want the country
For the Empire and the view.

The Yankees want the country for
A Yankee barbecue.
The Compact want the country
For their merrie green domain.
They'll all play finders-keepers till
Mackenzie comes again.

Mackenzie was a crazy man,
He wore his wig askew.
He donned three bulky overcoats
In case the bullets flew.
Mackenzie talked of fighting
While the fight went down the drain.
But who will speak for Canada?
Mackenzie, come again!

DENNIS LEE

SEPARATE INSCRIPTIONS FOR THE GRAVES OF LOUNT AND MATTHEWS, NECROPOLIS CEMETERY, TORONTO

I, Samuel Lount, coming from Pennsylvania
to find work, live a free man,
found work but no freedom.
So, fashioning a pike in the forge,
I walked down Yonge Street, proud of it as a banner.
Though the hand was struck down,
I hope that metal still glows.

I, Peter Matthews, having fought the Yankees
with the Brock volunteers, sniffed out worse tyranny
thickening here, an insufferable cesspool.
Reluctantly, turning my plough into a sword,
I hacked at the leg-irons chaining us all,
but found only justice
dangling from a British noose.

RAYMOND SOUSTER

EVENTS: 1841 – 1899

1841: The United Province of the Canadas is created and the capital moved from Toronto to Kingston.
1842: The streets of Toronto are lit by gas.
1843: King's College, later the University of Toronto, opens its doors.
1844: Editor-politician George Brown, a future premier and

Toronto's own Father of Confederation, founds *The Globe*, at first a radical Grit journal but later the voice of Toronto Liberal businessmen.

1849: St. Lawrence Hall is completed, ready for such stars as Swedish soprano Jenny Lind.

1853: The railway age arrives in Toronto, as the first train leaves for Aurora. The railway is soon extended to Lake Simcoe and Georgian Bay.

1857: Toronto's population reaches 42,000 (doubled in a decade): 12,500 native born, 10,000 British, 14,000 Irish and the bulk of the rest from the United States.

1858: A storm opens the eastern gap and turns the peninsula into the Island.

1867: Toronto becomes the capital of the new province of Ontario.

1869: Timothy Eaton opens his store on Yonge Street.

1871: Free public schooling is made compulsory for the first time.

1872: The Toronto printers' strike is successful and Canada's first pro-union labour legislation is passed by Sir John A. Macdonald.

1876: John Ross Robertson, ace reporter, tireless local historian and founder of the Sick Children's Hospital, launches his *Evening Telegram*, Toronto's most influential daily in local affairs for the next 90 years.

1878: Beginnings of the Canadian National Exhibition, the world's largest annual fair.

1880: Dr. Emily Stowe, after a long battle, becomes the first woman authorized to practise medicine in Canada, and three years later her daughter, Dr. Augusta Stowe-Gullen, is appointed first woman faculty member of Toronto's Medical College for Women. Dr. Stowe and her daughter become the first and second presidents of the Women's Enfranchisement Association.

1883: Appointment of Toronto's first medical officer of health; incidence of smallpox and other dread diseases soon drops dramatically.

1884: North America's first commercial electric streetcar runs in the CNE grounds. Toronto Public Library founded.

1883–89: Areas added to Toronto include Yorkville, the Annex, Parkdale, Sunnyside and east of the Don.

1894: Massey Hall opens its doors and becomes the home of the Toronto Symphony Orchestra and Mendelsohn Choir.

1899: Population reaches 200,000. The E.J. Lennox-designed city hall opens at the head of Bay Street.

*The fish market on the Toronto
waterfront in 1842, looking west from
what is now the corner of Front and
Jarvis Streets. Note the predecessor of
the present Flat Iron building in the
background. The fish wives and
Indians in the foreground are situated
in the area which was developed during
the 1980s into the urban village called
Crombie Park. Engraving in*
Canadian Scenery Illustrated,
*London, 1842, from a drawing by
W.H. Bartlett.*

VICTORIAN
TORONTO
AND ITS VISITORS

A little ill-built town, on low land, at the bottom of a frozen bay, with one very ugly church without tower or steeple; some government offices built of staring red brick, in the most tasteless, vulgar style imaginable; three feet of snow all around; and the gray, sullen, wintry lake, and the dark gloom of the pine forest bounding the prospect; such seems Toronto to me now. I did not expect much; but for this I was not prepared. . . .

"There is no *society* in Toronto," is what I hear repeated all around me—even by those who compose the only society we have. "But," you will say, "what could be expected in a remote town, which forty years ago was an uninhabited swamp, and twenty years ago only began to exist?" I really do not know what I expected, but I will tell you what I did *not* expect. I did not expect to find here in this new capital of a new country, with the boundless forest within half a mile of us on almost every side—concentrated as it were the worst evils of our old and most artificial social system at home, with none of its *agrémens*, and none of its advantages. Toronto is like a fourth- or fifth-rate provincial town, with the pretensions of a capital city. We have here a petty colonial oligarchy, a self-constituted aristocracy, based upon nothing real, nor even upon any thing imaginary; and we have all the mutual jealousy and fear, and petty gossip, and mutual meddling and mean rivalship, which are common in a small society of which the members are well known to each other, a society composed, like all societies, of many heterogeneous particles; but as these circulate within very confined limits, there is no getting out of the way of what one most dislikes: we must necessarily hear, see, and passively endure much that annoys and disgusts any one accustomed to the independence of a large and liberal society, or the case of continental life....

Toronto is, as a residence, worse and better than other small communities—*worse* in so much as it is remote from all the best advantages of a high state of civilization, while it is infected by all its evils, all its follies; and *better*, because, besides being a small place, it is a *young* place; and in spite of this affectation of looking back, instead of looking up, it must advance—it may become the thinking head and beating heart of a nation, great, wise, and happy; who knows? And there are moments when, considered under this point of view, it assumes an interest even to me; but at present it is in a false position, like that of a youth aping maturity; or rather like that of the little boy in Hogarth's picture, dressed in a long-flapped laced waistcoat, ruffles and cocked-hat, crying for bread and butter. With the interminable forests within half a mile of us—the haunt of the red man, the wolf, the bear—with an absolute want of the means of the most ordinary mental and moral development, we have here conventionalism in its most oppressive and ridiculous forms.

ANNA JAMESON, Winter Studies and Summer Rambles in Canada
(1838)

You are at once struck with the difference between the English and the American population, system and ideas. On the other side of the lake, you have much more apparent property, but much less real solidarity and security. The houses and stores of Toronto are not to be compared with those of the American towns opposite. But the Englishman has built according to his means—the American according to his expectations.

The hotels and inns of Toronto are very bad; at Buffalo they are splendid; for the Englishman travels little; the American is ever on the move. The private houses of Toronto are built, according to the English taste and desire of exclusiveness, away from the road and are embowered in trees; the American, let his house be ever so large, or his plot of ground however extensive, builds within a few feet of the road that he may see and know what is going on. You do not perceive the bustle, the energy and activity at Toronto that you do at Buffalo, nor the profusion of articles in stores.... If an

American has money sufficient to build a two-storey house he will raise it up to four storeys on speculation...whilst at Toronto they proceed more carefully.

CAPTAIN FREDERICK MARRYAT, Diary in America *(1839)*

"The blue hills of old Toronto," so poetically spoken of by Moore, exist only in the imagination of the poet, as the land rises very gently and gradually into the back country, clothed with forest, eternal forest. "Blue hills," are, however, perhaps a good phrase, as the distant view in Upper Canada, in clear weather, is always, wherever there are woods, a blue one, and that blue so soft, so cerulean, and so unattainable even in painting, that it is useless to attempt it in poetry or prose. None of the towns in Upper Canada yet display much expense or taste in the public edifices, and Toronto has certainly not contended for the palm.... The public amusements in Toronto are not of a nature to attract much attention. There have been various attempts to get up respectable races, and to establish a theatre, and a winter assembly for dancing; but owing to the peculiar state of society, these attempts have always proved nearly abortive, as well as those of a much higher and more useful kind, which have been made by persons attached to science and the arts. A national Literary and Philosophical Society was by great exertion established; but, after being in a wavering state for about a year, it dropped.

SIR RICHARD BONNYCASTLE, The Canadas in 1841 *(1841)*

The country round this town, being very flat, is bare of scenic interest; but the town itself is full of life and motion, bustle, business, and improvement. The streets are well paved, and lighted with gas; the houses are large and good; the shops excellent. Many of them have a display of goods in their windows, such as may be seen in thriving county towns in England; and there are some which would do no discredit to the metropolis itself. There is a good stone prison here; and there are, besides, a handsome church, a Court-house, public offices, many commodious private residences, and a Government Observatory for noting and recording the magnetic variations. In the College of Upper Canada, which is one of the public establishments of the city, a sound education in every department of polite learning can be had at a very moderate expense: the annual charge for the instruction of each pupil not exceeding nine pounds sterling. It has pretty good endowments in the way of land, and is a valuable and useful institution.

The first stone of a new college had been laid but a few days before by the Governor General. It will be a handsome, spacious edifice, approached by a long avenue, which is already planted and made available as a public walk. The town is well adapted for wholesome exercise at all seasons, for the footways in the thoroughfares which lie beyond the principal street are planked like floors, and kept in very good and clean repair.

CHARLES DICKENS, American Notes *(1842)*

We have been to Toronto, and Kingston; experiencing attentions at each which I should have difficulty in describing. The wild and rabid toryism of Toronto is, I speak seriously, *appalling*. English kindness is very different from American. People send their horses and carriages for your use, but they don't exact as payment the right of being always under your nose.

CHARLES DICKENS, letter to John Foster, 1868,
Life of Charles Dickens *(1872)*

I had been accustomed to see hundreds of Indians about my native village, then Little York, muddy and dirty, just struggling into existence; now the City of Toronto, bursting forth in all its energy and commercial strength.

PAUL KANE, Wanderings of an Artist *(1859)*

It appears that a coloured man killed his would-be kidnapper in Missouri and fled to Canada. The bloodhounds have tracked him to Toronto and now demand him of her judges. From all that I can learn, they are playing their parts like judges. They are servile, while the poor fugitive in their jail is free in spirit at least.

HENRY DAVID THOREAU, The Journals of Henry D. Thoreau *(1860)*

Toronto is the handsomest town we have yet seen. Wide streets, good shops, lovely gardens, handsome public buildings, churches rich in spires and traceried windows, spacious hotels, and elegant equipages. We put up at the Revere House, and during our stay there was a grand Scottish gathering. Such piping and dancing, and throwing the caber! Glorious weather, bands playing, handsome women, wonderful calves (the men, I mean—that is, the men's legs). . . .

CHARLES HORTON RHYS, A Theatrical Trip for a Wager! Through
Canada and the United States *(1861)*

Toronto, with a neighbouring suburb which is a part of it, as Southwark is of London, contains now over 50,000 inhabitants. The streets are all parallelogramical, and there is not a single curvature to rest the eye. It is built down close upon Lake Ontario; and as it is also on the Grand Trunk Railway it has all the aid which facility to traffic can give it. . . .

Toronto as a city is not generally attractive to a traveller. The country around it is flat; and, though it stands on a lake, that lake has no attributes of beauty. Picturesque mountains rise from narrow valleys, such as form the beds of lakes in Switzerland, Scotland, and Northern Italy. But from such broad waters as those of Lake Ontario, Lake Erie, and Lake Michigan, the shores shelve very gradually, and have none of the materials of lovely scenery.

The streets in Toronto are framed with wood, or rather planked, as are those of Montreal and Quebec; but they are kept in better order. I should say that the planks are first used at Toronto, then sent down by the lake to Montreal, and when all but rotted out there, are again floated off by the St. Lawrence to be used in the thoroughfares of the old French capital. But if the streets of Toronto are better than those of the other towns, the roads around it are worse. I had the honour of meeting two distinguished members of the provincial parliament at dinner some few miles out of town, and, returning back a short while after they had left our host's house, was glad to be of use in picking them up from a ditch into which their carriage had been upset. To me it appeared all but miraculous that any carriage should make its way over the road without such misadventure. I may perhaps be allowed to hope that the discomfiture of those worthy legislators may lead to some improvement in the thoroughfare.

ANTHONY TROLLOPE, North America *(1862)*

As we approach Toronto everything looks doubly beautiful, especially the glimpses of blue Ontario's waters, sunlit, yet with a slight haze, through which occasionally a distant sail.

In Toronto at half-past one. I rode up on top of the omnibus with the driver. The city made the impression on me of a lively dashing place. The lake gives it its character.

Long and elegant streets of semi-rural residences, many of them very costly and beautiful. The horse-chestnut is the prevalent tree: you see it everywhere. The mountain ash now with its bunches of red berries.

We are off, off into Toronto Bay (soon the wide expanse and cool breezes of Lake Ontario). As we steam out a mile or

*On May 24th, 1854, Queen Victoria's
birthday, a huge crowd of more than
5,000 citizens, dignitaries, policemen,
firemen and members of the national
societies assembled on the grounds of
Government House (near King and
Simcoe Streets) to give cheers for Her
Majesty and to celebrate their British
heritage. A lithograph by J. Ellis of
Toronto from a drawing by Lucius
O'Brien who later became first
president of the
Royal Canadian Academy.*

so we get a pretty view of Toronto from the blue foreground of waters—the whole rising spread of the city, groupings of roofs, spires, trees, hills in the background. Goodbye, Toronto, with your memories of a very lively and agreeable visit.

WALT WHITMAN, *July 26...27, 1880,*
Walt Whitman's Diary in Canada *(1904)*

I am just off to the Art Schools and the University. Tonight I lecture as usual, will be home I don't know when. I must go to Japan, and live there with some little Japanese girls.

OSCAR WILDE, *letter to Norman Forbes-Robertson,*
written from Toronto, May 25, 1882

We strode down King Street together, past the corner of Yonge Street, below the windows of the hated Temperance and General Life Assurance Company where I had licked stamps, and on towards the Hub Hotel. The Toronto air was fresh and sweet, the lake lay blue beyond, the sunlight sparkled. Something exhilarating and optimistic in the atmosphere gave thought a happy and sanguine twist. It was a day of Indian summer, a faint perfume of far-distant forest fires adding a pleasant touch to the familiar smell of the cedarwood sidewalks. A mood of freedom, liberty, great spaces, fine big enterprises in a free country where everything was possible, of opportunities seized and waves of fortune taken on their crest—I remember this mood as sharply still, and the scent of a wood-fire or a cedar pencil recalls it as vividly still, as though I had experienced it last week....

A pine forest beyond Rosedale was my favourite haunt, for it was (in those days) quite deserted and several miles from the nearest farm, and in the heart of it lay a secluded little lake with reedy shores and deep blue water. Here I lay and communed, the world of hotels, insurance, even of Methodists, very far away. The hum of the city could not reach me, though its glare was faintly visible in the sky. There were no signs of men; no sound of human life; not even a dog's bark— nothing but a sighing wind and lapping water and a sort of earth-murmur under the trees, and I used to think that God must be nearer to one's consciousness in places like this than among the bustling of men in the towns and houses. As the material world faded among the shadows, I felt dimly the real spiritual world behind shining through....

The hours passed with magical swiftness, and my dreaming usually ended in sleep, for I often woke in the chilly time just before the dawn, lying sideways on the pine needles, and saw the trees outlined sharply against the eastern sky, and the lake water still and clear, and heard the dawn-wind just beginning to sing overhead. The laughter of a loon would sound, the call of an owl, the cry of a whip-poor-will; and then—the sun was up.

ALGERNON BLACKWOOD, c. 1890, Episodes before Thirty *(1950)*

COME TO THE VALE
OF THE BEAUTIFUL DON

Oh! come to the valley where the bright waters flow;
Where the maple encrimson'd and giant elms grow,
Oh! come to the woodlands 'neath their shades deep and free;
Where sings the lone wild-bird in the green linden tree.

Chorus:
Come! linger thy footfall where the waters flow on,
By the banks and the glens of the beautiful Don!

When the dew-laden sunbeams all gladly adorn,
Each leaflet and flower as it opens to the morn,
Or when the bright glory of summer's full hour,
Gems each wavelet of gold in a crystalline show'r;

When calmly the twilight, like an Eden on high,
Enhallows the whispers, which the young cedars sigh.
Or woo the pale shadow, when the moon's tender beam,
Is enshrining the vale in a magical dream.

G.A. GILBERT (1870)

HUMBER LOVE SONG

Heard ye of the Humber "Fairy"?
Know ye that her name is Mary?
Queen of beauty—light and airy,
*   Winsome, yet so shy;*
In a cottage by the river,
Where the green ferns nod and quiver,
There my fancy turneth ever,
*   For her smile I sigh!*

When the sun is slowly setting,
Then, my heart with fulness fretting,
All but love of her forgetting,
*   To my skiff I hie.*
Off to "my Fairy-land" I glide,

Each feather'd oar on either side
Like Cupid's wings, they skim the tide—
O'er the waters fly!

O'er the Bay the moon is stealing,
All her loveliness revealing,
Then to each fond heart appealing,
Love looks eye to eye!
Glide we up the Humber River,
Where the rushes sigh and quiver,
Plight our love to each for ever,
Love that will not die!
             J.K. JOHNSTONE

TORONTO
ON THE EVE OF
CONFEDERATION

*Once upon a time, many worlds ago, before there was a Germany or half the
earth's nations were thought of, when medieval emperors ruled Middle Europe
and all the Russias and a Napoleon governed France, when the pound sterling
commanded the commerce of the seven seas and the Pax Britannica protected it,
when the factories of Lancashire and the blackening Midlands were leading
mankind past the threshold of the industrial age and the young republic that
called itself the last best hope of earth had just freed its slaves and fought the first
total war in history, in a time before the lesser breeds of Asia had quite become
the white man's burden or the white man theirs, and before Livingstone,
vanished in the darkness of Africa, had been found by the first ambassador from
the new mass media, Stanley of the New York* Herald—*long ago in that far
distant age, on the first day of July, 1867, the Dominion of Canada was born.*

New Year's Day, 1867, was sunny, clear and cold.

From his rectory study overlooking Trinity Square in the northerly part of town, where he was already putting together notes for his book of reminiscences of early Toronto, Reverend Henry Scadding could look down over the town to the bay, which then reached the foot of Front Street.

That day it was scattered with ice boats and cutters and prancing horses. And the streets below were filled with the sound of sleigh bells and of sleighing parties bundled in their muffs and gauntlets and great caps and buffalo robes.

Even the Toronto Street Railway, whose horsecars pulled travellers as far north as the village of Yorkville, had switched from wheels to bobs for easier winter travel. Though the railway was prohibited by law from clearing the snow off its tracks, Toronto had not gone as far as Montreal, which imposed a fine for the use of wheels in the snowy months.

But winter was the time for travelling and entertaining, and it was easier for the dray horses delivering heavy loads than when they had to pull wagons through the deep mire of spring and fall. The absence of frost and snow in winter was a calamity.

The Toronto *Leader* of Wednesday, January 2, reported that great numbers of citizens had indulged in "the time-honored custom of paying New Year's Day calls" and that the public skating rinks had been even more crowded than usual with citizens who had donned "the magic irons."

The night before, the Methodist churches welcomed in the year 1867 with watch-night prayer meetings, the bells of St. James' Cathedral pealed out the old year in a long concert of chimes, and Toronto's several military bands blared out their gallant best.

That week the Holman Opera Troupe played *The Cobbler and the Fairy* and *The Bohemian Girl* to standing-room-only crowds, and the elite of Toronto looked forward to a splendid *Conversazione* on Sunday, January 6, at the Normal School, when Miss J. Beverley Robinson, among others, would sing, and Dr. May would entertain in the intermissions with "exhibitions of Canadian insects magnified by Oxy-Hydrogen Gas Microscope."

Even on winter days when it was fine, the young people of quality, and not a few of their elders, indulged in the practice of "doing King," which was to say, parading up and down the north side of the street on the 12-inch board sidewalk between the hours of 3 and 6 p.m., past such sights as the Chinese mandarin bowing at passers-by from the window of the East India Tea House, owned by the estimable Mr. Yates, who also, as president of the Consumers Gas Company, lit the streets of Toronto.

King Street was the place "where everybody meets everybody" and "the last quotations in the matrimonial market are exchanged." "Would you know," asked the *Canadian Illustrated News*, "how many young swells are doing nothing for a living? Would you have the latest imprudence of Young Harum Scarum related to you? Or the progress of Miss Slowcome's engagement? You are sure to find them on King Street."

Most of the people of course did work for a living in Toronto in 1867. The occupations listed in a census taken four years later reveal much about the sort of society it was. There were 2,872 servants, 2,184 common labourers, 1,413 clerks and 1,100 carpenters (these were the four largest categories). Among others there were 86 saddlers, 48 brewers and distillers, 302 hotelkeepers (more than the number of grocers or teachers), 683 shoemakers and 232 blacksmiths.

In the fields of crafts and culture, there were 70 booksellers, 381 printers and publishers, 56 carvers and gilders, 41 photographers, 40 engravers and 31 architects, and, in a new category listed a decade later, there were 78 "artists and

*Dr. Henry Scadding, first rector of
Holy Trinity Church and pioneer
historian of early Toronto, enjoying a
fine day in the woods on the site of
Castle Frank, Upper Canada's first
summer cottage, built by Governor
Simcoe, for whom Scadding's father
worked as estate manager. The site is
now occupied by
Castle Frank High School.*

literateurs.'' Sprinkled toward the top of the social pyramid were 109 clergy, 96 physicians, 206 lawyers, 20 bankers and 183 gentlemen. Incredibly, there was the grand total of 108 government employees.

The total population of Toronto in 1867 was about 50,000, though it was well over half as large again as Saint John, N.B., and soon to overtake Quebec as the nation's second largest city. Toronto was far smaller than such American cities as Cincinnati and St. Louis (approaching 20,000 each), Baltimore (nearing a quarter-million) and even Buffalo and the little northwestern city of Chicago.

Except for a few scattered families, the great numbers of Italians and other non-British peoples who were to transform the heart of Toronto in the twentieth century had not yet arrived. The chief exceptions to Toronto's overwhelming Protestantism were about 10,000 Roman Catholics (almost all of them Irish), exactly 157 Jews, 23 Quakers, 66 "without creed" and such odd lots as seven Tunkers and 72 Swedenborgians.

Among the leading citizens of Toronto, primacy of place belonged to the Right Reverend the Honourable John Strachan, DD, bishop of Toronto, in his eighty-ninth year, the original mentor in church and state of the whole Family Compact.

Toronto business leaders in 1867 included the merchant prince, W.P. Howland, soon to be lieutenant-governor of Ontario; the dry-goods czar and pillar of Jarvis Street Baptist Church, William McMaster, who had just founded the Canadian Bank of Commerce the previous year and was to found the university on Bloor Street, named after him 20 years later. And there was the Polish military engineer, Casimir Gzowski, who had become very rich in the act of building the Grand Trunk and bringing Toronto firmly into the railway age and who was later knighted by the Queen.

The most awesome presence next to Strachan was that of the Methodist founder of *The Christian Guardian*, Reverend Egerton Ryerson. As superintendent of education, he was nearing the climax of his successful 30-year campaign to bring free universal education and Prussian efficiency to the provincial schools (in spite of woeful predictions that state interference would utterly destroy the sacred teacher-student relationship).

One of Toronto's most colourful characters was the Ranger of High Park, John Howard, with his flowing white beard and long-tasselled toque. He had taught many of the city's leading citizens as drawing master at Upper Canada College. As city surveyor and, simultaneously, an engineer and architect in private practice, he had had a hand in building almost everything in Toronto—from his own handsome Colborne Lodge, which still stands in High Park, to Toronto's first sewers and the board sidewalks on King Street.

Perhaps the most esteemed amateur and advocate of all good causes was the Honourable George William Allan, PC, one of the original Family Compact Allans, whose father and uncle had stood in a Front Street doorway serenely watching several young bloods hurl the type and type cases of their nextdoor neighbour, William Lyon Mackenzie, into Toronto Bay.

In 1867 George William Allan had already been mayor of Toronto and was later to become Speaker of the Senate of Canada and chancellor of Trinity University. In his lifetime he was president of just about everything cultural and horticultural that ever happened in the city: the Historical Society, the Ontario Society of Artists, the Upper Canada Bible Society, the Toronto Conservatory of Music, the Toronto Horticultural Society and the Royal Canadian Institute.

He was the friend and patron of Toronto's first native artist, Paul Kane, that superb Indian painter who still would tell his fabulous tales of the west to all who cared to listen during his daily summer trips to the Island. But his most famous monument was Allan Gardens, which he bequeathed to the city so that his fellow citizens "could share with him his lifelong love of flowers."

Three of Toronto's greatest Victorian characters were just about to appear on the scene. They were Timothy Eaton, who moved in from St. Mary's in 1868 in order to establish his dry-goods business the following year on unfashionable Yonge Street, with the unheard policy of a single fixed price and payment in cash; Goldwin Smith, the city's leading intellectual and writer, formerly Regius Professor of Modern History at Oxford, who was to arrive, by marrying a Boulton, at the Grange in 1871; and John Fraser, who established the photography studio of Notman and Fraser in 1868 and spread the craze for hand-tinted miniature portraits that had made him the rage of Montreal.

Fraser's own magnificent landscape paintings so pleased him that he once exclaimed before a finished canvas: "The man who can paint like that ought to wear a gold hat." Many of the best Canadian painters—Homer Watson and Horatio Walker, for example—passed through Fraser's engraving and art department, and in the 1870s Fraser was the leading spirit in the founding of Toronto's oldest organization of artists, the Ontario Society of Artists.

Among those Torontonians on New Year's Day, 1867, with a future place in the city's history was Ned Hanlan, a 12-year-old schoolboy whose family had just moved to the Island, where he could practise more readily the skill that would make him the world's rowing champion. And there was Edmund Osler, elder brother of William and later to be a bank president, knight bachelor, member of Parliament and donor of a charming city park, who at 21 had just begun his career as a stockbroker.

Oliver Mowat was already a judge but had not yet begun that quarter-century spell as premier of Ontario that was so long remarked on as "the all-time record for British statesmen," until it was later eclipsed by another young Liberal named William Lyon Mackenzie King, whose early contribution to Toronto's history is chiefly remarkable for his leadership of a student rebellion against the president of the University of Toronto and the leader of the loyalist student minority, Arthur Meighen.

King's political patron, William Mulock, was a young law student at Osgoode Hall in 1867 and already 22 years along the road to becoming Canada's Grand Old Man, chief justice of Ontario until well into his nineties and chancellor of the University of Toronto until his death at the age of 100 in 1944.

My own great-grandfather, a considerable tanner and alderman who was pleased to have his mail addressed simply to S.R. Wickett, Toronto, used to refer rather scornfully to Sir William, who was his exact contemporary, as "old Moolock." I think what annoyed Grandpa Wickett most was that he suspected, quite rightly as it turned out, that Sir William would succeed in living to be 100 and he himself would not.

The most influential of Torontonians in 1867 was George Brown of *The Globe*, the man who captured the loyalties of both the farmers of Canada West and the businessmen of Toronto, mixed them with the old radical Grit tradition, and by the force of his personality and the power of his newspaper transformed them into the Liberal party. Brown's New Year's editorial looked forward to the passing of the Confederation bill that he as much as anyone had helped to make possible, and to a year which would be "the most important in the history of the British North American provinces."

The Globe devoted more space that week, however, to the aftermath of the major event of 1866, the Fenian invasion from across the Niagara frontier. For some oldtimers it had recalled vividly the American occupation of 1813 and the border raids of 1838. But the first Sunday in June, 1866, was still a sharp memory for even the youngest Torontonians. Not a sermon had been preached in York that day, but the churches were packed and couriers rushed in with the latest news from the front and "then a prayer would be offered by the preacher or the company would bow their heads in silent supplication." At 10 o'clock that night the steamer returned from Port Dalhousie with the dead and the wounded on its decks from the battle of Ridgeway. It was greeted at the Yonge Street wharf by an immense throng, and the following Tuesday, to the tolling of bells and bands playing the Dead March, the whole city lined the streets to watch the half-mile-long funeral procession of gun carriages, soldiers and mourners. As *The Globe* put it, "The autonomy of British America is cemented by blood shed in battle." It was of no consequence that the volunteers of the Queen's Own Rifles had suffered tactical defeat at Ridgeway at the hands of battle-hardened American Civil War veterans.

The battle, incidentally, gave young Colonel George Taylor Denison III (whose great-grandfather had settled in York in Governor Simcoe's time, and who commanded, like his father and grandfather before him, Denison's Horse) some of the experience that later enabled him to win the czar of Russia's essay prize on cavalry, against competitors from all over the world.

Short of the great question of nationhood, a major concern of *The Globe* was to lend support for the campaign that by the 1890s had made Toronto a place where the streetcars could not run on Sundays. *The Globe* was death on any breach of the new Sabbath Day laws: "A number of youths were enjoying themselves playing 'shinty' yesterday on Clare Street," it reported. "His Worship the Mayor saw their proceedings and instructed Constable Bradshaw to arrest them. He succeeded in taking a boy, but whilst conveying him to the station, an alderman discharged him. Justice should not be frustrated in this way. If the law is broken, the offender should certainly be punished as a warning to others.

"Alderman Ewart expressed his sorrow for having ordered the release of the young culprit on Sunday, but said he was a very small boy and crying as if his heart would break. The other boys who had been playing were older and ran away."

On another such occasion *The Globe* editorialized in that familiar tone of voice which has comforted generations of respectable Torontonians ever since: "Twenty-four hours in the cells would be a good means of stopping boys from practices of this kind on the Sabbath."

The Globe also took up the cause of abstinence, first espoused by such worthy papers as *The Christian Guardian* and *The Canadian Son of Temperance and Literary Gem*. Its columns of city news were daily full of reports of drunk and disorderly charges and stiff fines and sentences. There had been hope for one victim who "addressed the court with unmistakable brogue and eloquence" but, thank heaven, "justice was inexorable."

Considering the vast number of hotels, taverns and dram shops in Toronto, and what green rye whiskey by the dipperful did to the human constitution, there is some justification for sympathizing with *The Globe*'s conviction that drunkenness had reached the proportions of an epidemic, and was a serious enemy of public order and the efficient operation of the new railways and factories. Harsh Sabbath laws were not merely an industrial society's reaction to frivolity and boyish play as the enemies of profit and progress. They also expressed a new humanitarian concern to relieve the working classes from their otherwise continual round of labour.

There was a grandeur and gusto about even the sternest of our Victorian predecessors, and the gradual lessening of that spirit may explain why reaction against Toronto's Protestant mores arose not in 1867 or 1897, but later in the next century.

Certainly there was little thought of saving a few pennies per citizen by stinting on the glory of a new public building. No merchant considered his dry-goods emporium complete without the exuberant exercise of the designer's and sculptor's and painter's imagination upon it. A gargoyle or a wrought-iron grill was well worth the week's labor of a skilled carver or smith.

Above all, Toronto possessed a palpable and vital sense of community that it never entirely lost. The curving twin towers of our new acropolis, flanked by the sacred shrines of the law and the proud battlements of the old city hall, proclaim a concept of both liberty and order, and new possibilities of relationships between persons better than either Athens or Henry Scadding knew. And who knows? Toronto may yet find a way of letting Scadding's successor look out upon the skaters on Nathan Phillips Square without pulling down the best of our Victorian past.

FROM VICTORIAN TO GEORGIAN TORONTO: SEVEN SKETCHES OF THE CITY 1899–1950

THE BOERS AND THE EMPIRE

Bands blazed, Union Jacks waved, mothers wept, and suddenly Toronto was part of a wilder, nobler, more exciting world.

It was October 25, 1899, and our own volunteers were bound for a rendezvous with death and glory in the land of Rhodes and diamonds, soldiers of the Queen in the newest outpost of her Empire and ours.

The whole parade route, from the armouries to Jarvis Street, back on King and down to the station, was "one great shout of praise."

"One might have walked on the heads of the people all the way," said one witness. "Every window was white with faces. No page of the city's history records an outburst of enthusiasm to equal it."

It was the ritual climax to a week of lesser ceremonies and mounting passions. The name and regiment of each man who passed his fitness test were listed on the front page of the newspapers.

The headlines celebrated each evening "a splendid rush" by British troops or a levelled-bayonet charge against the Boers, and recorded the daily toll of British officers—by name again—picked off by sharpshooters, because it was still considered unbecoming for them to seek cover with their men.

City council debated the appropriate gift for each member of the Toronto contingent. The public, it was felt, would smother them with "delicacies," so council decided on a purse of £25 along with a revolver and field glasses for each officer, and five gold sovereigns for each man.

Their commander, Colonel Otter, formerly CO of the Queen's Own Rifles, had already led Ontario boys against rebels—the Indians and Riel's French-Canadian half-breeds on the Empire's northwest frontier. He was offered £150 and the adulation of the city.

The social notices recorded each little farewell party. The grandest was for the soldiers of "C" Company, who arrived in full dress uniform at the Princess Theatre for a performance of *Faust* and were presented to the audience. "An orchestral program of national airs" provided a stirring climax.

That week William Briggs' bookstore afforded the public a wide choice of Books for the Hour, ranging from *Imperial Defence* by Sir Charles Dilke to *Our Living Generals* and *Deeds that Won the Empire* and *Tommy Atkins of the Ramchunders*. The only discernibly Canadian item was *Canadian Battlefields and Other Poems* by Lieutenant-Colonel Wilkinson.

Another merchant advertised gas fixtures on a patriotic note: "The pick of our boys are off to lighten the dark of South Africa. Some of us are left behind to lighten the homes of Toronto—just let us smell powder, or in other words call in and see us."

The purveyors of Slocum's Expectorant did not attempt a martial metaphor, and the Electric Bitters people stuck to their hard sell about fermented food and gas attacking the kidneys, but a variety of other advertisers were appropriately patriotic. The Grand Trunk Railway offered first-class return passage—to see the South Africa contingent sail from Quebec—for the price of a single fare.

"The war, the war! there is nothing else discussed today," wrote The Gossip in the *Star*'s regular feature, "Topics for the Tea Table." "Tonight sisters will cling to brothers bidding them to stay, even as they push them away. Tonight lovers will stand with dulled eyes, teeth clenched and lips set hard."

But there was no question where duty lay: "The bluest blood of the Mother Country has already stained the dark veldt. Hot Irish blood has poured forth and staunch Scots hearts shed their last drops. And now Canada—our Lady of the Snows—is offering a thousand of her sons, the rich blood of loyalty flowing hot in her veins."

Torontonians had recently witnessed the conclusion of one satisfactory imperial adventure. "You furnish the pictures

Celebration of Boer War victory on
Yonge Street (near Adelaide), June 5,
1901, Pretoria Day.
Everybody wears a hat!

and I'll furnish the war," wired William Randolph Hearst to his reporter in Cuba. Through the rest of 1898 the papers satisfied a popular taste for stories of Anglo-Saxon triumphs over lesser breeds with dispatches from the Spanish-American War, though one Toronto newspaper warned the Americans against conquering the unmanly Latins and so undermining the "influence of Anglo-Saxondom" with alien racial stock.

For Toronto itself there still appeared no prospect of being anything but a British community. But Sir Wilfrid Laurier's hesitant compromise over sending troops in Britain's hour of need confirmed Orange doubts about electing a French-Canadian prime minister.

Although the *Star* cautioned against talk of taking rights away from French Canadians for showing Boer sympathies, the *Toronto News* flatly denounced our "French" rulers: "This Dominion is in the grip of foreigners who have no taste for British advancement. They would cast off their allegiance to Britain's Queen tomorrow if they dared. Only a whole-some fear of what would happen to them at the hands of the more virile people of Ontario and the West restrains them."

It was just over a month since Major John Shaw had spoken, at its opening, of Toronto's new and glorious, gargoyled, pink-stone city hall as the symbol of the people's aspirations and their moral calling. He now spoke with equal warmth, as he bade the Toronto boys godspeed, of "the high imperial destiny of the British race" and the righteousness of their cause. Both sentiments together perfectly expressed the Toronto of 1899. The Empire was the means to that rule of universal law and progress and the arts of civilization celebrated in the Romanesque splendour of the new building.

Perhaps the least enthusiasm for the war was shown by the churches, although predictably enough the newspaper summaries of the week's Sunday sermons included one denunciation of the Boers as a selfish, cruel and unjust race.

University students celebrated Trinity's fall convocation by burning Oom Paul Kruger in effigy. But one recent graduate found the war repugnant. He thought back to the grievances of Canada in 1837 and British failure to understand and act until it was too late, and wondered whether the Boers might not have been more amenable to reason and conciliation. His name was William Lyon Mackenzie King.

THE SOUTH AFRICAN WAR MEMORIAL, UNIVERSITY AVENUE

Old men come here, stare at the statue
of two young warriors walking into the drum-fires
with that easy look Canadians take to battle
MAFEKING
CAPE COLONY
BLOEMFONTEIN
pigeons light on the statue
defile it lovingly with their droppings
weather has stained the proud bronze a sickly green
but the young men still carry that sure look into the drum-fires
and the old men squinting up at them are suddenly young
    again, warriors,
fighting the battles that nobody remembers.
                    RAYMOND SOUSTER

1901: THE QUEEN'S OWN CITY

More than most towns in the realm, Toronto was very much the Queen's own—in mansions, morals and attitudes the epitome of High Victorian.

A fledgling three-year-old city that June morning in 1837 when the young princess was greeted with the news of her accession, by 1901 Toronto had grown up to riches and style in the long summer of Victoria's 64-year reign. There were few people left who could remember Family Compact Toronto, although such old names as Robinson and Denison were still prominent.

The toy-soldier town of colonial streets and plain little Georgian buildings had almost disappeared before such monuments of progress as the Flatiron Building wedged between Front and Wellington streets, the escalators of Timothy Eaton's store, the Romanesque campanile of city hall, and North America's tallest steeple (on St. James' Cathedral).

From the tallest vantage points downtown, *The Mail* and the Canada Life buildings, you could see all the way to the Crystal Palace in the grounds of the world's largest annual exhibition, the citizens' "carnival of instruction, business and amusement."

The Queen's Hotel was where all famous Victorian visitors stayed—from Jenny Lind to General Sherman and the

Prince of Wales. It was not itself the victim of progress until torn down to make way for the Royal York in the 1920s. Its handsome rates of $3 a day and up were justified not only by its clientele but by all its modern appointments: the first hot-air furnace, the first elevator, first electric bells, first baths and running water for bedrooms in a Toronto hostelry.

Progress itself was fashionable. Being a telephone operator was one job a girl of the better class could decently accept. And to accommodate the telephone, a forest of wooden poles and wires was springing up fully grown on the city streets. Adam Beck's Ontario Hydro, with its flickery 25-cycle delivery, began finding new uses for "white coal," and there was no stopping its spread. Chief harbinger of the electric age was the street railway, however, running again on Sundays after an enforced spell of holy rest in the 1890s. Radial cars were planned to link Toronto with a network of satellite towns.

At the foot of the Yonge Street hill you could start out for Holland Landing and the Lake Simcoe steamer on a Metropolitan car. The electric railway made settlement in a host of new distant suburbs feasible; between 1905 and 1910 the city annexed East and West Toronto, Wychwood, Bracondale, North Rosedale, Deer Park and the Baldwin Estate at the top of Spadina.

The open belt line car, round Sherbourne, Bloor, Spadina and back on King—an hour's ride for a nickel—was an entertaining way to cool off and do the town on a hot summer evening.

For the rich and adventurous, there was, of course, the splendour of the automobile—Toronto's homemade Russell car, for example, lovingly fitted by hand from crankshaft to shiny brass knobs and carbide headlamps. But driving was a matter of goggles and duster and the hazards of mounting the loose sand on the long Bloor Street hill by High Park or traversing the quagmires of north Yonge Street.

If you really meant business, you still had to get a horse.

The paddy wagon came flying down the street behind the police horses. The fire engines' huge tea kettle was pulled by animals trained to run into their traces at the sound of a bell. One newspaper's circulation manager bought a thorough-bred that had won several races at Woodbine in order to improve his image and outspeed his competitors.

Simpsons owned a stable of dapple greys and delivered parcels by sleigh in wintertime. For the comfort of exhausted travellers, Toronto's better hotels sent their stagecoaches with red plush seats to meet the incoming trains.

The way to pay a call at a good address—Jarvis or St. George or Queen's Park—was behind a coachman and a high-stepping pair. Take an open Victoria and black silk parasol in summer and bundle into the sleigh's buffalo robes in winter.

One of the sights of Toronto was the daily drive, during the racing season at Woodbine, of the daughter of Senator Sir Lyman Melville Jones. Lady Eaton recalls in her memoirs that people used to gather at points along her route just to catch a sight of the haughty, fair young lady, "not beautiful but with a complexion and an hourglass figure," driving her team of magnificent bays while the coachman sat stiffly perched on the tiger seat at the rear of the carriage.

In later years, as the wife of Reverend T. Crawford Brown, she remained one of those figures whose very presence would remind Toronto of its Victorian upbringing.

1914: PEACE YEAR AT THE CNE

None of Toronto's new millionaires accompanied the glittering generation of affluent Americans who went down with the *Titanic*, though Eaton's chief European buyer and three other Torontonians were lost.

But Sir Henry Pellatt sank spectacularly enough, in the great stock market crash of 1913. His Casa Loma, like the *Titanic*, provided a towering symbol—as well as a gravestone—to mark the pride and excess of a gilded age, and an omen of the greater doom to come in history's most terrible war.

Back in the halcyon days of the sculling king of the world, Ned Hanlan of Hanlan's Point, young Henry Pellatt cut a figure in Toronto by becoming North America's champion mile-runner. But only as a rising broker in the prosperity of the *Titanic* era could he make gestures the size of his desires. Whether the twentieth century would belong to Canada or not, there were new Toronto millionaires who clearly believed that at least a good piece of Canada could belong to them. In 1902 Pellatt spent one of his earlier fortunes on shipping the bugle band of the Queen's Own Rifles over to blow at the coronation of Edward VII. In 1910 he took the entire regiment to the Imperial Army's annual manoeuvres at Aldershot.

Sir Henry was but the most spectacular of Toronto's self-made men. Another was one of Laurier's financial wizards, Senator Cox of Canada Life and the Sherbourne Street

Methodist Church. Two were Upper Canada College school-masters: George Cockburn, who ultimately became president of the Bank of Ontario, and Edward Peacock, who rode the Ontario countryside selling bonds for E.R. Wood's Dominion Securities and who later became a director of the Bank of England.

Along with the western wheat and real estate booms, the great northern Ontario mining strikes of the 1900s—control of the industry had been captured from under Montreal's nose by Toronto financiers—helped build Toronto's preeminence in stocks and bonds. The climax of prosperity came in 1910 – 12 when dozens of old family firms were merged and refinanced by men such as Sir Edmund Osler, William's older brother, who had long since established his house, Craigleigh (now a quiet Rosedale park with only the gates still standing), as one of the social centres of Toronto.

Those who captured the imagination now were men of wealth or social muscle and bold deeds in business, the captains and the crews of industry. "Canadian's great artists to-day," said a *Globe* writer in 1910, "are not the whole busy bunch of story tellers and verse writers, but men like Mackenzie and Mann" [Sir William and Sir Donald, the contractor-knights, who were honoured for growing rich from building us an extra transcontinental railroad we didn't need] and those epic-minded workers who are writing a new kind of blank verse in townsites and railway iron."

Whether Toronto's working classes were epic-minded or not, there were certainly more of them—working a 60-hour, $20-week in the factories, as the boom and then the war replaced the small foundries and carriage shops with larger plants and the first assembly lines.

For the first time, Toronto's immigrants included not only the Irish labourers of Cabbagetown and the British clerks and artisans of the Danforth but people from all parts of Europe. Their numbers grew to 30,000 by 1910, and nearly 100,000 by 1920, which made them a sizable bloc of the city's 1921 census population of 521,000, a total that had itself more than doubled since the turn of the century.

In that decade there was no such thing as a "New Canadian." The "Fifteen Brawling Polacks" (*Star* headline, April, 1912) and the protesting "Hebrew" from the Ward whose cart was forcibly seized, paid for in full (this *was* a British city after all) and burned as part of the victory celebrations the night of November 11, 1918, these people were "foreigners"—the sort who, when they got the vote, joined the French and a lot of subversive Wobblies and unionists like that Reverend Woodsworth in protesting against conscription. Was not the war being fought for "Highest Beliefs"?

Another side of the same stern dedication to duty and ideals that could send whole battalions so bravely and blindly to slaughter in the quagmires of France was exhibited by the redoubtable dean of Toronto journalists, Ernest Sheppard, some years before the war.

In an article on the need for strict application of the death penalty, he wrote, "History, religious doctrine, everything, proves that mankind will always be either blood-thirsty or sensual. Of the two, give us blood-thirstiness.

"The man who does not care whether he lives or dies is less dangerous than the man who does not care what happens so long as he lives and can satisfy his desires. There are already too many people unfit to live. Let them be removed...and give the honest people a chance."

The age of the Casa Loma millionaire and the Cabbagetown labourer had little sympathy for mere human beings. And yet the lasting impression of Toronto on the eve of Armageddon is one of vulnerable innocence and contentment.

It was a school-days world of red readers and nib pens, boots and "breeks" and gingham; of girls' wand drill and dumbbells and much marching to the sound of the Victrola; of live tableaux swathed in gauze and jiggly movies like *Jessica's First Prayer*, improving to the soul if not the eyes. One Toronto schoolgirl who used to sail leaf boats in the puddles near Dundas and University was suddenly back downtown again—Mary Pickford as Tess of the d'Urbervilles or Little Lord Fauntleroy in long curls—crowding half the burlesque shows off Shea's Hippodrome stage.

It was a world of innumerable outings and excursions: on the paddlesteamer *Chippewa* to Niagara, the *Primrose* or the *Mayflower* across the bay to the old ball park on Hanlan's Point; for Sunday school picnics to the Beaches or one of the farms north of St. Clair; boating up the Humber to the Old Mill or on one of the Island lagoons; tramping for miles through the wild ravines in what is now the centre of Toronto; boarding the train to Mariposa and the cottage country at Parkdale Station.

Appropriately, 1914 was to be Peace Year at the CNE. But before the floral tributes and festooned buildings were in readiness to illustrate their theme, Toronto's volunteers of the first contingent were drilling at Valcartier in frenzied preparation for the long voyage overseas from which so many would never come home.

THE TWENTIES

Two suave and impossibly eminent physicians are deep in earnest conversation in the *Star* advertisement, watched from a respectful distance by a pair of adoring young things with bobbed hair and cloches.

"I want to congratulate you, Doctor, on the great success I hear you are having with your throat cases. Wish you'd take a look at mine."

"I guess, Doctor, I will have to introduce you to Formamints, an antiseptic with which you will keep the soft tissue in an almost constant antiseptic bath. . . ."

And so on, through talk of influenza, and how "they are certainly heading off a lot of tonsillitis, but I am interested in their prophylactic power. . . ."

The Toronto doctor in the '20s still had about him the sacred aura of the country GP who would harness his team for a two-hour drive at midnight. But he also inherited the new prestige of science: Einstein and Freud, the IQ test and the Aspirin, the Great War's new wonder drug.

The world's greatest doctor, Sir William Osler, was a Canadian. Pride of place in the Canadian *Who's Who* went to Colonel Dr. Herbert Bruce, later to be Ontario's lieutenant-governor, silver-haired and handsome in his Sam Browne and war decorations. And Dr. Jackson was preparing his stoic assault on the unscientific regimen of the Toronto stomach with his patented Roman Meal and Bekus Puddy— the production of which soon became a sizable part of the city's baking industry.

About the only thing a doctor couldn't readily command was research money. Fred Banting, the gentle, slow-spoken young MD home from the trenches, was given $100 worth of lab time and equipment in the summer of 1921. He was also given the help of a bright 22-year-old physiology graduate named Best—partly, it was suspected, to see he didn't waste anything. Together they chugged about downtown Toronto in their Model T, "The Pancreas," hunting for dogs at $1 apiece for their experiments. They ate eggs and sausages fried over a Bunsen burner to save time and money, and when they had proved a hunch about diabetic dogs, risked their lives by taking extract themselves before using other human guinea pigs. By January they made ready to announce perhaps the greatest single victory over a killer disease in medical history: the isolation of insulin, and new hope for diabetes sufferers.

Among the University of Toronto's other contributions to the community were its chancellor and later president, Archdeacon Henry John Cody, rector of St. Paul's, who had also recently been Ontario's minister of education; and such great teachers as the classicist Maurice Hutton, who retired after a half-century and wrote a book called *The Sisters Jest and Earnest*.

Lester Pearson was teaching history, and Harold Innis was working on a theory about civilization and the Canadian fur trade that later led straight into the approach of his most famous disciple, Marshall McLuhan.

On the national stage, the two young prime ministers of the '20s, Mackenzie King and Arthur Meighen, had previously confronted each other as the leaders, respectively, of the rebel and loyalist factions in the University of Toronto student strike.

Near the new Royal Ontario Museum, where Charles J. Currelly was being encouraged by such patrons as Sir Edmund Walker to bring the ages home, the Varsity rugby team, cheered by cutups in coonskin and peered at from the stadium roof by such pioneer wireless telephone broadcasters as Harry "Red" Foster, played a bony, unpadded sort of game that could win them a crack at another Grey Cup—if they beat Balmy Beach, Ted Reeve's spirited ORFU champs. The ultimate model of the gridiron was the Big Train, Lionel Conacher, who could play all the other popular sports, too, such as lacrosse.

After the game a coed might hope—with the help of rouge and fox trots and saxophones—to vamp a fellow who had his hair midparted and plastered down like Rudy Vallee's. She might even have been enticed by the movie ads to dream of "brilliant men, beautiful jazz babies, petting parties in the purple dawn" or "white kisses, red kisses, the truth."

It was easy enough to get "blotto," in spite of Ontario's prohibition of spirits and the detectives who boarded the Montreal – Toronto trains at Oshawa in search of liquor. Denunciations of the still-legal beverage rooms ("trap-doors to hell") by Dr. T.T. Shields of Jarvis Street Baptist Church made drink just that much more wicked and "smart."

But temperance, too, was just as thoroughly modern. The WCTU after all had been a magnet for radical women, and they attacked the male monopoly of the vote as furiously as the male's escape into the saloon.

Emancipation meant that wartime overalls and then the knee skirt replaced the boa and big hats and the flowing line and yards of petticoats. It also meant household science— save labour with an electric iron and a Hoover; forget about home preserves and shop by phone for canned goods; beautify your kitchen with an "iceless refrigerator."

The ice wagon, like all the other horse-drawn vehicles, was slowly disappearing from the streets of Toronto. No one paid much attention when the closed motorcar was denounced as "a house of prostitution on wheels." By the end of the decade there were more than a million of them in Canada and you could travel around Toronto without making each trip into a hazardous adventure—all the way up Yonge Street to the far northern suburb of Lawrence Park, or across the new Prince Edward viaduct beyond Bloor Street East, which ended the old isolation of the Danforth. Or even down into the filled-in land on the bay, where water used to lap at the shore just below Front Street.

By 1920 the Toronto motorist no longer had to ship his car to Hamilton by steamer if he wanted to do some out-of-town touring. Canada's first paved highway was built between the two towns, and more highways quickly followed.

Toronto, for all that, was still in most ways a big market town. But even if we'd known, we probably wouldn't have minded that Ezra Pound's letters to a young *Star* reporter named Ernest Hemingway—addressed to Tomato, Can.— were all delivered.

We preferred our leader and seven-time mayor, Tommy Church (even though he was laughed at when he spoke in the House of Commons), to the one they had in Italy whose posturing was ridiculous enough but no laughing matter.

We had lots of culture for those who wanted it. The Group of Seven and the Canadian Authors' Association were winning their battles for a nationalism in the arts and letters, and Toronto was their headquarters.

In spite of Arthur Meighen's rhetoric, we were not so "Ready Aye Ready" any more to fight a war at Britain's side. The sort of border incident we were really interested in was closer to home: rum-running into Buffalo or Detroit. It was perfectly legal to make the stuff here even if we weren't supposed to drink it ourselves or sell it to the Americans. Besides, we could still believe that the last war really was the last war, or at any rate hope that, in the words of Conservatory pianist Ernest Seitz's popular song, the world was waiting for the sunrise.

The world's sunrises of 1929 and after were not exactly what Toronto's carefree '20s had in mind.

THE THIRTIES

The headlines got bigger and blacker as the decade progressed from the Lindbergh kidnapping to the burning of the airship *Hindenburg* at its mooring mast in Lakehurst, New Jersey.

The most exciting story was about the last gun battle of Red Ryan, the Toronto gangster whose going straight had received such support from local sports promoters.

But the biggest headline came in the *Star* the week of the Moose River mine disaster, climaxed by that one word, "Rescued," running down half the front page.

The daughter of the man who wasn't rescued went to our school. So did one or two victims of the annual polio epidemics that seemed to be as much a part of the times as the drought in Saskatchewan. The grim statistics in the newspapers of August and September could always be supplemented by graphic accounts of what it was like for a child to live and die in an iron lung. Every pathetic preventative, from never eating unpeeled peaches to staying over at the Island in September, was used to ward off the evil.

The news would veer drastically from death to life—the stork derby set up by an eccentric Toronto millionaire for the mother who produced the most children was continually in the papers. But the Dionne quintuplets were the biggest story of all. With the help of a Toronto reporter, who eventually became manager of the whole publicity and tourist operation up at Callander, and thanks also to Dr. Allan Dafoe's daily column of folk wisdom, the Quints lasted right through the decade, rivalling Niagara as the thing for which Ontario was famous, down to the day when they met Their Majesties on the 1939 royal tour of Canada.

As a child growing up in the centre of Toronto during the depression, my earliest memories include autumn streets smoking with dozens of bonfires, long-bearded men with rickety carts and spindle-shanked horses calling out "Dry-wo-o-od!" and "Rag-a-bones!"; occasional herds of cattle lowing through the city streets, and the day the British airship R-100 flew over Toronto. I remember my great-grandfather proposing a toast to the little New Year, 1931, and happy days that would be here again soon. My first weekly allowance was two giant George V pennies.

A lot of good things came for a nickel: a bunch of all-day suckers, a bottle of O'Keefe's stone ginger beer, and a trip to the Hollywood to see Silly Symphonies. Big Little Books and animal crackers cost a dime, but the best things in life were free: the BeeHive Golden Corn Syrup cards of all the NHL players and Al Leary's nightly sports broadcast on CKCL, with its theme song, "Smoke Gets in Your Eyes," played on a harmonica.

At the beginning of the decade, with the Royal York and the Bank of Commerce—largest hotel and tallest building in the British Empire—the Toronto skyline all at once went metropolitan and took a shape that it held for the next 30 years.

Eaton's expanded uptown to College Street. Art moderne, the angular new streamlined style of the decade, was featured in the auditorium of the new store, in the Eatons' new house on Dunvegan Road and in Conn Smythe's Maple Leaf Gardens. The style was more familiar as it appeared in the Airflow Chrysler, the new railway locomotives and the marvellous variety of planes in the comic strip "Skyroads."

The comics themselves reflected the times. Besides the old strips from the pre-war male world of the saloon and the barbershop—Mutt and Jeff and Barney Google—and that smart, emancipated young couple of the '20s, Toots and Casper, there were Winnie Winkle the Breadwinner and Tillie the Toiler.

Year after year we kept hoping that George Young of Toronto would beat Ernst Vierkotter in the CNE swim. The other gruelling test of endurance was for Doug and Torchy Peden in the six-day bicycle race. The decade also meant miniature golf, cars with rumble seats and running boards, Monopoly, neon signs, Dr. Blatz, Walter Damrosch, Sir Ernest MacMillan as Santa Claus at the Christmas Box Symphony, the radio variety shows such as Jack Benny and Charlie McCarthy on *The Chase and Sanborn Hour.*

At the Lakeview work camp, organizers persuaded the 800 men to strike for higher pay and better working conditions. They were concerned about reports of carpenters who got 72 cents an hour in Toronto being laid off by employers and replaced by work-camp labour at 20 cents.

Thirty-five Mounties were moved in to protect the handful of men still willing to work and the food supply of the rest was cut off. The local United Church collected $10—enough for hearty breakfasts for the whole camp. Truckloads of food

An Albert Franck oil painting of Strachan Avenue
looking north from Richmond St. W. (1962).
Thousands of late Victorian and Edwardian houses have been
the city of Toronto's greatest single physical asset.
Their rapid and wanton destruction by developers, planners and
politicians during the 1950s and 1960s has only been slowed down recently.
For more than 40 years, until his death in 1973, this superb
Dutch artist, "our Boswell of the back alleys," photographed
and painted his beloved houses so that one day his
fellow citizens might cherish rather than tear them down.
He never complained that his genius was so long unrecognized
or mocked by the fashion-makers of his day; only that
his best subjects kept turning into parking lots.

started coming in from all over Toronto. The Department of Defence struck back by declaring the camp closed and asking the men to leave. The organizers tried to persuade the men to stay on for a sit-down hunger strike, but by the end of the week most of them were seeking some other temporary solution on the streets of Toronto—a nickel could buy a bowl of soup at Bowles Lunch.

If a man had a job, the best salaries, according to the 1931 statistics, were in the civil service or as a railway conductor or an engineer. The average annual salary was $927 and the lowest was that of a domestic servant at $52.

No class of women got more than $1,000 a year, but teachers came closest. Soap sold at a dozen bars for 49 cents, and meat ranged from hamburger at five cents a pound to the best sirloin at 25 cents.

A sturdy pair of boy's Oxfords went for 79 cents, but silk chiffon stockings cost a small fortune: $1.35 a pair. For $745 a round-the-world cruise was available and $54.25 would buy a trip to Vancouver and back—although a lot of men, riding the boxcars, managed to make that trip for free.

THE FORTIES

The war came early to Toronto. There were Toronto boys and girls coming home from a summer in Europe, along with the first British war guests, aboard the *Athenia* when she was torpedoed just 48 hours after Hitler's blitzkrieg struck Poland in 1939.

Toronto's Number 100 squadron was the first RCAF unit overseas. The soldiers who left in the fall of 1939 were gone for six years. As early as 1940, *Saturday Night* was speculating on the possibilities of "victory by Christmas," and when Christmas came, a bit more cautiously, "victory by summer if. . . ."

But the total war effort was only beginning. The Island airport was filled with Norwegian flyers, and on the streets of Toronto there were men from all over the Commonwealth on leave from one of the bases of the air training plan.

Wartime Toronto meant city hall with its tall red thermometer keeping track of the latest war-bond drive; Sunnybrook Farm, Toronto's finest Sunday walk, taken over for the hospital; Toronto businessmen on the train to Ottawa to run the wartime Prices and Trade Board, and some of them, such as E.P. Taylor, torpedoed in the chilly North Atlantic during production trips to England.

There were victory gardens and blackouts and ARP wardens, Quonset huts and grandmothers going to shift work in bandanas. The Inglis plant was producing Bren guns, and de Havilland, besides all the trainers and Ansons, turned out 1,000 Mosquito fighter bombers.

Rationing meant one bottle of liquor a month; books of stamps for sugar and most other staples; a stay of execution for Toronto's horse-drawn fleets of milk and bread wagons; and the disappearance of appliances and new tires from the stores.

Wartime styles took "inches off skirts and pockets off coats and the drip out of women's fashions." There were salvage drives for everything, from paper and coathangers to wrought-iron fencing, some of which was bought and resold as it was by a junk dealer with an eye for aesthetics and profit.

In advertising, everything bad, from dirt to lost time, was "a silent saboteur" or "a secret fifth columnist." Other bad things included zombies and gremlins and black-market profiteers.

And from the dark, deep voice of Lorne Greene on the 10 o'clock news came the toll of Dieppe and the raids over Germany, of Monte Cassino and Normandy, and the long battle of the North Atlantic, where the convoys were chiefly protected by Canadian corvettes.

It was the last period of close ties with Britain. The national song was "There'll Always Be an England," our national hero, Winston Churchill. Toronto papers kept close track of Princess Elizabeth in her ATS uniform. Amid power dimouts and hot-water shortages we were encouraged by reports of the low level of bath water at Buckingham Palace. And there were Bundles for Britain—never has so much public knitting been done by so many.

The later 1940s brought us the Cold War, refugees and DPs and a lot of initialed organizations, from UNRRA to NATO. At least one prominent Torontonian, Professor Leopold Infeld, returned to his native, now socialist, Poland to seek a better society than he found in Toronto. Lister Sinclair wrote, and Andrew Allan put on *CBC Stage*, a play call *We All Hate Toronto*. Our heroes included Mayor Bob Saunders, Whipper Billy Watson, the Leslie Bell Singers, Syl Apps and Just Mary. Mart Kenney brought his Western Gentlemen to town. Brock Chisholm wanted us to tell the truth about Santa Claus, and in Maple Leaf Gardens, Charles Templeton asked 17,000 Youths for Christ if they would have George Drew's cocktail bars and they roared back, "No!"

With the Club Top Hat and its 50-cent cokes, a new phenomenon, the night club, arrived in Toronto.

Among our postwar styles were the drape shape and the zoot suit and the first new cars in half a decade, led by the '47 Studebaker; the lavish yards of clothing known as the New Look, heavy red lipstick and bobby soxers listening to *Juke Box Saturday Night* or Dizzy Gillespie's new bebop sound, though the ultimate idol of that new breed of people called teenagers was still Frank Sinatra.

Veterans swamped the campus, and the university had to acquire an annex out at Ajax.

The first hideous strawberry-box suburbs sprang up but there weren't enough of them to take care of the war brides and the baby boom.

Toronto had never been so politically radical as during the 1940s. The CCF managed to frustrate Conservative leader Arthur Meighen's attempt to get a seat in the House of Commons in York South in 1942, and came within a couple of percentage points of electing a government for Ontario in 1943.

For years we had two Communist MPPs, A.A. McLeod and Joe Salsberg, and another Labour Progressive, as they had to call themselves, Stewart Smith, who was a perennial and often successful candidate for city council. But in 1945, CCF leader E.B. Jolliffe's Gestapo charges against Premier George Drew backfired, and Mackenzie King stemmed the socialist tide in the federal elections by stealing much of their program.

When CCFer Bill Temple gave George Drew a personal drubbing in 1948 in High Park riding it was because he had mobilized the temperance forces against the coming of cocktail bars to Toronto the Good.

THE FIFTIES

Toronto became a big city in the 1950s—the fastest-growing in North America. With the move of the Ford plant to Oakville to balance GM on the other side at Oshawa, Toronto came closer to being the Canadian Detroit than ever.

With the erection of the CBC television tower on Jarvis Street, the head offices for oil and religion in the Imperial Oil building and the United Church Vatican on St. Clair, with the growth of the harbour facilities into those of a full-fledged ocean port to meet the opening of the St. Lawrence Seaway, and with its expanding ad agencies and stock market and publishing industry, Toronto became the New York of English-speaking Canada.

In its role as magnet for people on the move from poorer parts of the nation, for new industries producing objects such as the Avro CF-100 jet fighter, and in the growth of smog and traffic jam, suburbs and expressways, Toronto became the Canadian Los Angeles.

The metropolitan area's population jumped during the decade from 1,100,000 to 1,800,000; salaries and wages in our manufacturing industries moved from less than $400 million to nearly $900 million a year, and the most spectacular advances of all occurred in new service and electronics industries that had scarcely been heard of in 1950.

The Golden Mile of new factories that was in the hinterland in 1950 seemed well on its way, a decade later, to being part of the older central city. As suburbia rolled outward over land that was once concession roads and orchards and country stores, millionaires were made in real estate. A 400-acre farm in North York that sold for $60,000 after the war had a three-and-a-half-acre piece carved out of it for $300,000 a decade later, and the rest of it went into lots for mass-produced strawberry boxes at $5,000 and up.

Toronto's posh suburb, Forest Hill Village, became a case study for North America's new affluent society in John Seeley's *Crestwood Heights*, a book whose popularity was itself a sign of a new breed of readers concerned with problems of status or worried about why, in the blandness of our school system, as Hilda Neatby asked, there was So Little for the Mind.

The counterpart to split-level, picture-window living, to the barbecue pit and patio and swimming pool, arrived downtown in the tombstone architecture of University Avenue offices and the first highrises. But the heart of Toronto was saved from death of the spirit by such developments as Canada's first subway and the beginnings of the vulgar vitality of the Strip north of Dundas on Yonge.

Certain functions of the wider city were placed in the hands of a Metropolitan Federation in 1953 and its chairman, Fred Gardiner, who appeared to run it "more like a construction company than a government."

The mayor of all the people, Nathan Phillips, had already set a record for longevity as alderman and was on his way to doing the same as mayor and official greeter. But it was he who took Professor Eric Arthur's noble vision of a civic square and city hall to rival the great urban public spaces of the old world, and, by his tireless efforts on the banquet circuit, routed the political old guard who denounced it as an extravagant Taj Mahal.

As Toronto's first Jewish mayor, he soon found himself presiding over one of the world's larger Italian cities. A third of the decade's 1,500,000 Canadian immigrants came to Toronto. Half the Hungarians who fled to Canada from the counterrevolution of 1956 settled in Toronto. Kensington Market became the heart of a Portuguese community, replacing a Jewish community that had moved north.

The city of Toronto, once the stronghold of the Orange Lodges and King Billy's parade, was by 1961 more than half Roman Catholic. People of British descent became a minority. And Toronto's immigrants were transforming the parks and shops and supermarkets. They even helped Torontonians to loosen up and enjoy themselves.

The 1950s brought Toronto a new culture that included transistors and beatniks and going steady, the Hula-Hoop and hi-fi, chrome furniture and 5BX exercises and do-it-yourself, Elvis Presley, rock and roll, Oscar Peterson and Glenn Gould, Nathan Cohen and Harold Town, a revival of folk music and jazz, the Crest Theatre, *Spring Thaw* and the pilgrimage to Stratford. New art galleries such as the Isaacs brought commercial success, as well as high standards and abstract expressionism, to the art world. The Royal Conservatory began producing great singers—Lois Marshall and Jon Vickers and Maureen Forrester to name only three.

On television, Canadian variety artists such as Jackie Kane and Jackie Rae and Shirley Harmer flourished, as well as the great perennials Wayne and Shuster.

Our nightly town meeting of the air was Ross McLean's *Tabloid* with Joyce Davidson and Percy Saltzman. But right to the end of the decade a lot of serious people still managed to pride themselves on not having an idiot box in the house.

On radio, Old Rawhide's little theatre group flourished, as did such sources of his raw material as the ubiquitous Kate Aitken.

Casualties of the decade included the Avro Arrow, the Centre Island cottages, the Edsel (launched the same month as Sputnik), Canadian ownership of old firms such as Moffat's of Weston, Li'l Abner's bachelorhood and the Toronto Argonauts under Harry Sonshine.

The 1950s brought the doldrums to the Leafs hockey club. Detroit ended Toronto's three-year-grip on the Stanley Cup in 1950 and Rocket Richard and Gordie Howe took over the

NHL.

The biggest sports story was Marilyn Bell's conquest of Lake Ontario. Jack Kent Cooke, of CKEY and *Liberty* magazine, managed to keep us entertained with his baseball team.

Toronto in the 1950s became an exciting though not yet a highly civilized place to live. That New Year's Day in 1950, when the citizens went to the polls to vote in favour of Sunday sports—against stern warnings from the three newspapers and most of the candidates for civic office, plus full-page ads sponsored by the churches—seems part of another and far-distant era.

EVENTS: 1903 – 1984

1903: A silver strike at Cobalt launches the northern Ontario mining boom, which makes the Toronto Stock Exchange the world's busiest in mining shares.

1904: Toronto's Great Fire burns out the heart of the downtown business district and leads to brick or stone requirements for future city buildings.

1905 – 12: East, West and North Toronto are annexed, the last major boundary changes until Swansea and Forest Hill are added to the city as part of the 1966 Metropolitan reform.

1907: The elegant Royal Alexandra, the world's first air-conditioned and completely fireproof theatre, opens. Saved in 1963 from demolition and refurbished by discount king "Honest Ed" Mirvish, it became part of a west downtown renewal in the 1970s.

1909: The first Grey Cup football game, between Varsity and Toronto Balmy Beach, is played in what is now Rosedale Park.

1910: Eminent sage and invective journalist Goldwin Smith, who acquired his property by marrying one of the Family Compact Boultons, bequeaths the Grange, Toronto's earliest surviving brick mansion, to the city for use as an art gallery (now part of the Art Gallery of Ontario).

1911: The census reveals nearly 4,000 Italian-born citizens of Toronto and sizable Chinese and Macedonian communities. But Toronto's most important new group is the 18,000 Jewish refugees from eastern Europe. The city's total population has nearly doubled in a decade, to more than 400,000.

1912: The Toronto Harbour Commission begins its vast landfill project in the bay south of Front Street.

1914: The Royal Ontario Museum opens.

1917: The viaduct over the Don Valley ends the Danforth's

isolation.

1921: The Toronto Transit Commission is formed to take over a variety of streetcar lines, with a single fare for any one trip.

1927: New Union Station opens.

1931: Maple Leaf Gardens is built.

1932: The Guild of All Arts founded in Scarborough by Rosa and Spencer Clark. Over the next half-century, sculpture and other features of the many superb buildings demolished in Toronto are relocated on the Guild's grounds at the edge of the Scarborough Bluffs.

1930 – 45: Fifteen years of depression and war stop Toronto's building boom and hold down population growth (to about 650,000).

1949: The world's first commercial jet, built in Toronto, makes its first run to New York City.

1950: The world's first cardiac pacemaker is given to a patient at Toronto General Hospital. Led by Mayor Lamport, against the opposition of the daily newspapers and church leaders, Toronto voters opt for Sunday sports.

1951: The National Ballet Company founded by Celia Franca, followed in 1959 by the National Ballet School, under Betty Oliphant.

1953: The city is federated with 12 surrounding municipalities into the 200 square miles of Metropolitan Toronto, led by its first chairman, Fred Gardiner.

1954: The Yonge Street line, Canada's first subway, begins operation.

1955: Marilyn Bell, the first person to swim Lake Ontario, reaches the CNE grounds from the American shore.

1957: The Canadian Opera Company is founded, giving Toronto its own regular repertory season of opera.

1950s: Immigration from Europe and elsewhere transforms the city into a colourful, multicultural society.

1960: York University receives its first students.

1965: The opening of Toronto's new city hall, designed by Finnish architect Viljo Revell, winner of an international competition for the purpose.

1967: Toronto celebrates the centennial of Confederation with the construction of the St. Lawrence Centre, now home of two resident theatre companies.

1971: Plans for the Spadina expressway are cancelled by Premier William Davis, and Metro Toronto is forced to stress better public transportation instead of an inner-city expressway network. Phasing-out of the last streetcar lines is halted.

*An Organ Grinder on
Bay Street in 1922.*

1974: The new Toronto zoo is created amid the rolling hills of the Rouge River Valley.

1975: The CN Tower, at 1,815 feet the world's highest building, is ready for broadcasting and sightseers.

1978: Major league baseball arrives with the Toronto Blue Jays.

1979: The galleria of the Eaton Centre, designed by Eberhard Zeidler, architect of Ontario Place, is completed and soon becomes Canada's chief tourist attraction.

1983: The $50,000 McLuhan Teleglobe Canada Award in Communications, named after Toronto's best-known citizen of the global village, is established by the Canadian Commission for UNESCO, to be awarded for contributions toward understanding media.

1984: Toronto celebrates its one hundred and fiftieth birthday.

TORONTO
THE
GOOD

Toronto is known as Toronto the Good, because of its alleged piety. My guess is that there's more polygamy in Toronto than Baghdad, only it's not called that in Toronto.

AUSTIN F. CROSS, Cross Roads *(1936)*

Toronto as a city carries out the idea of Canada as a country. It is a calculated crime both against the aspirations of the soul and the affections of the heart.

ALEISTER CROWLEY, c.1906, The Confessions of Aleister Crowley: An
Autohagiography *(1970)*

No one should visit Toronto for the first time.

Anonymous

The inhabitants do not possess the finest character.

LE DUC DE LA ROCHEFOUCAULD-LIANCOURT (1795)

THE IMMIGRANT

"Too many churches, not enough bawdy houses,"
this frank young Englishman
fresh from the London flesh-pots
wrote to a friend after spending
his first week in Toronto (1885).

But later that year

was seduced in his own room
by the daughter of an Anglican minister,
and the next spring opened up the first
all-night mission ever seen on Yonge Street.
                                    RAYMOND SOUSTER

THE SUNDAY CAR

1. The car is one of the most insidious of Sunday invasions. It is a public convenience. It facilitates social visiting, outings, visits to the graves of the dead and the beds of the sick. It becomes even a convenience for getting to church. The evil it does is not at once apparent. The convenience of it is manifest. Even the very elect are therefore easily deceived into minimizing the harm it does and magnifying the ends it serves.

2. As a quiet, constant secularizer of the Lord's Day, it has few if any equals. Its educational influence is its worst feature.

The public of course does not recognize this. We leaders of religious thought and life ought to do so.

3. It will inevitably be followed or accompanied, once the Company's right to operate on Sunday is conceded, by an aggressive effort to make it a business success.

This is the invariable experience.

4. The Sunday car, therefore, in a community like yours, is an enemy of religion, morality and church life, and tends to break up what remains of the blessed unity of family life.

5. It also necessarily deprives a growing number of men of their Sabbath rest and opportunity to worship, and thus results in not a few immortal souls being eternally lost. There are at present, in the Dominion, 150,000 Sabbathless toilers.

6. It prepares the way for other public Sunday conveniences.

The selfishness of an unthinking public is never satisfied. These other conveniences are logically defended on the same specious pleas, and regularly follow in the wake of the Sunday car. This has been the uniform experience in Europe, the United States, and already in some parts of Canada.

Memoranda furnished by the Secretaries of the Lord's Day Alliance of Canada
                                                              (1893)

TORONTO THE GOOD

They tell of a city, Toronto the Good,
With beautiful children and fair womanhood;
They sing of its noblemen, honest and true,

142

Its elegant mayors and aldermen, too.
They boast of its churches on many a street,
Where multitudes gather with hurrying feet;
And yet there's a wrong thou hast not well withstood,
There's somewhat against thee, Toronto the Good.

Chorus:
O beautiful city, Toronto the Good,
Awake to thy danger, and do as you should.
If thou wouldst no longer be misunderstood,
Then close up thy bar-rooms, Toronto the Good.

Thou art a fair city, thou Queen of this land,
And yet thou has stretched out thy delicate hand
To shelter the Monster that's wringing the blood
And tears from thy children, Toronto the Good.
That revenue plea never, never will count,
Thy hand must be washed in the penitent's fount;
Then hold it out free from suspicion of blood
To rescue thy children, Toronto the Good.

The record is darker as year after year
These pestilent dens by thy sanction are here;
Their powers of evil sweep on like a flood,
To sink thee forever, Toronto the Good.
Before the wide world thou are surely no saint.
While drinking goes on with but little restraint;
And, how shall thy sons reach the noblest manhood
'Midst two hundred bar-rooms, Toronto the Good?

I trust we'll remember those alderman fine
Who voted against bar-rooms closing at nine;
Their heads, when again at the polls they have stood,
We'll drop in the basket, Toronto the Good.
O city, lead on in the battle for Truth,
And strike to the Death this destroyer of youth.
My city, I love thee, and would, if I could,
Sing, "Thou art all lovely," Toronto the Good.

J.M. WHYTE

The mayoralty of William Holmes Howland from 1886 to 1888 was an early example of reform politics in Toronto. His supporters, as Goldwin Smith wryly observed, "told the electors that they had to choose between Christ and Barabbas": if the promised millennium was delayed in transit, some consequences of the Howland era were lasting. The city's slightly dated nickname of "Toronto the Good" was an enduring tribute to the mayor's campaign for moral purification. To a degree without contemporary precedent, municipal authority was used to uphold the spiritual and moral values preached from the city's pulpits.

Fashions in reform have altered as dramatically as Toronto itself. Perhaps a few present-day reformers may be slightly chastened to discover how transient were some of the issues for which their ancestors did passionate battle. If reformers in the 1880s expressed a thoroughly modern contempt for capitalism and industrialism, if they often sympathised with trade unions and the struggling poor, they also tended to see such personal weaknesses as intemperance as the central cause of social malfunction. Whiskey and gin were evils; the sanctity of the family was a sublime good. On the other hand, neither Howland nor his supporters saw any sin in rapid development and Toronto experienced some of its fastest growth during his years in office. Just as modern reformers must somehow reconcile the elevated preaching and the economic self-interest of their middle-class constituents, Howland had to serve the moral fervour and the material concerns of his prosperous Methodist backers. A century later, Toronto reformers might feel more comfortable with the old guard politicians who sympathised with the city's drinkers and wondered where Toronto's mushrooming expansion would end. Typical among them was the well-known Orangeman, school trustee and pillar of his Tory ward organization, Marcellus Crombie.

DESMOND MORTON, Mayor Howland *(1973)*

It was not merely that I found myself back in the Biblical and Victorian atmosphere of my boyhood—that would have been hard enough to someone bent on emancipation—but it was the dead uniformity that I found so tedious: one knew beforehand everyone's opinion on every subject, so there was a complete absence of mental stimulation or exchange of thought.

Life in Toronto was in many ways very pleasant. Curiously enough, one partook of cultural activities more than in London. There, where so many were always available, one had to make an effort to find the necessary free time. In Toronto there was only one serious centre, the Massey Hall, and everything that came there did so only for a week. So it became always a weekly habit to attend, and it was very rewarding, since the most celebrated artists of the musical and theatrical world always included Toronto in their American tours.

From the memoirs of Ernest Jones, Freud's biographer and disciple, who lived and worked in Toronto, 1908 – 1912

Toronto (pronounced *T'ranto*, please) is difficult to describe. It has an individuality, but an elusive one; yet not through any queerness or difficult shade of eccentricity; a subtly normal, an indefinably obvious personality. It is a healthy, cheerful city (by modern standards); a clean-shaven, pink-faced, respectably dressed, fairly energetic, unintellectual, passably social, well-to-do, public-school-and-varsity sort of city. One knows in one's own life certain bright and pleasant figures; people who occupy the near middle distance, unobtrusive but not negligible; wardens of the marches between acquaintanceship and friendship. It is always nice to meet them, and in parting one looks back at them once. They are, healthily and simply, the most fitting product of a not too perfect environment; good sorts; normal, but not too normal; distinctly themselves, but not distinguished. They support civilization. You can trust them in anything, if your demand be for nothing extremely intelligent or absurdly altruistic. One of these could be exhibited in any gallery in the universe, "Perfect Specimen; Upper Middle Classes; Twentieth Century"—and we should not be ashamed. They are not vexed by impossible dreams, nor outrageously materialistic, nor perplexed by overmuch prosperity, nor spoilt by reverse. Souls for whom the wind is always nor'-nor'-west, and they sail nearer success than failure, and nearer wisdom than lunacy.

But Toronto—Toronto is the subject. One must say something—*what* must one say about Toronto? What can one? What has anybody ever said? It is impossible to give it anything but commendation. It is not squalid like Birmingham, or cramped like Canton, or scattered like Edmonton, or sham like Berlin, or hellish like New York, or tiresome like Nice. It is all right. The only depressing thing is that it will always be what it is, only larger, and that no Canadian city can ever be anything better or different. If they are good they may become Toronto.

RUPERT BROOKE, Letters from America *(1916)*

The typical Torontonian is about five feet nine inches high, with fairly broad shoulders, and a dolichocephalic head with an ear on each side of it.

STEPHEN LEACOCK, My Discovery of England *(1922)*

I have always found that the only thing in regard to Toronto which faraway people know for certain is that McGill University is in it.

STEPHEN LEACOCK, My Discovery of the West *(1937)*

I like very much the city of Toronto. People a little cold from that of Montreal but I was obliged to give one encore more than the last city. I was taken by the steam heat, which make me nervous. A newspaper published a critic and not so nice like everyone else. But there were other newspapers answered the one which was not satisfied.

ENRICO CARUSO, Enrico Caruso: His Life and Death

Meanwhile my Toronto comrades kept on insisting that I was wanted in their midst. They had never believed that their city could respond so warmly to anarchist propaganda. They urged that I make Toronto my permanent home or that I remain there several years at least. They offered to foot all bills and I should consider myself engaged, they declared.... Nor could I think of spending the rest of my life in Canada. But I would risk it for a year.... The public and university libraries in Toronto were lacking in modern works on the social, education, and psychologic problems occupying the best minds. "We do not buy books we consider immoral," a local librarian was reported as saying.

EMMA GOLDMAN, Living My Life *(1931)*

I remember in the 1930s when the police chief General Draper stationed constables with stopwatches in the wings of the Royal Alexandra Theatre, timing the kisses in the Lunts' production of *The Guardsman*, ready to ring down the curtain if they lasted more than 20 seconds.

JOHN GRAY (1974)

Long ago a moth imprisoned in a musty purse invented the Toronto mind. It is a mind poured in a mould made of narrow building laws and red brick and the scarlet letter and the white feather and of people who, when challenged, wrap themselves in Union Jacks and sing "God Save the Queen" like hell. It is a mind of pump organs in the parlour and drapes drawn so that the rugs don't fade—and what if they also shut out the sun?

SCOTT YOUNG (1955)

I remember having breakfasted with a French Canadian in Montreal and having dined with an English Canadian family in Toronto on the same day. The contrast was quite a shock to my senses. It was like experiencing the different pressures in a diving bell. Involuntarily I thought of the uncompromising formula of Maurice Barrès: "Prayers that do not mingle."

ANDRÉ SIEGFRIED, Canada (1937)

Since "Toronto the Good" had given me my first steady job, had kept me in funds, had provided a rehabilitation centre for my father and had proved for me the gateway into Canada, I was disinclined to take a poor view of the city. Not so my friends, all of them Torontonians. The silent venom which they poured on the city, the loud splenetic rancour with which they cursed it, used to astonish me. I thought Toronto was a bit smug and self-complacent, a bit hypocritical and certainly a great place for a humbug to make an easy living. But these were the virtues (or characteristics) of Anglo-Saxon and Anglo-Celtic Protestants of the middle class, especially in new countries. Having lived in Melbourne for over a decade I didn't think Toronto had much to teach me about humbug and self-complacency. But my friends thought otherwise. They just hadn't a good word to say for the town. Montreal was exotic and Gallic; Quebec was history; Winnipeg was brash and vigorous; Vancouver had the scenery. But Toronto, Toronto the Good, Hogtown, Babylon-on-the-Humber, what did it have?

Well, I thought it had quite a lot. Its 750,000 people supported by far the best symphony orchestra in Canada; in fact for a while they had two of them running in competition. It had the biggest and best museum in Canada and a very fine art gallery. It had four daily papers and was the centre of the Canadian publishing business. It had, in those days, deep tree-choked ravines where a man could wander in silence without sight of a house for miles down rustic lanes and watch the squirrels and chipmunks and listen to the birds much as they must have been in Fenimore Cooper's America or the country of Ernest Thompson Seton's *Lives of the Hunted*.

Of course certain of the publicized virtues were harder to live up to. Toronto was "a city of churches," and indeed you could hardly help seeing them, for they were on almost every other corner. But did this imply piety or churchiness? Toronto was "a city of homes" in contrast to sinful Montreal where people, one was told, dwelt in apartments. True enough; but the homes, especially in the west end and off the Danforth, were of a paralysing sameness. The city struck me as worthy, hardworking, self-centred, shrewd and pretty pleased with itself. It wasn't like Paris or New York or London; but then it wasn't like Adelaide or Belfast or Cleveland either, though it was more like them than it was like the first three. It was perhaps a frustrating place for a young man to spend seven years of his life, but not a stifling place. The reason for this was that, even as Paris sums up France, so Toronto summed up the virtues and drawbacks of the pioneer society of Upper Canada from which it was descended. And although the drawbacks were distasteful—censoriousness, smugness, frugality—the virtues were not inconsiderable either, hard work, tenacity, shrewdness, reliability.

GRAHAM MacINNES, c. 1935, Finding a Father *(1967)*

This city is said to be the most American of Canadian cities; but it is a mournful Scottish version of America (union with which it yearns for dismally).

This is a province: but with a provincialism that has not equal for exclusiveness and jealousy.

When I first arrived I had the sensation of being a dog who had strayed into a farmyard, and had there discovered a dozen indigenous dogs standing fiery-eyed and softly growling around one very lean bone indeed.

A prominent bookseller, unsolicited, took me aside the other day and said: if he might venture to give me a little advice if I thought of publishing, it would be much better to have published in New York or London.

This distrust for anything Canadian extends to anything appearing here, or even to any stranger stopping for more than two or three days!

As [for] a visitor like myself, from another planet—bringing with him a great reputation—they sniff at him suspiciously. They ask each other—"What the heck is he doing here?" For just as there is something degrading about a book having itself brought out here, so there is presumably something degrading about being here. . . .

I feel that someone is sitting on my chest—having to start with gagged me—and singing Moody and Sankey all day long.

Oh for a half-hour of Europe after this sanctimonious icebox.

WYNDHAM LEWIS, The Letters of Wyndham Lewis, *edited by W. K. Rose*

And then all round Paris lies France, furrowed with one-way roads, and then the seas dyed blue or black, the Mediterranean blue, the North Sea black, the Channel coffee-coloured, and then the foreign lands, Germany, Italy—Spain white, because I did not go and fight there—and all round the cities, at fixed distances from my room, Timbuctoo, Toronto, Kazan, Nijni-Novgorod, immutable as frontier points.

JEAN-PAUL SARTRE, The Age of Reason *(1945)*

Gilbert Harding, who bred a reputation for iconoclasm in the '40s when he represented the BBC in Canada, was once asked where he lived in Toronto. "Jarvis Street," he said. "Oh, but Mr. Harding!" said a snob, "Jarvis Street is hardly a good address!" Gilbert bridled, with a magnificence only he was ever able to muster. "My dear man," he thundered, "Toronto is hardly a good address!"

ANDREW ALLAN, A Self-Portrait *(1974)*

It took the Molsons 150 years to decide that Toronto was a worthy site for one of their breweries, and even then it was a reluctant move. When Hartland Molson tried to persuade Bert Molson to attend the new plant's opening, he shook his head and replied, "I went to Toronto once. Didn't like it then, and I have no intention of going back."

PETER NEWMAN, The Globe and Mail *(1983)*

That's just it. We *all* hate Toronto! It's the only thing everybody's got in common. You hear a dreadful quarrel start up between two Canadians, and French Canadians, or Maritimers and Manitobans, or some such thing. Just when they're going to cut each other's throat, *somebody* mentions Toronto.

LISTER SINCLAIR, We All Hate Toronto, A Play on Words and Other Radio Plays *(1948)*

It is not as easy to hate Toronto as it used to be. It can still be done, of course. If you put your mind to it. But you are no longer struck, the moment you step off the train or the plane, by a wave of offensiveness.

ERIC NICOL, The Canadian *(1966)*

The problem with poor Toronto is that the city is without any interesting topographical features. A city, to have character, must have some inclines, some vistas. Spend all day in Toronto and all you can see is the city. You cannot lift thine eyes up unto anything but man-made mediocrity. There are no hills to look down from, or up to. The soothing sight of water, of Lake Ontario, is virtually prisoned off from the city. It's a debilitating experience just to be an inhabitant. "Inmate" may be the more appropriate word.

It is completely understandable, therefore, that when you have a city that is visually sterile, there is a need to erect a phallic symbol as an attempt at mechanical machismo. The rationale is obvious. A global psychiatrist, if asked to take a look at Toronto's rather unhealthy obsession with the CN Tower, would advise the city to take a cold shower and lie down on the couch for a spell.

ALLAN FOTHERINGHAM, Maclean's (1975)

Toronto does not have to devote all its energies and resources to seeking remedies for yesterday's problems—slums, ghettos and unemployment. Free of these major constraints, it can be a truly future-oriented protypic city.

BUCKMINSTER FULLER (1968)

If one is rich enough, the best cities for permanent residence remain London, Paris and New York. For those who cannot afford to live in these cities the second-best choices are Toronto, Rome and Sydney. It is possible to live a fairly civilized life in Vancouver, San Francisco and Cape Town though the intellectual climate in these places is somewhat insular, enervated and xenophobic.

McKENZIE PORTER, Toronto Sun (1971)

On Monday, Mayor Nathan Phillips gave me a pair of gold cuff links. On Wednesday they gave me a pair of steel handcuffs. I wonder which of these is the proper credentials for a writer. The cuff links are an honour. The handcuffs show I'm not a statue yet.

Toronto will be a fine town when it is finished.

BRENDAN BEHAN, on being arrested in Toronto,
quoted by Ulick O'Connor in Brendan (1970)

RUNNER

As Pindar long ago in Greece was proud to hail
Thessalian Hippokleas, even so
It is meet we praise in our days fleet-footed
Bruce Kidd from Toronto.

W.H. AUDEN, City without Walls (1969)

Personally I always think of Toronto as a big fat rich girl who

150

has lots of money, but no idea of how to make herself attractive.

ROBERTSON DAVIES, The Table Talk of Samuel Marchbanks *(1949)*

Torontonians don't give a damn what anybody says about Toronto, possibly because few of us think of ourselves as truly Torontonian. Most of us come from somewhere else.... In the eyes of the rest of the country Toronto is a kind of combination Sodom and Mecca.

PIERRE BERTON (1961)

Toronto is an excellent town to mind one's own business in, and a lot of the writing and drafting [of *Fearful Symmetry*] was done in its restaurants, pubs and street corners as well as in my office.

NORTHROP FRYE, Pelham Edgar's Across My Path *(1952)*

The hard routine of a strict monastic rule may be very good for the soul. The orderly, unexciting, strict Toronto life... cannot distract me, cannot give the illusion of gay living, and if the flesh groans the spirit may grow strong.

...I have tried wandering into other cities, and pressing on to distant shores, and have found after a few weeks in a strange place, the urge to move on grows strong, the old weariness gripping me, makes me believe that each new place will be charming because it is new. Well, a writer can stand only so much of this restless boredom; he will go on and on, once he starts wandering, seeking the unexpected scene, the new lovely face, with the charm of novelty always pulling him on and finally wearying him to death. If you stay in Toronto, the longing remains deep in the soul, and since it can't be satisfied you can't be wearied, and your mind and your imagination should become like a caged tiger. O Toronto! O my tiger city!

MORLEY CALLAGHAN in A Sense of Identity *(1954),*
edited by Malcolm Ross

TORONTO'S PAST:
A CANADIAN EXPERIENCE,
NOT AN AMERICAN DREAM

At first glance, Toronto will pass for an American city. But a better appraisal of its history and character will tell you clearly that it is not.

In the United States, from the Puritan Fathers, Virginia planters and William Penn to Abraham Lincoln, Jimmy Carter and Ronald Reagan, the realities and the idea of the city have been profoundly suspect. The American dream involves the sovereign individual shedding the old clothes of civilization—literally, "citification"—and finding freedom and virtue in the new land, "the last best hope of earth." The ideal polity has always been that of the small self-governing rural community—a town meeting or even a PTA. Thomas Jefferson believes that the growth of large urban populations would spell the doom of the republic.

When large American cities did form, most of them became places to be used but not loved, or even lived in permanently, except by the un-American effete, social dropout or very rich, or by the not-yet-American rural immigrant from Europe, the Deep South, Puerto Rico and Mexico. The city was where you escaped from community into anonymity. City society is, literally, "urbane," and you don't really get to know an urbane person. Society and high culture are masks for the soul. The soul and heart of America are still in the suburbs, the town and the country. The idea of amalgamating groups of such communities into large metropolitan districts like Toronto's was briefly fashionable in the 1950s.

*The Toronto skyline remained
unchanged from the 1930s through the
1950s. This Nicholas Hornyansky
etching, which looks east from Fort
York, shows the Royal York and the
Bank of Commerce which were always
touted to visitors as, respectively, the
largest hotel and tallest building in
the British Empire.*

No attempts to do so succeeded, and by the late 1960s the president of the American Political Science Association was arguing that humane and responsible government was impossible in political communities larger than 200,000 people.

Many Americans have yearned for a home-grown London or Paris, just as some of them now idolize Toronto. But the city core—except perhaps for Manhattan—is not about to become the cherished and humane focus of American life. Increasingly the great affluent majority of Americans live in exurban communities, and increasingly these communities are not merely bedrooms and living rooms, but economically and culturally self-sufficient, and only tenuously related to any particular city core. "The 'natural' configuration of the American city," Irving Kristol has argued, "is that of a doughnut." Each has a hollow centre of institutional and office buildings; people live in the surrounding ring, and most of them find their work, shopping, recreation and community concerns somewhere in the ring rather than the core. Even avant-garde bohemia now tends to settle on-campus and off-campus in the suburbs, rather than in a Greenwich Village downtown.

The thrust of Canadian history is different. It comes more from the metropolis than from the grassroots. The institutions of law, religion, commerce and finance were planted before most settlers arrived. Typically Canadian, Toronto was begun not by a Mayflower Compact, a Declaration of Independence or a Bill of Human Rights, but by a military governor and a colonial aristocracy. Their authority was later tempered and shared, both by their recruits and by rebels, within the established structures. Over the years, Toronto annexed its inner suburbs, and was amalgamated with 12 outer ones, by a stroke of the pen of the sovereign's provincial governor on the advice of his premier.

Unlike the land around American cities, early Toronto's immediate surroundings were not cleared for farming. The Family Compact kept their estates and trees in Rosedale and Spadina, and maintained a continuous tradition of residence in what eventually became the centre of town. Toronto's recent history has reinforced this tradition, and city policy is deliberately aimed at building new housing in the urban core. The residential density of the city (excluding the rest of Metropolitan Toronto) is nearly 20,000 persons per square mile—double that of comparable American cities like Cleveland and Detroit. Most of our new economic and cultural institutions—bank towers, theatres, the ball park, new symphony hall and metropolitan library—are still being located in the core rather than beyond it, with all the dangers of over-centralization that this involves.

There have been resemblances to the American pattern in all large Canadian cities: an immigrant reception area, with the next generation moving outward to the suburbs; active citizen groups with something of the vigour of an American town meeting. But these have developed within a larger European and Canadian context different from that of the American urban experience.

Toronto in the future, just as Canada itself, could well become so absorbed by American culture that it loses touch with its historic character. But like a number of her country-men, the American urbanist Jane Jacobs has moved here and became a citizen in the hope that Toronto would not change. "When my family and I settled in Toronto," writes the author of *The Death and Life of the Great American Cities*, "we soon learned the flat we had rented was perched on the putative edge of the Spadina Expressway, variously described to us as elevated, no, depressed; six lanes wide, no, eight; with a subway underneath, no, without; to be built soon, no, not for a long time. Whatever it was, it was not imaginary. Up at Highway 401 we could see what Marshall McLuhan called the launching pad, a big, confident interchange poised for imminent attack upon a wide swath of raw earth, and for the subsequent invasion of still unviolated ravine and pleas-ant communities to the south. In the mind's eye, one could see the great trees and jolly Edwardian porches falling before the onslaught.

"As a relatively recent transplant from New York, I am frequently asked whether I find Toronto sufficiently exciting. I find it almost too exciting. The suspense is scary. Here is the most hopeful and healthy city in North America, still unmangled, still with options. Few of us profit from the mistakes of others, and perhaps Toronto will prove to share this disability. If so, I am grateful at least to have enjoyed this great city before its destruction."

3

PEOPLES AND PERSONS

Wasps and Celts

JOHN TORONTO: VARIATIONS ON STRACHAN

*One insolent Bishop of Toronto, triumphant
Canadian*
— Thomas Carlyle

H e is our only patriarch
first-class, the founder-in-chief of Upper Canadian society.
For a parallel one must go back to New France. The Scottish
stonemason's emigrant son is a cruder version of Laval, with
a touch of Talon, Frontenac and Mother Superior Marie de
l'Incarnation thrown in.

For nearly seven decades, from his arrival in the wilderness
until his death in the year of Confederation, Strachan was a
prodigy of willpower and accomplishment, even in defeat.
He educated two generations of the ruling class in his own
private schools. He founded public-school education in the
province. He badgered the British into granting him charters
for two universities in Toronto and persuaded his brother-in-
law, James McGill, to found one in Montreal. He wrote
prodigiously—tracts, texts, letters and bad verse; he built the
province's first science laboratory; organized its early chari-
ties; he was a founding director of the first bank and hospital;
led the assault on cholera personally, as if it were a Yankee
virus; and planted his elegant palace on Front Street, with its
shade trees and carriage sweep and liveried footmen, the
town's first brick residence and prototype of a thousand
more.

As a churchman, his purpose was to "preach civilization"
as well as the gospel. Strachan was under no illusions about
the odds against his plans for the colony—five educated
clergymen in 1812 among a scattered population of 70,000,

The Right Reverend the Honourable John Strachan, D.D.,
first lord bishop of Toronto, the dominant presence in church
and state, education and society, in Little York and early
Toronto for half a century, from the day he threatened the
American commander who captured the town with the vengeance
of the British navy, through his many battles against the forces
of democracy, secularism and the bureaucrats of the British
Colonial office. He called King George III a paragon amongst
men, and President Thomas Jefferson a mischief-maker.
Mezzotint with stipple and line engraving on wove paper by the
artist George Theodore Berthon, 1847.

most of them uneducated American frontiersmen looking for land.

Under Governor Maitland in the 1820s, Strachan was the closest thing Upper Canada ever had to a prime minister. He became the first advocate of Confederation (in 1822)—chiefly as a means of keeping the elite in control of British North America. Then, after his gradual withdrawal from politics, Strachan at 61 began a new career, as first bishop of Toronto.

I first encountered him at Trinity College, where his portrait hangs above the high table. For four years he watched us: grim-mouthed, iron-masked, blunt little being, his bearing and robes adding a foot to his stature, Captain Ahab in drag, the soul in arms, episcopal. Epi-skopos: on-looking, over-seeing. With an eye that could tell a goat's hair from a sheep's at 40 paces and a mind honed to split either down the middle.

Not that we took much notice of him up there on the wall. But this was very much his college still:

> Orthodox, Catholic
> Crammed with Divinity,
> Damn the dissenters!
> Hurrah for old Trinity!

With the passion that has now channelled itself into very different expressions of student power, we would yell down and hustle out any Trinity man who dared to enter Strachan Hall without a gown, or we would spoon the tables in deafening approval of some returning college hero.

John Strachan had another epiphany in college. As Father Episkopon, he resided in the lantern of the highest turret among Trinity's towers, like the reserved sacrament, God's body, a ghostly but real Presence. Once a year his chosen Scribe visited the Father to receive word of his children's behaviour, the men of Trinity. We processed through the dark halls singing very low:

> Are you ready?
> Yes, we're ready, ready as can be.
> With sword in hand,
> We'll march through the land,
> At the Order of the Golden Key.

Then, by the guttering candlelight, in the presence of a skull and crossbones, the Scribe would read out the anonymous judgments upon the behaviour of members of college submit-ted by their fellows, some witty, some cruelly accurate.

I learned later that at his first school in Cornwall, John

Strachan had a black book of shortcomings which consisted of extracts from daily registers kept by the monitors and himself, and each month would read out the choicest excerpts to his assembled pupils and comment upon them. There was also a book of merit. As an old man he still had one of the books and brought it out occasionally when his old students came to pay their respects. At one of these gatherings, he called them to order—chief justices, merchant princes and the rest, none of them under 60—with the stentorian command, "Boys!" They came to attention and fell silent, instantly back at school, as they had been 50 years before.

Even for some of us in 1948 this ancient Scot was a compelling authority figure, a father to be coped with. The confrontation I remember best was not during Episkopon but at a ceremonial dinner in Strachan Hall where members of the leaving class could speak their minds to the assembled college. The nimblest and quickest of us, class rake and rebel (he had played Mercutio brilliantly at Hart House), leapt onto the high table, glass in hand, and proposed an insulting toast to Strachan's portrait. I forget exactly what rich invitations he extended to our founder (with all Don Giovanni's panache to the graveyard statue of the *commendatore*), but he ended up by railing at the portrait, "You old bastard!" He was the first of our class to be killed, run down by a British lorry while on duty against the Mau Mau in Kenya.

Strachan, as Bagehot said of Lord Eldon, believed in everything it is impossible to believe in. For Strachan, the hope of the world lay in British institutions. By that he meant King, Lords and unreformed House of Commons, rotten boroughs and all; an established Church, the Common Law as it stood in the eighteenth century, and of course Empire, not Commonwealth. The doctrine of responsible government was "an insane paradox," "a phantom"; the secret ballot was "the most corrupt way of using the franchise"; free trade was against all "common sense."

There was no hope for mankind in either the democratic dictatorship of Napoleonic France or the republican anarchy of the United States. The Declaration of Independence was a pernicious document to be refuted, point by point. George III was a paragon among men, Thomas Jefferson a mischief-maker. Any sane political doctrine required that duty be placed before liberty. True authority derived from rank, age and experience, from the few, not the many, from the past, not the whim of the passing present. Fear was as necessary an influence in the classroom as in the body politic, and the manliest virtues were to be learned through struggle and adversity. A sound education and the Protestant faith were inseparable. The possibility of world peace lay in the power of the British navy. The future of a stable Canada called for the gradual absorption of the French population and influence.

In Strachan's Upper Canada the contest lay between tories and radicals. But since 1841 Canada has been run by men of the centre: conservative Reformers like Baldwin, Liberal-Conservatives like Macdonald, Liberals who swallowed the progressives like King, Conservatives turned progressive (dubbed the Forwards Backwards party by Stephen Leacock when they changed their name in 1942) and all the rebels and outsiders who have joined the established parties in hopes of taking them over. Ours has been a politics of the extreme centre. We are a people of the law, not the prophets, hewing diligently, as the Irishman put it, to the straight and narrow path between right and wrong.

Strachan died in 1867 in his ninetieth year. The century that followed turned most of his fears for Canada into a reality. Why then is he interesting again after 100 years of neglect? Why are we fascinated with such an anachronism? Perhaps Strachan's style and posture are relevant once more. Certain of the older virtues are attractive again. Excellence and the remarkable individual. Plain speaking and a contempt for the press and popular conventional wisdom. An imprudent urge to bring the cutting edge of ideas to politics.

In the age of McLuhan, liberalism and the linear mode were no longer adequate. Tribal community became more comprehensible. The canons of secular academic education were questioned for their lack of moral content and commitment. Tory and radical have always shared a fierce rejection of the American way of life. Strachan is the patron saint of Yankee-baiters, the first and most successful anti-New Roman. No Canadian has ever confronted the American military more effectively or with greater effrontery. In 1813, after the British general had withdrawn with his troops to Kingston, Strachan was the governing presence in enemy-occupied Toronto. When he was through giving General Dearborn a piece of his mind—an act that led to the prompt signing of the articles of truce—it was difficult, as one historian has said, to tell who was the conqueror and who the conquered.

But Strachan will not be remade into a long-lost great-uncle to the new left. The Family Compact and the Vertical Mosaic and the monarchy may be in retreat (as they were in his day), but they are not dead yet. The Union Jack still flies in the Ontario flag—and in the Ontario mind. The provincial coat of arms proclaims our loyalty. We do not like rebels. The final assault on Mackenzie's followers at Montgomery's Tavern was planned in Strachan's front parlour. The editor of the Hamilton *Spectator* in his denunciation of student rebels in 1969 might just as well have been using words uttered by Strachan on rebellion night in 1837. "There is some danger," said the *Spectator*, "of righteous wrath focussing on too limited a target." (Of one troublesome assemblyman Strachan said, "Never mind the law, toorn him oot!" And out he went.)

There are ambivalences still. This admirer of England never set foot there until he was 46, a quarter-century after he had first visited New York. The British objected to his charter for King's College, Toronto, on the grounds that it was too liberal. He had no use for English gentleman-clergy who could not rough it on the frontier the way he did on his prodigious travels. He was snubbed many times as a young man in Scotland because of his rough manner, broad accent and lack of pedigree. Appointed without salary to the episcopate in 1839 after half a lifetime of lobbying for the position, he became the first Church of England bishop in generations not born a gentleman. He then turned Toronto into the first self-governing diocese in the Empire and provided that future bishops were to be elected by clergy and people rather than appointed by the Crown.

Strachan's ruling principle was that of the family. He believed church or school or college should be run according to "the principles of a well-regulated family." His former pupils were aptly named the Family Compact. When he was seven years old in Aberdeen, his own family held a council that decided he should go to school rather than be apprenticed like his brothers. The oldest boy argued for a scholar in the family; his father, sensibly, that there was no hope of a position in the Kirk without a rich or influential patron. His mother settled the matter by recalling the miraculous circumstances of his birth—at the twelfth hour on the twelfth day of the first month of spring, when the sun and moon were full, and the tide was high, "and the sacrament dispensing in the city."

Many years later his old friend Mrs. Sibbald recalled visiting him: "There he sat in an armchair with a tabby cat as big as a dog on his knees. 'You know, my lord, why I am here?' 'No, but I am glad to see you.' 'Well, this is your eighty-third birthday and I am come to congratulate you.'

'O, then I must have a kiss.' So up he jumped for the purpose, tumbling poor pussy to the ground.''

In terror of the dominie's disciplinary rages, a student once wrote home, ''Mr. Strachan is very passionate.'' But Strachan himself spoke of true discipline as springing from a certain ''civility of the heart.'' He was in the habit of whistling huskily to himself—Scottish airs and tavern songs usually, and louder as he grew older and deafer. He whistled at meetings, on the street, in the cathedral during a dull sermon, and even at the funeral of Mrs. Sibbald. O rage repressed!

Strachan died on All Saints' Day, November 1, 1867. Business was suspended throughout the city. The streets of Toronto were draped in black and lined with people as the funeral cortege moved by to the beat of muffled drums toward the gaslit gloom of St. James' Cathedral. The procession included the officers of six militia units, the city council, the magistrates and the police, the benchers of the Law Society, 150 clergy of various denominations, the faculty and students of Trinity and the University of Toronto, the masters and boys of Upper Canada College and Toronto Normal School, members of the patriotic societies—St. Patrick's, St. Andrew's and the rest—and a host of private citizens.

Strachan had outlived all his children but one, as well as his dearest friend and former pupil, John Beverley Robinson, and his beautiful invalid wife, Anne, whom he had watched over tenderly for so long. During his far journeys across the diocese he always wrote her loving letters—but signed them formally with the name he had long since assumed and earned: John Toronto.

UPPER CANADA
COLLEGE
AND ITS
OLD BOYS

Its red brick clock tower is no longer the highest point in Toronto and Upper Canada College has long since ceased to be a central issue in the politics of education. Gone are many of its oldest traditions: caning, fagging, the hazing of new boys, the compulsory cadets in their archaic uniforms, the strict code of classroom dress and manners. The two immediate past principals, an Anglican clergyman and a former officer in the Gurkha Rifles, both British schoolmasters, have been succeeded by a Canadian university professor. But on the green acres of playing fields in the heart of Toronto young men in whites play cricket while the swarm of rush-hour traffic makes a wide detour around them. The great cathedral of elms still arches over the ceremonial avenue beyond the front gate, as if protected by some magic spell from disease and the designs of traffic commissioners. If Upper Canada College no longer dominates, it still stands aloof, a place apart. The inner quadrangle, the groves and paths among the college buildings, speak of an older and half-forgotten society. And in an age when almost all the bastions of masculine exclusivity have fallen—the Anglican priesthood, English colleges and schools, the Empire Club of Toronto, the RCMP—there are still, at Upper Canada College, no girls.

What on earth are Tom Brown's school days doing in postmodern Toronto? Can a North American democracy tolerate an English public school, with its connotations of class and privilege and discipline? Should such a place as Upper Canada College exist at all?

From its beginning in 1829 the college sought to train an elite, the future leaders of a British colony in the wilderness. The Family Compact sent its sons there, and in every generation since one can find their descendants in the school. Of the economic elite identified in John Porter's *The Vertical Mosaic* no less than one-third came from the private schools, and of these Upper Canada College supplied the largest number. Conrad Black, Ken Thomson, John and Fred Eaton are Old Boys. Yet the college never achieved the preeminent political place of its English models such as Eton, or even the status of the classical colleges in Quebec. No prime minister of Canada has graduated from UCC, and none of the recent chief executive officers of the five great chartered banks. The best known Old Boys are not those one might expect. Vincent Massey, who did so much for the school, attended Jarvis Collegiate, among other places, but not Upper Canada College. But Stephen Leacock did attend, and actor Melvyn Douglas; philosopher George Grant and novelist Robertson Davies; the artist Michael Snow and the composer (of *Hair*) Galt MacDermot; Father Dan Heap, MP, who worked for years as a shop steward in a box factory; editor and author Peter C. Newman, who came to Canada as a young refugee from Europe; Canada's leading Marxist historian, Stanley Ryerson; and Toronto's iconoclastic mayor and self-proclaimed friend of the lunch-pail voter, Allan Lamport. While it never really fulfilled the role originally (or even still) widely expected of it, the college in a century and a half has been a rich cultural haven, and sometimes a hated prison, to a great many exceptional young men.

In the 1980s it finds itself in excellent financial shape, better able than ever to pick and choose from a long list of aspiring applicants. But what makes 180 pairs of anxious parents compete fiercely for the 30 places open annually for new entrants to the Upper School? People who already pay a heavy municipal school tax are eager to put out an extra $6,000 (day boy's fees) or $10,000 (boarder's fees). Some of them are not affluent and must dip into savings, or work at an extra job, to keep a son at the college. Is it the discipline, the schooling in manners, athletics for all, the special quality of teaching? Or is it something as mundane as the procuring of future contacts for their boy—or association with elite parents for themselves?

The original Upper Canada College
buildings on King Street, opposite
Government House. The college moved
to its present location in Deer Park
during the 1890s.
Engraving from the
Canadian Illustrated News,
November 8, 1879.

Major General Sir John Colborne, who still gazes upon the school in bronze effigy from his founder's pedestal in the quad, was a remarkable man. Not the most powerful character who has shaped the college's destiny, he was not even a very good politician, and certainly no intellectual or academic. But while he may not have known much about education, he knew what he liked. As soon as he arrived at Little York in 1828 as the new lieutenant-governor of Upper Canada, he determined to found a college. Defying or ignoring the wishes of both his superiors in London and the little clique who were accustomed to having their way in the colony, he used every resource and connection at his disposal to provide funds and to recruit a "cargo of masters" from English universities. Within a year of the college's opening in a temporary quarters he had completed a handsome set of buildings on the square beside Government House at King and Simcoe streets. Colborne's headstrong ways had been apparent early in his career. At the Battle of Waterloo it was the young Lieutenant-Colonel Colborne who, without orders from headquarters, wheeled the entire Fifty-second Regiment and broke Napoleon's Imperial Guard.

Sir John had acquired and practised his daring and determination at Winchester College, one of the great English public schools. After the war, as lieutenant-governor of Guernsey, he refounded the Channel Islands' decaying Elizabeth College on the Winchester model. In Upper Canada he decided to build a similar school. It was particularly needed, he felt, to counteract democratic and American influences in the province, as well as to prepare its best young men for the professions and for leadership in politics, society and the army. His goal took precedence over the projected university that John Strachan, leader of the Family Compact, had set his heart on, and also over expanding the motley collection of public grammar schools already in place. It inevitably diverted public funds from both. Fees of £8 for day boys and £25 for boarders were not exorbitant, but they helped establish UCC's reputation for exclusivity. So did the provision of salaries large enough to lure excellent English masters to the staff—most of them Anglican clerics from Cambridge—when there were already a number of teachers available locally.

In the provincial assembly, William Lyon Mackenzie tried to have Governor Colborne impeached for endowing the college so extravagantly—"by the sweat of the brow of the Canadian labourer." Bishop Strachan, determined to get his university, was more diplomatic. He confined his criticisms of UCC to the "preposterous" frills, such as hiring drawing masters. He recognized the quality of its classical curriculum, however, and enrolled his sons. So did Chief Justice John Beverley Robinson, and the Jarvises, the Boultons, the Ridouts and the Baldwins. For the next couple of generations most of the leading families were represented at UCC. Even Egerton Ryerson, creator of the province's public school system, rather ruefully decided to send his sons to Upper Canada, because of its superior teaching. And in 1850, on returning from his post-rebellion exile, so did William Lyon Mackenzie himself.

The boys enjoyed a special niche at the great ceremonies of church and state. They were paraded along King Street to St. James' Cathedral every Sunday morning; at the opening and closing of the legislature there was a place reserved for them. They begged a half-holiday of the governor to watch the trooping of the colours. In 1838, they were given another one so that they might surround the scaffold at the public hanging of the rebel leader Samuel Lount.

The rebellion itself had been part of their education. As Toronto panicked at the rumours of rebels marching down Yonge Street in early December of 1837, the boys almost in a body waited upon Lieutenant-Governor Francis Bond Head and offered their services to Queen Victoria. The governor thanked them warmly, gave them each a piece of cake and told them to go home. Instead, some of them decided to cut northeast through the bush beyond Queen Street. Sure enough, they found the rebel front lines near the Yorkville tollgate on Yonge Street and stayed to spy on a few "rough men riding about, apparently much excited," as one of them wrote in his diary. The boys were spotted and taken prisoner. The contrast between the rumoured massing of bloodthirsty rebels and the dismal reality was something they were "aching to get back and tell about." The sight of a rebel aiming his rifle at one prisoner deterred them for a while, but they finally pried a window open and eluded several rebel horsemen by diving into the thick woods between Yonge Street and what is now Avenue Road. Back at headquarters in Archdeacon Strachan's living room they told their story and were lionized as "the little heroes of the hour" by the attendant crowds.

As the colony grew into a prosperous province, the Old Boys of UCC took their place as lawyers, financiers, judges and MPs. Ontario's first minister of education, a former head boy, took office just in time to save the school from a particularly bad patch of financial difficulty and attacks upons its privileges in the legislature. Nor was Colborne's military tradition forgotten. One of the first Victoria Cross winners (in the Crimean War) was from UCC. Like the heroes of G.A. Henty's stirring imperial tales, Upper Canada boys fought in the Northwest Rebellion, on the Nile and in the Boer War. One hundred and seventy-six of them died in France in 1914–18 and 26, including Chief of Staff General H.D.G. Crerar, achieved brigadier status or higher in World War II.

The apogee, as well as the ultimate parody, of the college's and of his family's fighting tradition was Septimus Julius Augustus, seventh son of George Taylor Denison II, whose father organized the cavalry troop, Denison's Horse, and ruled over 100 tenants on his country estate. "A perpetual adolescent whose exploits were largely confined to ceremonial and to the dispersion of civil riots," as historian Carl Berger described him, Septimus finally came into his own on the South African veldt: "Just as the sun had risen I heard the first gun," he wrote in his memoirs, "and thanked God I had found at last what I have been searching for for twenty-three years, viz., an enemy."

His older brother, Colonel G.T. Denison III, who became chairman of the UCC board of governors, was of more consequence. Founder of the Canada First movement and a leading spokesman for British imperialism, he won the czar of Russia's prize in 1879 for his *History of Cavalry*, still one of the definitive works on the subject. He, too, lent himself to caricature, because of his exaggerated military bearing in the post of Toronto's police magistrate, his spirited public defence of UCC ("Have the rich no rights?" he once demanded), and his virulent anti-Americanism. He threatened, if they erected the planned statue of George Washington in Westminster Abbey, to go there just to spit on it. After the repulse of the Fenian raiders, who crossed the Niagara River in 1866 to "liberate" Canada, he picked up a Yankee sword from the battlefield and kept it as a poker to stir his grate. (The college cadet corps was attached to the Queen's Own Rifles during the Fenian Raids, and all living members were later given active service medals for guarding the Toronto armouries.)

The archetypical nineteenth-century Old Boy was not a military man nor a member of the Family Compact but the editor of the *Evening Telegram*, John Ross Robertson. Later to become the founder of the Hospital for Sick Children, a member of Parliament and president of the Ontario Jockey Association, Robertson devoted his college career to the integration of football, gymnastics and rowing into the school's activities, and to creating *The College Times*, Canada's first school paper. Though one of his editorials attacked the college authorities for planning to sell some of their King Street property, he managed to evade being caned or closed down. At 16 he invested the $50 given to him by his father (for being wounded during an election riot) in his own printing business. He set type himself and ran off his paper on an old hand press at the *Globe* office.

In later years, Robertson's *Telegram* could be relied on to defend the college in a continuing controversy over its right to public funds. As editor of *College Times*, his successors have included B.K. Sandwell, editor of *Saturday Night*; the Anglican primate of all Canada, Archbishop T.C. Macklem; Broadway playwright and founder of the Shaw Festival Brian Doherty; Ottawa mandarin A.F.W. Plumptre; publisher and critic Ivon Owen; typographer and book designer Paul Arthur; and Stephen Leacock and Robertson Davies. The earliest major figure among college masters was John Howard, a young surveyor-architect-engineer who came out to Canada in 1832. A letter of recommendation to one of the Robinsons and a meeting with Governor Colborne led to the position of drawing master at UCC. The boys respected his skill and their parents became clients for his buildings. His masterpiece was the 1846 provincial asylum on Queen Street, which was destroyed by the Ontario government in 1976. As Toronto's first mayor, William Lyon Mackenzie appointed Howard city surveyor, and in that role he began the transformation of Muddy York by laying out the city's first plank sidewalks. Howard bought High Park, built himself the elegant Colborne Lodge, which still stands there, and eventually bequeathed it all to the citizens of Toronto.

In the later nineteenth century the masters included the Reverend Charles Gordon, who as Ralph Connor wrote *The Man from Glengarry*, George Johnson, composer of "When You and I Were Young, Maggie," and E.R. Peacock, who as Sir Edward became a director of the Bank of England. Stephen Leacock was 17 years at UCC, as both student and teacher, and it is not difficult to find the sententious cadence of the schoolmaster's wit in his later prose.

For the benefit of parents who were overly helpful with a son's homework, Leacock would remark: "Tell your father, young man, that he must use the ablative after *pro*." For a colleague who wished to complain to the board of governors, he drafted a letter: "Unless you can see your way to increasing my stipend immediately, I shall reluctantly be forced"— and then, over the page—"to continue working for the same figure." In later years, Leacock expressed his sympathy for "the many gifted and brilliant men who spent their lives in the most dreary, thankless and worst paid profession in the world." Like many of his colleagues, Leacock got out as soon as he could—to be a professor at McGill.

For its inmates, the most memorable figures of the college were usually the masters who devoted their lives to the place. Few early graduates would forget the mathematician George Maynard, a Cambridge clergyman and petty eccentric, who played first violin in the college orchestra, made the boys rattle off their arithmetic problems as fast as he could gabble morning prayers, wore a magnificent gold chain and velvet waistcoat and a cape and hat, and spent more than 20 years feuding with another senior colleague until the demise of them both.

The most beloved figure on staff, still held up as a model nearly a century after his retirement, was probably John "Gentle" Martland, the first master to make of the boarding house something more than a bleak detention home. He tempered the spartan regime of long study drills, chilly dormitories, dreary diets and the bullying of the weak by the strong with an easier discipline for all, swift punishment for gross offenders, occasional feasts, civilized recreation and much fatherly counsel and encouragement. His nickname derived from his habit of emphasizing the "gentle" as he addressed his young gentlemen, and from the mild, sweet manner he taught by example. To Toronto's fashionable hostesses, Martland was a modest, reliable extra man to fit into a formal dinner at short notice—a dear "old worldling," as one of them put it, a good "afternoon man." But to many of the boys to whom he gave his life, he was their first formal acquaintance with the graces of civilization and the meaning of kindness. He set a pattern that has not been without a glimmering of renewal in every UCC generation since.

The better the college became as a place for its students, the more it attracted public attacks on its special character and privileges. In 1869 its government grant, though smaller than in Colborne's time, was still 25 times as large as that for the average of the 104 small grammar schools in the province. UCC's downtown Toronto site was worth a small fortune.

"This illegitimate offspring of Sir John Colborne's scheming brain," cried one critic, "born of fraud and nurtured by spoliation, should be called to strict account." A backbencher in the legislature moved that it be abolished entirely. Well-placed Old Boys, including Robertson of the *Telegram*, defended the school with just as much gusto and hyperbole. In the 1880s however, the government was forced to compromise by reducing staff salaries and in 1891 by arranging to move UCC entirely onto cheap land on the heights of Deer Park north of St. Clair Avenue.

From the outset the turmoil had taken its toll of college principals. The first one retired to the peace of an English country vicarage, taking with him Governor Colborne's sister-in-law as his wife. The second, Reverend John McCaul, as soon as he could decently leave, became vice-president and then president of the University of Toronto. The strongest, a brilliant Scot named George Cockburn, retired at the age of 47 in exhaustion and disgust after 20 years of battle—eventually to begin a new career as a Toronto business tycoon and a member of Parliament. In the 1880s and '90s the school more than once seemed on the verge of extinction. It required two great public figures to steer UCC into the safer paths of independence and give it the character it possesses today.

The first was Sir George Parkin, the renowned evangelist for the British Empire and its virtues, who ended his career back at Oxford in charge of the Rhodes scholarships. The son of a New Brunswick farmer, Parkin was converted to the glories of English culture by a year at Oxford and the friendship of a great British headmaster at Uppingham. Back home in Fredericton he established a boarding school modelled on the lesser English public schools. He also wrote books, became a correspondent of *The Times* of London and began a series of triumphant lecture tours of Britain and the Empire.

His appointment as principal of UCC in 1895 gave him a more secure base and he in turn determined to give the school its independence of the state. It helped greatly, of course, that Parkin received his knighthood and quickly became the foremost sage of Toronto. Prime Minister Wilfrid Laurier came to dinner; young Winston Churchill, like all important British visitors, sought him out for counsel. Sir George put it sternly to Old Boys and Toronto business magnates alike, starting with Timothy Eaton, that they must give him funds that would allow him to cut off provincial control. In 1900 his goal was achieved. And though the teachers' salaries took another beating, Parkin also managed to find capital funds to add some buildings and playing fields. In educating his young men, his first concern was the training of Christian character and the formation of general culture. He regularly preached sermons that—his son-in-law recalled—"never quite got God and Oxford and the British Empire" wholly separated.

That son-in-law, William ("Choppy") Grant, was himself the son of Canada's foremost educator, George Grant, principal of Queen's University. After teaching history at UCC, and at Oxford and Queen's, Grant arrived back from war service in 1917 to take over as principal. Even the statistics show just how much the college depended on strong leadership. Not long after Parkin left to run the Rhodes Trust in 1902, enrollment began declining—to a nadir of 214 during the regime of a brilliant English schoolmaster who simply could not cope with the board of governors or his teaching staff. When Grant arrived the total began to climb—to more than 600 in the 1920s.

Although he was an academic who had written some of the better Canadian history books of his day, Grant, like Parkin, put the formation of character and manners ahead of narrow academic training. He loathed the examination-ridden regime favoured by the Ontario system and its pedagogues, men who in his view were "devoured by the birds of Pedantry and Philistinism." For his staff he sought out teachers of passionate conviction, usually combined with remarkable personality traits, who could both discipline and inspire the students. He expected a modicum of intelligence, and preferably some experience in the school of life, but he never worried about what university degrees or teacher training the men had taken.

The quintessential Grant appointment was J.M.B.P. ("Jock") de Marbois, CBE, Légion d'Honneur, a naval officer and adventurer, fluent in 20 languages, who was born on the island of Mauritius in the Indian Ocean. He had married the daughter of the czar's commander of Horse Guards, the Countess Tatiana, for which he was hunted through Russia with a price on his head in the days following the October Revolution. De Marbois' unorthodox modern language classes were exciting and he tested his charges with a great variety of extracurricular activities. Along with another young teacher and refugee from the Russian Revolution, Nicholas Ignatieff, he began the practice of taking UCC boys on adventure tours in the Canadian Rockies. De Marbois was one of the first to promote the sports of skiing and archery in Canada; his efforts at teaching polo, however, for which he devised a wooden horse in a high wire cage, came to grief. At the outbreak of war in 1939, he was called to Naval Intelligence in Ottawa and eventually became a commodore in both the Royal Navy and the Royal Canadian Navy.

To aid him in his war against Canadian Philistinism, Principal Grant enlisted the services of a brilliant young Canadian organist and conductor, Ernest MacMillan, and of Ettore Mazzoleni, who followed MacMillan as principal of the Royal Conservatory of Music. There had been some form of visual arts teaching at UCC since the days of John Howard, but Grant was the first to insist on drama as a necessary part of a young man's education. From the beginning of his regime amateur theatricals were part of school life. Productions of Gilbert and Sullivan have long since been commonplace fare in Canadian high schools, but they were a rarity in Toronto in 1929 when they became a annual event at UCC. Arthur Gelber, energetic and perpetual chairman of one major Canadian cultural operation or another, began his days at UCC as Buttercup; his brother Shalom, a giant of six foot four who went on to a rabbinical career in New York, played the Fairy Queen in *Iolanthe*. Grant took young Arthur aside at the age of 18 and told him that he had a great future ahead of him in Canadian theatre.

Robertson Davies has written that it was Grant and a couple of other UCC mentors he had in mind when portraying Dunstan Ramsay in the Deptford Trilogy—"men of character, old warriors, ripe scholars." Grant went out of his way to enliven a boy's interest in history and literature from his own personal experience. One day, as Davies was walking the Oval, "the Headmaster seemed to rise out of the ground at my side. 'Walk with me,' he said, 'and I'll tell you about the Oscar Wilde scandal.' Therewith he proceeded to do so, in such a richness of detail, and with the use of words that I thought only boys knew, that he left me stupefied and elated."

Grant even managed to make Christianity exciting. One night in Prayer Hall, his charges were electrified to hear him shouting, "Live in the large! Dare greatly, and if you must sin, sin nobly." In scripture class Grant would transfix some bland youth by demanding what he thought he would have been doing at the time of Crucifixion if he were standing within 100 yards of the cross, and when the reply was noncommittal, he would mutter the words "a clod, unen-lightened by a spark." To an oversolicitous mother he is reported to have said, "Take your son out of this school and never let me look upon his face again."

The principal was just as capable of challenging everyone else he had to deal with. He stood up to the board of governors when they demanded better first-class teams at the expense of sports participation for all, or asked him to stop his "socialist" speakers from the Student Christian Movement from polluting young minds. Grant blasted parents who allowed their sons to enjoy Toronto's social rounds to the detriment of their studies. And when his own Canadian history text was banned from one school system for being "anti-British" and "pro-French," he responded by insisting on an even more prominent role for French at the school and pressing in his public addresses for a greater understanding of French Canada.

When Grant died in his prime in the winter of 1935, of pneumonia exacerbated by war wounds, it was perhaps comparable to the shock that went through Rugby at the death of Dr. Arnold. A moral force had ceased to emit its energy upon the Canadian public; people who had never met him felt a personal loss. The Ontario Legislature stopped its business and kept a silent vigil upon receiving the word. The Parkin-Grant dynasty continues, of course—not only in the philosopher George Grant (named for both his grandfathers) and his son-in-law George Ignatieff, chancellor of the University of Toronto, but in many remarkable daughters, in-laws and grandchildren.

When I was informed by my parents some three years after Grant's death that I was to be sent to the preparatory school of Upper Canada College, I wept quietly to myself. I was 10 years old, had been through eight classes in three different schools, and was by now thoroughly afraid of change. Worse, I had intimations, from cousins who were there, of the college as a place of rough boys, severe masters and mysterious, ominously cruel customs. I was a bit of a cream-faced loon anyway. My father was gentle and compassionate about my predicament but absolutely firm. He believed I would get a richer curriculum and the sports I had missed in public school (since I wasn't very good at them). He was right on all counts, and to my surprise, toward the end of my stay seven years later, I even got to like the place.

Principal Grant had been able to dominate the college. He

could resist far better than his successor the Philistinism of powerful members of the board, the fancies of influential parents and the sophisticated barbarism of their offspring. Compounding the school's troubles, the Depression had cut into the number of families who could afford the $250-a-year day boy's fees and thinned the already sparse ranks of rich people willing to make donations. The school was not full to capacity, and there was no waiting list for any boy with a modicum of intelligence. Though discipline was strict in a haphazard sort of way, I had the impression that it would be difficult to get oneself expelled. Conrad Black managed it 20 years later—for his entrepreneurship in the field of final exam sales to classmates. But in my day, even that might have escaped official action, if any of us had the gall or the imagination to try it.

After 1939 the school lost some of its best young masters to the armed services and other war duties. Many of the senior ones who remained were well into the full flower of their eccentricity. Indeed, they seemed to us boys not ordinary adult human beings at all, but creatures of a different species. In varying mixtures they were one part wise old magician, one part irrational tyrant, and one part boy like us—not a bad recipe, of course, if you want to command attention and stir the imagination. With some of them, it seemed at times as if we were at school with the Marx Brothers.

The most memorable aspect of my education was the shared suffering through various compulsory rituals and ceremonies of college life: rifle battalion drills in our heavy blue serge uniforms; the terrors of the annual boxing tournament; the chest-stabbing agony of the cross-country steeplechase, which always seemed to be scheduled for a day of driving rain or sleet; the long tables at lunch presided over by a master who initiated things with the sort of quick, obscure ceremony that Huckleberry Finn used to call "grumbling over the vittles"; the extra tasks imposed for breach of school rules or lack of zeal in studies.

Compared to these, interhouse sports every afternoon and the bellowing out of hymns at 9 a.m. school prayers were requirements I positively exulted in. We loved to raise the roof with what we thought of as the school hymn: "To Be a Pilgrim" by John Bunyan. "He who would valiant be/ 'Gainst all disaster/Let him in constancy/Follow the Master." But our favourite, and that of the classics master who died in harness in his fiftieth year of teaching at the school, was "O Quanta Qualia" by Peter Abelard. As we sang the

Latin of his 800-year-old celebration of the joys of the heavenly Jerusalem from our struggling exile here below, we could gaze at the great polished dark boards on the walls above us with the gold-lettered names of our predecessors who had run their course—medallists, scholars, head boys, war dead—glowing up there in the high gloom around us. We were indeed "encompassed about by so great a cloud of witnesses," as the scripture lesson reminded us, and linked at that place and moment to the living, the dead and the yet to be born, whose names would in their day join the others on the walls. Frequently, as the war dragged on toward its seventh year, the principal would gravely announce at the beginning of prayers that another of our number, often one who had been a boy among us a few months before, was missing or killed in action.

On arrival at the Upper School at the age of 12 or 14, whether he came from the exalted ranks of Upper Remove One in the Prep or from the most benighted of public schools, every new boy was adorned with a crinkly blue and white barred tie to go with his necessary white shirt, jacket and flannels. At the howl through the halls of "Nyooooboyyy!!" from any of the school prefects he was expected to scurry toward the source of the cry and await fagging instructions. These might be fetching grub from the tuck shop to one of the house common rooms at mid-morning break or tidying up the sergeants' mess, or running a message to the masters' common room. For evasion, or even a slothful response, the penalty would be something like seven times round the oval—"*on* the double!" If only one or two minions were required, first arrivals usually got off scot-free.

New boys were also drilled by their seniors in college lore and custom and were required to practice the unofficial school song: "We never stagger, we never fall, we sober up on wood alcohol." To the question, "Where and when did the UCC battalion win its battle colours?" one of our number with a little more local history than the rest of us essayed, "Montgomery's Tavern, sir, 1837?" and was swatted for being cheeky, though his answer was just as serious, if no more accurate, than the stern enjoinder, "Battle of Ridgeway, Fenian Raids, boy, and don't let me have to correct you again."

To become a prefect you participated in everything for four years and awaited your reward in the fifth. Half a dozen prefects were chosen for each of the five houses from among young men with proven qualities of leadership, or failing that, simple endurance. Even more exalted were the stewards, who were officers of the whole school and consisted of the first team captains of the three major sports, the editor of *College Times*, the lieutenant-colonel of the battalion, the five head house prefects and the two senior scholars, the Head of the House from the ranks of the boarders and the Head of the Town from among the day boys.

I was Head of the Town in my last year (sixth form), but prouder of having been chosen a prefect in my house (for persistence in athletics, I think), since scholarship was at best suspect among the qualities valued by the crude, smart young men who set the tone of the place. Heads of Town and House did get to do certain enviable tasks, however, such as leading the great procession of notables, governors and masters into assembly on Prize Day. The two of us were drilled in the niceties of a double slow march devised to accommodate the laborious shuffle of the nonagenarian university chancellor, Sir William Mulock, who delighted in pausing altogether from time to time in order to bow to any particularly beautiful white-haired lady he spied in the audience.

Attending the first team games was a different affair in each of the three major sports. Football on the oval against one of the other Little Big Four—Ridley, Trinity or St. Andrew's—was usually witnessed by, besides the boys from the other school and ourselves, a number of masters and parents and—in their ugly grey and maroon but leggily gratifying uniforms—girls from nearby Bishop Strachan School. We ripped into the rawest of our school yells as much for their benefit as the team's:

> *Nigger nigger hop-a-trigger*
> *Half past alligator*
> *Ram ram bulligator*
> *Chickawanna duck*
> *College! College! Rush 'er up!*

By contrast, at first team hockey in Maple Leaf Gardens, courtesy of Old Boy owner Conn Smythe, the favourite pastime of UCC spectators, uninhibited here by guests, masters or the role of host, was fighting the enemy in the stands. Our chief hockey rivals were the University of Toronto Schools and St. Michael's; they were deemed particularly alien and contemptible for being, respectively, scholars and Catholics. (We had quite a few of both at UCC, of course, but they didn't exactly flaunt it.)

For first team cricket we changed roles again, from city toughs into imitation English gentlemen, commenting over tea on the daring positioning of silly mid-off or clapping evenhandedly the elegant stroke of either our own batsman or theirs.

The biggest ceremonial of the year was Battalion Inspection Day. With drums rolling and bugles blaring, the long ranks of silver-bedizened navy blue uniforms and berets, black leather spats and boots and swinging white gloves, officers in sword and Sam Browne, sergeants in red sash, the colour party in the centre as solemn as if their flags were the Ark of the Covenant itself, we manoeuvred and paraded formally for hours under the blazing sun. To prepare the occasion there had been months of platoon and company drill, turning, wheeling, quick march, slow march, eyes right, marking time, numbering, standing motionless at attention, shouldering arms, slapping the rifle butts in unison. In case your rifle, that Great War brute of an old Ross .303 whose misfiring had undoubtedly killed at least some of those young men named in gold on our memorial boards, should slip and fall, you must drop with it, to be born off on a stretcher—no disgrace to faint, but God help you if you did not fake it when necessary.

The best part of the battalion year, except for those who simply loved doing the drill for its own sake or yelling orders at their inferiors, was the Battalion Ball, an occasion of splendour and one of the rare chances we got to take the young women of our choice into one of the messes or some other holy of holies. The worst part, I think, was the long church parade to St. Paul's on Bloor Street and the sweating and itching through morning prayer and an intolerably long sermon when we got there.

After three years in the battalion you were allowed to become a civilian again if you could face the shame of it. Many who clearly were not destined for a commission as lieutenant, captain, major or whatever did so. I became neither officer nor civilian, however. I stubbornly soldiered on through everything, the only member of my class to spend a whole year in each rank, attaining finally in sixth form the workhorse position of platoon sergeant of the third-year malingerers. These were simply doing their minimum three years' time until they could get free of the whole dreary business. They were a standing joke in the school and the bane of the smart young officers from my own year who were continually punishing them for sloth and evasion. We took our revenge, however, by doing our drill well-nigh perfectly on Inspection Day for the visiting Colonel, while the platoons

Private Kilbourn, age 12, of the Upper
Canada College Cadet Batallion.

of smart young officer-candidates got fouled up in their nervous eagerness to please. To their astonishment and chagrin, we walked off with the honour of the platoon shield. The Dirty Dozen never had a sweeter reward.

Besides military, athletic and religious life at the school, there were *The College Times*, edited in the tower and hand-set in the basement print shop; little theatre directed by the chemistry master, Captain F.J. Mallett, husband to the delicious Jane; the annual Gilbert and Sullivan, as well as extra music from Dr. Arnold Walter, who had been finagled into Canada as a refugee by the school authorities and later became dean of music at the university; the college tree farm at Norval, whose planting parties I passed up in favour of required labour on our family Victory garden; the Curfew Club for Sunday evening discussions with an interesting visitor on anything from postwar world affairs to eugenics.

There always seemed to be time, if you really needed it, to explore the maze of rooms and passageways in the old building and its tower or to contemplate the silence of the Prayer Hall at dusk, or to walk about alone on the college grounds. Though there doubtless were such things at the school, most of us were quite ignorant about homosexual love affairs. I can remember talk of casual mutual masturbation in the boarding houses at night. But basically sex was something that happened off campus with girls or, for the more daring of us, was attempted in dark recesses or secret rooms on the nights of school dances. Our development suffered, I am sure, for lack of feminine participation in our everyday academic and social life. The one really significant female figure at UCC—for more than 40 years, as it turned out— was the vivacious and hail-fellow college nurse, Miss Barrow, who was buddy and mother-confessor to all in need, but especially to the military and athletic types. She also entertained a continual stream of Old Boys on their first or fortieth trip back to the school. I kept away from her infirmary throughout my college career, mainly, I think, for the same reason I cherished weekends and holidays: I felt gauche and uncomfortable in the company of boys older or more sophisticated than myself. On the whole, in fact, I hated school.

In a number of our academic subjects the same rather casual approach prevailed as in our optional extracurricular activities. I cannot be sure, for example, whether it was under the formal rubric of history, geography or English or all three, but in lower form classes Reverend John Davidson shared with us his interest in arcane lore, personal reminiscences and the basics of half a dozen subjects not approved by the minister of education. We were shown how to give close textual analysis to the New Testament Gospels; we learned about the interpretation of dreams and paranormal communication, such as he and his wife experienced when miles apart during their courtship. We were told how Lake Winnipeg got its name (Muddy Waters—from heroic mythical defecations) and other Nanabush legends, from his anthropology thesis on Indians. From his experience of China, he gave us the adventures of innocent Western visitors such as the one who asked for a supply of milk and months later discovered that the pailful he received each morning was being furnished by the women of his village. To help liven up the downtown political meetings of Father John Frank of Holy Trinity Church, our Mr. Davidson, who was also an early CCFer, would dress up in old clothes, smudge his face a bit and act as a heckler in the crowd. In his more formal classes we produced reviews of a weird variety of books and studied geological eras and the development of life on earth, from the Precambrian to Neanderthal man. If we were willing to give up some weekly spare time, we learned enough rudimentary Greek to labour through bits of Xenophon and Herodotus and, more important for most of us, to possess forever the key to one of the sources of the English language.

English literature was the subject I liked best, and for four years I was fortunate enough to have a superb teacher. He was perhaps a bit vain and self-absorbed, and when provoked gave to the more Philistine of his colleagues and students the benefit of his withering tongue. He was not warmly or widely appreciated at UCC and eventually left for another ill-paid job, in publishing. But for those of us who came green to Shakespeare and Milton, Coleridge, Dickens and Browning, J.J. Knights was wonderful. He also introduced us to contemporary writers nobody had ever heard of, some of whom even lived in Toronto—literature, it seemed, was not just the work of dead Englishmen. He helped us delight in the spoken word and trained us in choral recitation of poetry. It sank home to us in his classroom that literature could speak directly to our feelings and change our minds forever about how we should live our lives.

But nothing, except odd rumours, quite prepared us for Owen Classey, the ancient French department head. We did not know it until long after, but in his youth he had been private secretary to H.G. Wells. In our day he inhabited a set of attic chambers (formerly boarders' or maids' rooms) high up in the main building; some boys believed that he never left them. We were required to ascend to him by running up a double flight of stairs two steps at a time; how he knew accurately which boy to send down for a second attempt we were never sure. Latecomers would be hurled down for a second run. We soon got into the practice of arriving ahead of him. Sharp on the hour we would hear a faint, distant cry from another part of his attic, "Werrrk, ye bums!" then the slam of a door; then louder, closer, "Werrrrk, ye bums!" and slammm! and finally, "Werrrrrk!" a third time as he entered, coasting in like a figure on a merry-go-round with a mysterious grin on his chalky face. He was a wiry, wrinkled little man with grey-white skin, a Fuller Brush black moustache and a thick fringe of black hair round his bald pate. He was by then nearly deaf and, except when he put his ear close to a boy or used one of his uncanny extra senses, he could hear hardly anything. He would take attendance by calling out our names with the rapid fire command: "Signify-your-presence-by-raisin'-your-left-hand-at-the-same-time-not-disturbin'-the-index-finger-of-your-right-hand-which-is-engaged-in-follerin'-your-place-in-the-book."

Then he would begin with a stream of preposterous commentary on the French literature to hand. He obviously did not take all his own words seriously himself, but we were expected to pretend to. Mr. Classey relied on surprise and throwing us off balance. He would instruct us to read *Maria Chapdelaine* incessantly: "Take her to bed with you. Every night!" When he was pleased with us he would patrol the aisles as we scribbled, cooing softly, "Werrrk," like one of the pigeons under the eaves out the little window. But if the eyes in the back of his head spotted someone talking or exchanging something with his neighbour he was down on him instantly, cuffing heads in a flurry of blows. His anger seemed to fuel itself and he would then accuse the larger and more loutish of us of being "draft dodgers." Mr. Classey's nickname was Buzz, perhaps from a grinding sort of throat-singing he would do when leafing through the book for a piece of prose to spring on us. He invented such devices as a little silent air pistol that he used on dogs, which he loathed, and even on one occasion upon the rear end of a particularly large and pompous master. In those of us who were going around a second time with him, either because they had failed their senior matric the year before or were repeating it like myself in sixth form, he tolerated forms of behaviour that were not allowed to students in his class for the first time. Taking advantage of this, I would occasionally play my mouth organ in class—"A la Claire Fontaine" or "Au Prés de Ma Blonde" or the Marseillaise. He seemed never to hear it at all—except once when I strayed into a poor attempt at Glenn Miller, and was stopped immediately.

We loved Buzz. He was the ultimate anarchist, and he seemed to be a parody of everything that the school stood for. If the place made you miserable, he was an ally, however distant. Although I never attempted a conversation with him—any more than you would expect to have an intimate dialogue with the March Hare or the Cheshire Cat—I believe he recognized that until my last, repeated year I had been unhappy at UCC. He treated me, in his remote way, as a kindred spirit.

If Buzz Classey was the gargoyle on the academic structure of UCC, then Butch McKenzie was its cornerstone. To move from one class to the other was to shift from the surreal into a world of mad, total commitment. Lorne McKenzie was a figure of absolute terror for all but the most brilliant of scholars who took mathematics from him. He was said to be the best mathematics teacher in the province and certainly inspiring young men with his own passion for mathematics was the great mission of his life. He was possessed of a kind of divine frenzy. But he could not tolerate any failure to follow him, no matter how zealous you were or how hard you worked, although if you didn't show zeal or hard work it was even worse for you.

His hair was iron grey, his eye keen and penetrating, and his large face round, smooth and red-cheeked. He insisted on having us for a double period every day. He would begin calmly enough in his mellifluous high tenor voice, but he was soon scribbling a hint of some formula on the blackboard and then, with his chin resting on the great metre stick propped on his desk and an ominous smile on his face, slowly pronouncing the words, "There's not a boy here who can tell me. . . ." His whole form quivered and he leaned so hard on the metre stick that it would often skid a few inches on the shiny desk top. That slip of the stick always gave me a start, though I prepared for it a thousand times. Then he would suddenly throw both arms in the air and leap off his little podium as if his tubby frame could fly. This was the signal for us to jump up from our desks in a body with the completion of the formula on the tip of our tongues.

Invariably there were some hapless souls who remained bound to their seats in a spasm of mental paralysis. They knew the penalty for rising without the right answer. Butch would then single out each of them with sad, scornful remarks of a personal nature, heaping shame on their heads one by one. To one of three brothers who had been at the school he would say sadly, slowly shaking his head: "Oh, Stewart, Stewart, the youngest and the dumbest!" To another boy who had been at a public high school for a couple of years, with withering scorn, "Boy, you have been too long at school with *girrrls*." If it was a simple problem and few rose to answer, his fuse lit and he exploded. He would bellow at us dumbs and then come barrelling down one of the aisles to grab the nearest victim by the ear or the collar and throw him out of the room. Most terrible of all, he would go white in the face and say in an almost inaudible little voice, pointing at one after another, "Way out you go, boy, waaaayyy out," and these wretches one by one would go and stand in the hall to face more particular and excruciating torture after hours. We got through very few double periods in my four years under his rule without at least one of us standing outside in the hall. On some occasions almost the whole class was there.

Another of his tricks was to get us to stand at the blackboards, about a dozen at a time, and chalk up certain basic trigonometry formulas at lightning pace, wiping off with the chalk brush in our left hand almost simultaneously what we had written with our right. He rarely needed to look: "I can tell by the ticking of your chalk, boy, whether you've got it right." The first dozen would dash back to their seats and be replaced by another group attacking the board with their chalk sticks and brushes, Butch orchestrating the performance at a more and more furious pace until we finished.

He told us this would prepare us for the great day of reckoning, the provincial Grade 13 exams, when we would get into the examination hall and see the question paper. We would be so well prepared—and here he positively screamed in high soprano delight—"All the little formulas will come rushing before you, crying out, 'Use me! Use me! *Use me!*'"

My cousin John was the only boy in our class who had the temerity to replace one of his three mathematics with Grade 13 history; the timetable was such that those of us who took all three maths that year were not able to do history. Butch never forgave him for his foolish choice and used any device for torture that came to hand. There was often a mixed drill in all three maths and we would be sent to the board with a piece of paper bearing a problem in any one of them. John had the bad luck to pick up a formula in analytical geometry, the subject he wasn't taking, and he tried to bluff it out. He pretended it was something in algebra and after fooling about with it a while he finally wrote down the whole thing upside down on the board. Butch kept him up there a full 90 minutes, twisting in the wind, and finally hurled him out of the room just before the bell rang.

It was his towering repute as a disciplinarian and a teacher who got results that prompted the board of governors to appoint Butch McKenzie principal when his predecessor, T.W.L. MacDermot, left for government war service. The board was also reacting against MacDermot. A brilliant McGill history professor, an accomplished linguist and musician, he had fought in World War I, won a Rhodes scholarship, and taught for a while at Lower Canada College and a posh American school. His broad culture and his views on education seemed to make him a perfect replacement for Grant. The pattern of his career was almost identical. But MacDermot had also been brought up in proud poverty as a padre's son, and the Depression and his friend F.R. Scott had focused his Christian sympathies on pacifism and left-wing politics. He found the dominant group of governors, parents and boys at Upper Canada College smug and selfish. "What a cheap, vulgar, uncouth lot they are," he wrote in his diary. He loathed parents who tried to wheedle for their sons "opportunities which they have not earned"; and he called one group of Old Boys a lot of "tiresome, commercially bastardized clothes horses." The governors' "cheese-paring" at the expense of staff salaries reminded him that they belonged to the "hard, acquisitive, owning class." They in turn found him an erratic administrator and, though he kept his real views of them to himself, not a man they could warm to. I experienced MacDermot as a dry, remote figure who was not interested in us, though our masters seemed to respect him and enjoy his company. He went on to a brilliant diplomatic career and to bring up a son named Galt who was an even finer musician than he was.

When told by the board that it was his war duty to take over the college, Butch McKenzie replied that he was not their man. They insisted, however, and he reluctantly agreed. He was right. He found it almost as hard to work with the governors as he would have found sharing the rule of a classroom with students. He resigned in sorrow or in cold fury several times over the next five years, until the board finally took him at his word. He found it difficult to communicate and almost impossible to compromise. I still cannot readily reconcile the manic Mr. Hyde of the classroom, who harassed and terrorized me into scraping up first-class exam marks at the cost of any real understanding or enjoyment of mathematics, with the kindly Dr. Jekyll who took me aside as a sixth former to share his feeling about the burdens of office, ask me to be our class valedictorian, and tell me that my name would be up on the boards as head boy when I departed the college.

With the departure of McKenzie, whose appointment he had disapproved of, Vincent Massey resumed the interest in UCC that he had taken during Grant's regime. Grant had been his chief mentor in life since his student days, and when Massey married another of Sir George Parkin's daughters they became brothers-in-law. Massey sought his mentor's assistance in the founding of Hart House at the University of Toronto and with the work of the Massey Foundation, which became UCC's chief benefactor in the 1930s. Back in Canada after 12 years in London as Canadian high commissioner, Massey was appointed in 1949 to the three-man search committee for a new UCC principal. Although a Canadian was initially sought for the post, the choice fell upon an experienced British headmaster, who was also an old Oxonian and an Anglican priest, Reverend C.W. Sowby.

Through his years as governor general, Massey took a close personal interest in Upper Canada College and often discussed its circumstances with Sowby. Together they arranged for a stream of distinguished guests to inspect the place and speak to the boys. Prime Minister Louis St. Laurent laid a cornerstone and Field Marshall Bernard Montgomery inspected the battalion, pronouncing it the best cadet corps he had encountered in his career. The medieval office of Visitor, commonly filled by a bishop in the Oxbridge colleges, was revived at UCC in the person of Prince Philip. In memory of his wife, Alice Parkin, Massey donated a superbly appointed chapel, designed after the manner of Christopher Wren and richly decorated by Canadian artists. Sowby arranged for the donation of a piece of the altar cloth used at the coronation of Elizabeth II in Westminster Abbey and his friend the dean of St. Paul's gave marble from the ruins of his bombed cathedral.

On one of the governor general's unannounced little visits to the school, Principal Sowby was escorting him through the quadrangle when the two ladies in their party spotted the letters "F-U-C-K" chalked upside down under one of the tower windows and began to giggle. Massey peered up and exclaimed, "It looks like Russian to me." After more giggling, Massey put on his spectacles and looked again, then hastened to assure the principal that this sort of thing happened in the best of schools. As soon as his visitors had left, Sowby summoned a special assembly and demanded that the culprits repair to his office immediately. Two abject 14-year-olds owned up to the crime and each sent the governor general an apology. The chapter in Sowby's memoirs that he devoted to the incident concludes: "It was typical of Vincent Massey that in the midst of his many responsibilities, hating as he did all vulgarity and ugliness, he took the trouble to write immediately to the boys. 'I hope you didn't feel I had made heroes of them,' he said to me later."

No real harm was done by the indulgence of Massey's fantasies about the school. Certainly without him, its fabric would have been incomparably poorer and much less interesting. His efforts probably reinforced the perception of UCC as a place of patrician stuffiness in the minds of those who thought that way in the first place—another chapter in the long and continuing history of the Family Compact in Canada. On the other hand, for many who thought of sending their sons to UCC or of following the example of Massey's philanthropy, what he did for the school added an element of panache and encouragement.

The school prospered under Sowby and his English successor, Patrick Johnson. They were adept at getting on with governors and parents without necessarily giving in to them. Like their staff, they took a deep and effective personal interest in the development of their young charges. The academic calibre of teaching improved, and the eccentricity quotient declined. By the 1970s more university scholarships were being won by UCC graduates, and for the first time almost all of them were going on to higher education. The school was filled to capacity, and the waiting list grew. The percentage of Old Boys' sons in the Upper School dropped to as low as nine. Funds were found to provide more bursaries for bright students from poor families.

When the 1891 main building (though not the buildings erected since) was condemned as unsafe in 1959, a potential disaster that could have closed the school forever was turned to advantage—in a successful $3-million building fund campaign and in the communal struggle to survive the years of demolition and construction. Since that time UCC has ceased to rely on fees alone, along with the occasional wealthy benefactor, and has been partly funded by donations from alumni and parents. One of the governors' first acts in the 1959 crisis was to raise masters' salaries by 10 percent, in recognition of their loyalty to the school and of the fact that they could command better pay in the public system.

When the pattern of education in Ontario changed radically in the 1960s, to allow students a multiple choice of subjects, UCC stuck to its core curriculum. English, French, history, maths and science were required of everyone—and in the lower grades Latin as well. The other thrust of change in public policy in the 1960s—toward educating the whole person—was an ideal UCC had been committed to long since. Besides UCC's curriculum, its code of dress and discipline was attractive to parents who hoped to prevent their sons from becoming drug-addicted flower children. Fees doubled and redoubled, but still the waiting list grew.

In some respects the school changed with the times. The practices of fagging new boys, caning miscreants and using the prefects as enforcers of discipline were stopped. Pressure from the student body brought some relaxation of dress standards. The battle of long hair was fought to a draw. The cadet battalion was a casualty of the Vietnam War. The students would have abolished it in the 1960s if they had had their way, but the majority of parents supported it fiercely until well into the 1970s. By 1976, there were almost no war veterans' sons left in the school, and the spirit and discipline of the battalion were in a poor state. With no great resistance in the end from those Old Boys who held it dear, it became voluntary in 1976, a decision made by the new principal, Richard Sadleir, a former vice-president of Trent University and the first Torontonian to head the college.

UCC under Sadleir has sought to adapt its program to the needs of an increasingly sophisticated and academically select student body. Within the required subjects, courses such as Explorations in Mathematics, Science and Society, and Canadian Literature in English have been of benefit to those who found the standard drill in physics, math or grammar uninspiring or too simple. Language labs and immersion programs have improved skills in a way my generation of students would scarcely recognize. Half the graduates who have been through the new four-year art program are at present working full-time in the arts. In athletics the three major sports have been replaced for many students by a great variety of individual sports and a fitness program. Music at the school now serves as preprofessional training for some and provides a high standard of amateur participation for more than a quarter of the others. The passion among younger boys for Dungeons and Dragons, a complex and often addictive game, has been channelled and contained by creating a club overseen by a master and allowing club members the use of the school's computers.

Under its 40-year veteran headmaster, R.B. Howard, the UCC Prep (for eight- to 14-year-olds) has generally been more innovative than the Upper School. This is partly because the department of education is at the higher levels increasingly fussy about variations from its curriculum and its norms of pedagogy. (In my time its inspectors never seemed to check up.) But it can be chiefly attributed to the remarkable staff that Howard has assembled, which is quite unlike any other Ontario private school's. Most of them have worked in their specialty beyond the BA level. The ex-director of UCC's nature centre at Norval, Ontario, and now history head, Bruce Litteljohn, for example, did his MA on Quetico, a region he knows intimately from many summers there as a professional guide; he has published articles and books in ecology, and as a photographer has teamed up with well-known Canadian writers in a couple of magnificent books about Lake Superior and the Gulf of St. Lawrence. There was a great fuss from a certain group of parents a few years back when Litteljohn substituted for one of the two British history courses then required in the curriculum a course in environmental studies, which has proved to be excellent and subject to no further criticism.

The UCC staff have had to cultivate a talent for breaking the news to some Old Boy that his son does not quite meet the academic standards of the school, even though the boy may be twice as bright as his father. The waiting list is large and the school is committed to a size that will keep classes small and the playing fields and clubrooms uncrowded.

Since the Upper School body includes an Old Boy component of only about 10 or 15 percent, where do the others come from? Two of the most consistent sources have been the sons of Old Boys of other Canadian private schools and also boys from those same schools, especially those who want to take Ontario Grade 13. There have always been British immigrants' sons; many of these never aspired to get a boy into one of the major English schools such as Eton, for which the competition is fierce and the effective entry standards—some combination of brilliance, character and birth—are daunting. But UCC is just possible, and if their boy is accepted, the parents, since most are not rich, simply work harder to pay his fees.

There has for many years been a number of foreign students at UCC, usually from affluent families in Latin America or the Orient. Another large group of boarders are sons of Canadian professional and business people from small towns and cities or living overseas. A particular effort has been made recently to recruit Quebec francophones to UCC. There have been a number every year on some sort of bursary, three have graduated as head boy, and in 1982 the top three scholars at UCC were Québecois.

But UCC is not predominantly a boarding school, and boarding at the Prep, in fact, was abolished entirely in 1980. It is chiefly a day school for wealthy Torontonians. Although there is now generous financial assistance available for the less affluent and serious attempts have been made to recruit boys from Toronto's cultural minorities, few have applied. The chief exception to this is the large numbers of Chinese, East Indian and Japanese Canadians now entering the Prep: 42 out of a total student body of 361 in 1983, prompting one Old Boy to remark that the place was looking "east of Suez." For other groups the cultural and class barriers are still obviously formidable, but at least there is little evidence today of the ostracism of boys with strange accents or manners that was the experience of "foreigners" at UCC in my time. There was a quiet, pleasant young man called Weisheit in my house whom the Housemaster appointed prefect, but he was an object of covert mirth among some of his fellow prefects, who nicknamed him Wee Shit. These same school "leaders" would not likely be admitted to UCC now, if only because they could not pass the entrance test. If there are such prejudices at the school today their owners are smart enough to keep them in the closet.

The main reason I did not consider UCC a viable option for our three boys was, I thought at the time, financial. We could afford to send only one of them at best. But the oldest did agree to write the scholarship exam at the age of 12, was successful, and then persuaded us that he should stay with his class in public school. We had strong reservations anyway about a school that excluded girls. I have since come to accept the view that for some children between about 10 and 15, separate education is preferable. The chief argument seems to be that classroom competition to put on a show for the opposite sex is time-consuming and at that age too hard on the psyche. Though the school's long-range planners are discussing coeducation seriously, a number of UCC students have told me that if it were put to their vote, it would be overwhelmingly defeated.

Those who do not like things that way usually just leave. The sons of three of the most brilliant couples I know, all of them private school graduates themselves, were persuaded to let their boys leave UCC and attend a public high school, Jarvis Collegiate. The boys told me later that they were pleased with their decision. The main reason given was that life at Jarvis was more "real" (more like *Welcome Back, Kotter,* said one), that there was more unsupervised free time, and above all that it made more sense for both sexes to be at school together.

When Stephen Lewis, the Ontario NDP leader, and journalist Michele Landsberg came to see the headmaster about sending their son to the Prep, he was naturally delighted. Not only were the Lewises articulate, intelligent and famous, but they were also known to be connoisseurs of children's literature and education. Their son Avi proved to be a brilliant student and a leading member of his class in every way. He was the obvious person, along with a French-Canadian boy, to conduct the Visitor on his sesquicentennial inspection of the Prep in 1979. His Royal Highness got clear and thorough answers to all the questions he asked and some he hadn't. But to the school's regret, like the other three boys just mentioned, Avi left the next year for a public high school.

There is a story about a dear old Mr. Chips who was asked the secret of his successful teaching career and replied with a mixed metaphor that said more than he realized or intended. "Whenever I see the spark of genius," he enthused, "I water it! I water it!" Not a tale that could be told of a typical UCC master, and yet I can't but wonder if the worst thing about the college's recent history has not been its very success: it has been good at turning out its ideal end product, the well-rounded boy. It has not been a particularly good place, I suspect, for the brilliant, the eccentric or the rebellious. Sometimes when I see a couple of young gentlemen of the college, effortless and easy in their well-groomed look and lord-of-all manner, their beautiful bonding unsullied and unshared with the female half of the race or with anybody who was born and bred underprivileged, I want to shake them. No wonder Butch and Buzz and the rest got so enraged at us, especially those who were too comfortable to catch fire under *any* teacher, let alone one as peculiar or outrageous as they were.

But the smug we shall have always with us; I don't think that attacking the subspecies that flourishes at our private schools provides any fundamental answers to the problems of education. Indeed, as a university teacher exposed to a couple of thousand freshman over the past 30 years, I have been grateful for a certain independence of mind that I detected in the UCC graduates in my classes: any and all kinds of grit are welcome in a bowl of blandness.

The general argument for the existence of UCC and other independent schools is that a democratic society must clearly allow variety and excellence to flourish; it must encourage such values in the education of its young. Its teachers must have alternate ways of practising their craft. If they choose to work longer hours as the price of being more involved in the education of their students and of being freer of the state's requirements, that choice must be given them. Parents, too, should be allowed to maintain schools that encourage students to acquire a heritage, such as the French schools for anglophones, or to preserve one, such as the Hebrew or Dutch Reformed schools. Some independent schools practise a unique educational philosophy, like Montessori schools, or maintain special standards, such as the French government *lycées* in Montreal and Ottawa or Pearson College in British Columbia; some are strictly for cramming or immersion, to meet special requirements, some for students incapable of certain mental or physical tasks but able to excel in other things; some stress residential experience and learning from an outdoors life, others use a city and its resources as their campus and curriculum; and some, such as the cathedral choir schools or the National Ballet School, are for children who are already practising or training for a professional discipline.

That these alternatives exist is splendid. But except for the most enterprising, fortunate or desperate parents, they remain impossible. Clearly it would be helpful if these schools' existence were made less of a struggle, and they were enabled to do better by a larger number of students. The answer for the majority of children damaged or unchallenged by our public system, however, lies not so much in the proliferation of better independent school alternatives but rather in using the independents as laboratories whose most valuable experiments and experience can be adapted and used by the public systems.

My deepest feelings about UCC, however, have little to do

with such arguments and considerations. The college for which I feel affection is a bit like the country I grew up in: the Canada that had a real navy and not just armed forces personnel in green, the Dominion of the Red Ensign and "The Maple Leaf Forever" and Hand's fireworks on the Queen's birthday, of CPR dining cars and chateau hotels and plain cottages on lakes plied by rowboats and steamers, of electric radial cars rocketing through the Ontario country-side, of stooking wheat till you ached, of backyard raspberry patches and strawberry socials, of travelling circuses and factory picnics and horse-drawn wagons in the city.

Once in a while I go back and walk the empty halls of Upper Canada as the dusk settles, or pace the fields on a sultry summer day, encountering nobody. I listen and the stillness is alive with voices. Mr. Orr is singing us the Odes of Horace to the odd accompaniment of his tinkling piano; a distant bell is tolling; out of the rush of many spirits comes the choral recitation of our English class, J.J. Knights conduct-ing:

> *The angels keep their ancient places: —*
> *Turn but a stone and start a wing!*
> *Tis ye, tis your estrangéd faces,*
> *That miss the many-splendoured thing. . . .*

As it rides on into a world remote from the British colony in the wilderness where it began, blessedly removed from that world's pettiness and frustrations and raw savagery, I rejoice that the old place is still here. Not for my sons nor for my friends' sons, but for those young men and women of the future who will suffer their growing and learning here, and here better than anywhere, and who will love the college in their day, and make better a good tradition.

BETTER AND PURER: THE PETERBOROUGH METHODIST MAFIA AND THE RENAISSANCE OF TORONTO

BY MICHAEL BLISS

The strange title of this lecture may become a little clearer if I explain that I am not a native Torontonian. My hometown is in southwestern Ontario, and I first came to Toronto to go to university here in the late 1950s. At that time, of course, it seemed that all of small-town Ontario was migrating to Toronto. Almost everyone in the city seemed to have come from the hinterland areas, so much so that native Torontonians were rare creatures. They had either left town, been ruined for most useful purposes by their education at UCC or Bishop Strachan, or were rewriting their family histories to claim respectable origins in places such as Goderich, Kingsville or Peterborough.

This was not a new development, for Toronto has always been a city of newcomers, of immigrants, and when I was first given the job of putting together a historical talk about Toronto, my thoughts rather naturally turned to a small group of these newcomers who came to Toronto in the 1880s and '90s. They were mainly Methodists and mainly from Peterborough, and they did more than anyone else to transform Toronto from a sleepy provincial city into a national economic and cultural centre. This is why you're getting a talk about the Peterborough Methodist Mafia and the Renaissance of Toronto.

The other part of the title, "Better and Purer," comes from a letter one of these Peterborough Methodists wrote back to his wife on the day in 1887 when he leased their first house in

Toronto, just before making the move:

"So now I can fairly call myself a citizen of this growing city. I bow my head, darling bow yours with mine and pray the Father that we may leave it better and purer than when we came, because we have walked in righteousness and truth."

The writer of this letter was 30-year-old Joseph Wesley Flavvle, a provision merchant who was trying his luck in business in Toronto because he thought the established provision men on Front Street weren't doing a very good job. And also because he was very unpopular in Peterborough because of his leadership in the recent attempt to enforce local prohibition (his unpopularity led to a boycott of his business by Peterborough hotelkeepers, a rock through the front window of his store and an attempt to set fire to George Street Methodist Church.)

Flavvle was worth about $10,000 when he came to Toronto in 1887. His first few years in business here were uneven—the major setback coming when the teetotaller contracted the typhus that was endemic in the city's water supply—but generally successful. The great turning point in his career, however, came in 1892, when he was invited to become general manager of the William Davies Company, the pork-packing company located at Front Street where it meets the Don. Davies, a British-born Baptist, was operating the first modern pork-packing factory in Toronto, a complete disassembly line taking in live hogs and turning out cured sides of Davies' premium "pea-fed" bacon for export to England. Davies took Flavvle into the business because his own sons were dying of tuberculosis; he sold him a 45 percent interest in the company for $95,000, most of which Flavvle borrowed.

Under Flavvle's management, the William Davies Company suddenly found itself wallowing in profits. The reasons are too complicated to go into—they involve breeds of swine, American tariffs, the price of grain in Denmark and Ireland, brine versus dry salt cures, Flavvle's earnest management and a brilliant selling agent in Britain nicknamed "the Bismarck of the bacon trade." In Flavvle's first year as managing director the shareholders received a 65 percent dividend on their investments. After a few relatively lean years of only 25 to 45 percent dividends, the big payoff came in the later 1890s—110 percent in 1897, 100 percent in 1898, 120 percent in 1899 and 82 percent in 1900—with virtually no reinvestment required, and, of course, no corporation or personal income taxes to pay in a country that had not yet introduced them.

By 1902 Joe Flavvle's $10,000 had swelled to approximately $1,500,000, proving that there was indeed a kind of relationship between sows and silk purses. On land leased from the University of Toronto in Queen's Park, Flavvle was building one of the finest mansions in Toronto—he named it "Holwood"; the man in the street called it "Porker's Palace"—and, of course, he was pronouncing his name according to the original French, Flavelle. In 1902 Flavelle was also beginning to cut back on his business activities to devote more time to public service, more time to help make Toronto a better and purer city. I'll have more to say about that in a few moments, but first must double back and describe the careers of other Peterborough Methodists, most notably the man who was obviously the godfather of the group.

In 1868 10-year-old Joe Flavvle had been given his first job delivering telegrams for the local Grand Trunk telegraph agent, George Albertus Cox. Cox was another young Methodist for whom a Dun credit reporter was already predicting great business success if he didn't overextend himself. In addition to his telegraph agency, Cox was also the local agent for Hamilton's Canada Life Assurance Company, preaching very successfully the "gospel" of life insurance, and quickly became prominent in local politics, eventually serving six terms as Peterborough's mayor. In the late 1870s and early 1880s Cox seized his main chance when, as president of the faltering Midland railway network, he managed to reorganize and finish it and then lease the system to the Grand Trunk very profitably. He used his profits to buy shares in the Canada Life, to buy shares in Toronto's Bank of Commerce, and to set up his own Central Canada Loan and Savings Company in Peterborough. One of Central Canada's earliest employees in that town was 18-year-old Edward Rogers Wood, another Methodist boy who moved over from the telegraph agency. Cox's three sons also worked in the family businesses, and more talent was brought into the family in 1887 when a Cox daughter married a Methodist minister's son from Lambeth, Ontario, Alfred Ernest Ames.

Cox and the Ameses emigrated to Toronto in 1888, a year after Flavelle. By then it was probably more convenient for Cox to handle his business affairs out of Toronto, but he had been the other leader in the battle to enforce prohibition in Peterborough and had received almost as much criticism as Flavelle. It's significant that neither Flavelle nor Cox in their later years showered parks or public buildings on Peterborough in the way that hometown boys made good so often did.

Cox was already president of the Central Canada Loan and Savings Company. By 1890 he had become president of the Bank of Commerce, rising quickly in the bank's time of troubles following the death of its Baptist founder, Senator William McMaster. From 1892 Cox was also the most powerful shareholder in Canada Life, indeed probably held a controlling interest in the company. In 1899 he brought about the removal of its head office from Hamilton to Toronto—much against the wishes of the Hamilton directors and an act very symbolic of Toronto's final ascendancy over its old rival—and in 1900 he became president and general manager of Canada Life. In that year, then, the Honourable George Cox (he had been appointed to the Senate in 1896) was president of Central Canada, the Bank of Commerce and Canada Life, controlling combined assets of about $70 million, an enormous sum of money in 1900. Cox was the single most powerful businessman in Edwardian Toronto. His companies formed an identifiable "family," doing a great volume of business with each other. Cox and his associates were held together by complex ties of family, hometown, church, marriage and business interest (thus my comparison with a Mafia family—I do not intend the usage to include a connotation that they also looted their enterprises).

Although the leading ex-Peterboroughians worshipped together at Sherbourne Street Methodist Church (now St. Luke's United), it was not until the late 1890s that Flavelle, fresh from his success at meat-packing, joined the Cox family enterprises. Then he became very deeply involved—he joined the boards of Central Canada, the Bank of Commerce and Canada Life, of course. But more important, in 1898 he became the founding president of the National Trust Company, the institution Cox formed to handle trust and other agency business. In 1898 Flavelle was also one of the three Sunday school teachers from Sherbourne Street Church who, for $135,000, bought the Robert Simpson Company from the Simpson estate. Flavelle's partners in that deal were Henry Harrison Fudger, a brilliant wholesale merchant (who actually had been born in Toronto, but had grown up in Paris, Ontario), and A.E. Ames, who by now was managing his own stockbroking business, A.E. Ames & Company. As owners of Simpsons, Ames, Flavelle and Fudger were competing directly with yet another Methodist merchant who had come to Toronto from small-town Ontario some years earlier, Timothy Eaton.

In the good years of the late 1890s and early 1900s every enterprise touched by the Coxes, Flavelles and their associates seemed to turn to gold, and their golden touch seemed to be everywhere in Toronto and across Canada, with tentacles extending to Europe and South America.

Flavelle's William Davies Company was the largest pork-packing company in the British Empire. Its business was mostly for export, but in passing Flavelle had also created Toronto's first chain of retail stores, the William Davies meat markets, as a sideline. I have also looked into the use of the word "Hogtown" to describe Toronto. It apparently comes into use between 1900 and 1910, and it seems likely to me that it was the 500,000 piggies flowing down the Don Valley on the Grand Trunk line to the William Davies Company bacon factory on Front Street every year, making Toronto a hog-butcher to the Empire, that gave the city its enduring nickname.

Canada Life, under the energetic management of George Cox and his sons, extended its operations through the British Empire and into the United States, becoming a major life insurance company. The Bank of Commerce, whose general manager, Byron Edmund Walker (a Hamilton boy), had linked his fortunes to the Cox "family," more than tripled its assets between 1896 and 1906, becoming transformed from a provincial bank into a national financial institution. A.E. Ames & Company prospered selling stocks. At Central Canada Savings & Loan, managed by E.R. Wood, bond-trading became such a profitable sideline that a new company, Dominion Securities, was spun off in 1901 to carry on the Cox group's bond business. Wood became its president and DS soon became the largest bond dealer in Canada—even despite the 1905 withdrawal from the firm of G.H. Wood (no relation to E.R.) and J.H. Gundy, to form Wood, Gundy and Company. Both Wood and Gundy were Methodists; Wood was more or less a native Torontonian.

The Cox "family" also formed alliances with other entrepreneurs to launch new ventures. Various Masseys—Methodists to a man—became involved as directors in several Cox enterprises and were, with Cox, the key spirits in the great bicycle merger of 1899 that created the Canada Cycle and Motor Company out of the Massey bicycle division plus four American branch plants. Another Cox-Massey-Ames-Flavelle venture in 1899 was the refinancing of the Carter-Crume Company. It manufactured merchants' duplicating and triplicating sales books under patents held by a former printer, S.J. Moore, who was being brought into the Cox corporate family through this refinancing. Moore was a Baptist, not a Torontonian; when the Carter-Crume and several other companies were amalgamated in the 1920s the resulting firm was named Moore Corporation, which has since become a giant in the business forms industry.

In the early 1890s the Bank of Commerce had helped William Mackenzie, a Presbyterian from Kirkfield, Ontario, finance his purchase and electrification of the Toronto street railway system. By the end of the decade it was backing Mackenzie and his partner, Donald Mann, in their creation of a great new railway network in western Canada, the Canadian Northern, to service the exploding wheat economy. As Mackenzie and his associates expanded their activities in railways and electricity, the Commerce, Central Canada, National Trust and Dominion Securities all became deeply involved in the financing of railway and utility ventures abroad—the web of their interests eventually stretched from Birmingham, England, and Barcelona through Havana, Trinidad, Rio de Janeiro, Mexico City, Detroit and Minneapolis-St. Paul. The group's most enduring success was the Cox "family" promotion in 1900 of Sao Paulo Tramway, Light and Power Company, which survives today as Brascan.

I could go on tracing this web of companies and interlocking interests almost endlessly. At one time or another, for example, George Cox was a director of 46 distinct companies, but I think I've established my point that the Cox group of Methodists—Cox himself, Flavelle, E.R. Wood, A.E. Ames and others—had come to dominate Toronto business by the early 1900s. Older Toronto families such as the Gooderhams, Mulocks and Cawthras did not figure significantly in Toronto business life after 1900. Almost none of the great wholesalers of the 1870s and '80s had built up enough wealth to found a business dynasty or even ride out the hard times of the mid-1890s. The Eatons and Masseys—both Methodist families—had come earlier and they did remain prominent, the Masseys linking up with the Cox group, the Eatons tending to mind their store. The extent to which Methodists dominated Toronto business life by 1900 is extraordinary.

(I'm very tentative about the precise linkages between the group's Methodism and its success in business. There is, I believe, a common ground in concepts of accounting, or accountability, and of individualism. It can be shown that most of these Methodists specialized in precise accounting and learned how to departmentalize their companies, creating in their organizations an ideal combination of individual initiative and accountability, which John Wesley, who was also an organizational genius, would have found very familiar. From a quite different angle, I am more inclined to relate the success of Flavelle and the Cox group to the often unnoticed revolution in Ontario agriculture in the last third of the century and to see these entrepreneurs, and Toronto as a whole, as a city whose prosperity was linked much more closely to the prosperity of Central Canadian agriculture than we usually think.)

So big business in Edwardian Toronto was dominated by Methodists who had moved in from the hinterland. They soon became attached to their adopted city and were conscious that they were helping create a business centre to rival Montreal. Flavelle, for example, was very explicit in his suggestions that the spirit of Canadian enterprise had left the Bank of Montreal and the CPR and had moved to Toronto.

Toronto was to rival Montreal in other ways, to become as rich in civic institutions as it was becoming in bacon and bonds. Flavelle, for example, had hoped to make it "better and purer." After he had made his first million or two, he devoted much of his time and money, as did many of his associates, to trying to improve his new hometown. By 1904, as chairman of the board of trustees of Toronto General Hospital (replacing a Gooderham on the board), he had determined that the decrepit hospital building at Gerrard and Parliament streets—so badly heated that doctors claimed it was a menace to their health, let alone that of the patients— had to be rebuilt, and that it should be rebuilt in a more central area of the city, closer to the university. For the next nine years Flavelle devoted an enormous amount of his free time to raising the funds, lobbying for the legislation, and supervising the details of construction of the new Toronto General Hospital at College Street and University Avenue. When the new Toronto General opened in 1913, Toronto suddenly found itself possessing one of the world's great hospitals. All of the energy and more than half the money had been supplied by private citizens (and no community groups had opposed the expropriation and demolition of 200 downtown houses to clear the site for the new hospital). The largest donations had come from the Eatons, Masseys, Cox and Flavelle himself. The one old Torontonian who pledged a substantial contribution, Cawthra Mulock, welched on his promise, and despite several threats to take him to court to get the money, TGH did not get the last of Mulock's pledge until after his death, when his estate paid up.

Another fairly decrepit institution being reformed by public-spirited private citizens was the University of Toronto. Flavelle had a Grade 9 education, but had always been a generous supporter of such Methodist educational projects as Victoria College—whose bursar and the key figure involved in its move to Toronto from Cobourg was George Cox. Victoria's migration to the provincial metropolis paralleled the movements of many of its supporters, and it was the $90,000 that Cox, Flavelle and Ames gave Vic in 1900 that equipped it to compete on something like equal terms with University College for the best undergraduates in the university. Broadening his concern to the whole university, Flavelle in 1901 founded a travelling fellowship to support study at Oxford that anticipated the later Rhodes scholarship program. Then in 1906 he was appointed chairman of a provincial royal commission to investigate the troubled affairs of the university. Its report led to the establishment of a new governing structure, centring on a board of governors, which freed the university from the dead hand of political control. The province also agreed to give the university a fixed percentage of the succession duties, which were rising steadily; and with the appointment of Robert Falconer to the presidency in 1907 the University of Toronto entered into a golden age that lasted until sometime in the 1960s. The greatest of all the university's patrons were the Masseys, of course, but E.R. Wood also left Wymilwood and Glendon Hall to the university, and when Flavelle died in 1939 he willed Holwood to the university to be used as a social centre for women staff and students. (His second choice would undoubtedly have been the history department, which did possess the house in the late '40s and early '50s, but then lost it to the law school; in our wretched quarters in Sidney Smith Hall the only relic we have of the department's great days in Flavelle House is Sir Joseph's dining-room table in our common room.)

The other prominent businessman on that 1906 royal commission, someone even more identified with the university than Flavelle, was Byron Edmund Walker, the general manager of the Bank of Commerce. Walker, a nominal Presbyterian but in fact an agnostic, was prominently identified with everything that would better the educational and cultural life of Toronto. He was the key figure in the 1901 founding of the institution that became the Art Gallery of Ontario. Its other founders, who contributed $5,000 each, were Cox, one of his sons, Flavelle and a Massey. And in the years before the war Walker was also the moving spirit behind the founding of the Royal Ontario Museum, which opened its doors in 1914.

A complete study of these businessmen's contributions to Toronto's cultural life would involve looking at a great many more institutions. The gift of Massey Hall immediately comes to mind, and I think I can detect both the money and the moral support of Flavelle and Walker during the early years of the Mendelssohn Choir. For now, though, we can be satisfied with having noticed their role in the creating of the art gallery, the museum, the modern university and the modern Toronto General Hospital. Possessing institutions like these in 1914, Toronto was immeasurably richer— immeasurably better—than it had been in 1900.

Whether it was a purer city is another question. The Methodists built a lot of churches, of course, with substantial help from their generous laymen, and the YMCA was their chosen instrument for the promotion of healthy minds in healthy bodies. Cox and Flavelle continued to give generously to prohibition campaigns—although they were never again quite the ardent prohibitionists they had been in their Peterborough days. In 1905 Flavelle did enjoy a brief opportunity to help the cause when he was appointed one of the city's three liquor licence commissioners. The reforming trio began a crackdown on licence evasion by hotelkeepers and on public drunkenness, but their work was quickly undone when the provincial secretary, upset by the vigour of their attempt to enforce the law, fired their inspection staff. They resigned in protest.

As well, in 1902 Flavelle began a unique experiment in Canadian journalism when he bought a newspaper, the Toronto *News*, installed as its editor J.S. Willison, who was then Canada's most prominent English-language journalist, and told Willison to devote the paper to advancing the public interest. In an age when newspapers pandered to political parties, the lowest common denominator of public taste or the financial interests of their owners, it was an extraordinary gesture on Flavelle's part, so extraordinary that few believed he was sincere. His associates learned how sincere he was when the *News* regularly and pointedly attacked William Mackenzie, who was the single best customer of National Trust and the Bank of Commerce, but who Flavelle and

Willison also believed was directly responsible for Toronto's wretched streetcar service. When his friends complained about the editorials, Flavelle threatened to resign his corporate positions rather than reign in Willison.

The main aim of the *News* was to raise the level of political morality in Canada. Flavelle and Willison's greatest achievement was the prominent role the *News* played in Ontario's great fight for clean government, a crusade that in 1905 swept the decadent Liberal party out of office, replacing it with honest progressive Conservatives—who quickly discovered ways to stay in power forever and ever. The *News* had much less luck tilting at other windmills, though, was far too preachy and sanctimonious to be readable, and could not compete with more dynamic evening powers, such as the *Star*, run by another Methodist, Joe Atkinson, who had moved into the city from Newcastle in the 1890s and been given early support from George Cox (Atkinson and Flavelle were the two men Torontonians nicknamed "Holy Joe," by the way, and Atkinson had been for a time a member of Flavelle's young men's class at Sherbourne Street Church. They were not friends, however, and I think each thought the other's Methodism was one part sincerity and three parts hypocrisy). Flavelle sold the *News* in 1908, writing off $350,000 to $400,000 as the cost of his effort to purify Canadian politics.

It would take the rest of the evening to do more than touch on other aspects of the careers of these businessmen whose lives helped make the Horatio Alger novels plausible. They tend to live on in popular memory, of course, as the robber barons of Canada, the purple-faced, paunchy men with diamond stickpins and big cigars who prayed in church on Sundays and preyed on their customers the other six days. In fact they usually looked and dressed more like Methodist ministers than Peterborough plutocrats. They did often literally end a day at the office with first a board meeting and then a Sherbourne Street prayer meeting. Their ethical standards in business were higher than those of most of their contemporaries and would compare favourably with those of politicians, journalists or professors today. They lived very comfortably in splendid homes, but would have been mortified at the accusation of being ostentatious parvenus. To them the only vulgarly ostentatious parvenu in Toronto was Henry Pellatt, with his silly grab for social status through play-soldiering in the militia and his even sillier house, Casa Loma. Pellatt was an Anglican and a native Torontonian.

I can also only touch upon the inner history of the Cox "family" and its enterprises, which is really the raw material for a Canadian Forsyte sage. There was the crisis in CCM, for example, when it turned out that the bicycle company's directors had been far too free-wheeling and had lost most of the money that Methodist ministers and widows had invested in their stock promotion. The directors voluntarily made restitution. There was also A.E. Ames's great break with the Cox family in the early 1900s, when, in alliance with S.J. Moore and some of the Masseys he founded his own bank, the Metropolitan; bought his own life-insurance company, Imperial Life; and appeared to be about to create his own "family" of enterprises. But A.E. Ames & Co. was caught holding too much Twin Cities Traction on margin in the market panic of 1902 and was forced to suspend operation. Senator Cox had to step in and bail out his prodigal son-in-law, a rescue operation that included buying Ames's shares in Simpsons. Flavelle also seems to have helped Ames get back on his feet and reopen his business. This was only a prelude, however, to the great nepotism struggle at Canada Life, when Flavelle, Walker and the Cox "family's" brilliant lawyer, Zebulon Lash, decided that the old patriarch had gone too far in his determination to hide his son's business incompetence and conceal what for one of them was an unmentionable moral problem (probably drink). In 1911 the dissenters finally resigned from the board of Canada Life in protest against the Cox family's abuse of its power, but in a last act of loyalty to the old man they did not choose to make the issues public. Then there was the trauma of railway nationalization during the Great War, when Mackenzie & Mann's Canadian Northern collapsed, threatening to drag down the Bank of Commerce with it—and the Canadian Northern's harshest critic in the Borden government turned out to be W.T. White, the minister of finance, who had spent his whole business life deep in the inner circles of the Cox group as general manager of National Trust. (White probably did more than anyone else to create the modern Canadian National Railways—in the early 1920s Flavelle turned down repeated requests that he become the CNR's first president.)

Finally, in Joe Flavelle's life there was the great honour of being awarded a baronetcy in June, 1917, in recognition of his wartime service as czar of the Canadian munitions industry through his chairmanship of the Imperial Munitions Board—followed six weeks later by charges that the William Davies Company was unconscionably profiteering in its bacon business. In the summer of 1917 Holy Joe Flavelle, the

Methodist baronet, became Old Black Joe, the Methodist bacon bandit (also a baconet and a baconeer and several species of hog), his reputation tarred with rumours of scandal and tainted meat that persisted, without foundation, into the 1970s (a further attack came in the 1930s from the Conservative cabinet minister, H.H. Stevens, who as a young boy had been a member of Flavelle's Sunday school at George Street Church in Peterborough).

George Cox died in 1914. Flavelle eased into semiretirement in the early 1920s. As the Cox enterprises became more diverse, required more capital and were taken over by younger managers, they gradually drifted apart, although some associations and common interests have been maintained to the present. Unlike the Eatons and Masseys, but like Toronto business leaders of earlier generations, none of the Peterborough group of Methodists sired enough male offspring who were interested enough in and good enough at business to create a family dynasty. Their female offspring who might have been interested and good enough were discouraged from going into business by their fathers and mothers and the whole society around them. Consequently, the commanding role of these businessmen in building the foundations of modern Toronto is largely forgotten today.

For all of its colour, diversity and vitality, Toronto at the turn of the century was still a small city whose business life and business lifestyle could be dominated by a small group of men. In the years before the Great War this closely knit circle of Methodists, raised in Toronto's prosperous agricultural hinterland on hard work, prayer and cold water, immigrated to the city, seized strategic opportunities and spearheaded Toronto's rise to rival Montreal as the economic metropolis of Canada. If we wish to commit sociology or historical geography, it's possible to understand Toronto's growth as the consequence of impersonal factors, particularly the city's relation to markets and natural resources. A full understanding of this process, however, leads to the realization that the most important natural resource for the Toronto economy was then, as it is now, people. Montreal suffered in these years, I suspect, from the inability—and in some part the unwillingness—of its Anglostocracy to revitalize itself with new men of talent. As the Canadian economy developed, Toronto had a number of advantages over Montreal that perhaps made its comparative progress a certainty. The most important of these advantages, I suggest, was Toronto's great good fortune in being located so close to such really productive municipalities as Peterborough.

A NEST
OF WASPS

W**e are trustees for the British
race. We hold this land in allegiance.

FREDERICK BARLOW CUMBERLAND, speech to the Empire Club,
Toronto (1904)

Superman was conceived by Toronto-born Joe Shuster, who
originally worked not for the *Daily Planet* but for a newspaper
called *The Star*, modelled on *The Toronto Star*. This makes his
assumed identity of bland Clark Kent not merely understandable, but artistically inevitable. Kent is the archtypical
middle-class Toronto WASP, superficially nice, self-effacing,
but within whom there burns a hate-ball, a would-be avenger
with superhuman power, a smasher of bridges, a breaker of
skyscrapers, a potential ravager of wonder women. And
(may those who have scoffed at Canadian culture in the past,
please take note) a universal hero.

MORDECAI RICHLER, Hunting Tigers under Glass:
Essays and Reports *(1968)*

Cabbagetown had one unique feature which has amazed
some people who haven't given it any thought. It happened
to be the largest Anglo-Saxon slum in North America. We
have Mexican slums; we have Negro slums; we had Jewish
slums; we had French-Canadian slums, St. Henri; but this
was an Anglo-Saxon slum; we were all English and Scots; we
all belonged to the Anglican or Presbyterian churches; we

*For more than a century one of the great events of
Toronto was the Orange Parade on the Glorious
Twelfth of July, celebrating the victory of the Protestant
succession and King William III's army over the
Catholic forces at the Battle of the Boyne. In the second
half of the 20th century, in a city whose population is
neither predominantly British nor Protestant, the
parade has become an odd vestige of a vanished era.
This photograph taken circa 1866 is at King Street
looking east from Yonge. Note that St. James
Cathedral still lacks its spire.*

were the establishment except that we were the freak-outs from the establishment. The foreigners, the immigrants, would come here and think, If I were only English I could be president of the Bank of Commerce. And here we were, we were as English as you could get, and sang in the Anglican choir and everything else, and we lived in a slum. So that was a unique thing. And so I wrote about Cabbagetown, I think, because of that.

HUGH GARNER in "An Interview with Hugh Garner,"
The Tamarack Review *(1969)*

We Beaches people, we *Telegram* readers, were loyal in the way that only the petty bourgeois can be loyal: we accepted England and the King as fixed stars in the heavens; when we sang "There'll Always Be an England," as we did on every conceivable occasion, we believed it firmly. When the Pearson government introduced the maple leaf flag in 1966—thus setting aside the Canadian Ensign, a major symbol of British allegiance—the literary monarch of the Beaches, Ted Reeve, was one of those who publicly mourned. It would have been astonishing had he done otherwise. In the Beach there was never any doubt that Canada was a British nation.

ROBERT FULFORD (1976)

In some west-end districts there are almost no WASP children left in the schools. A young person I knew was the only one in her class at a time when it was preparing for a multicultural school fair. The class president managed to assign each of her constituents to costume-making, cookie-baking, singing, dancing or whatever, to represent one or other of the two dozen ethnic groups in the school. Except my young WASP friend, she was clearly a problem for her. "Well," she concluded thoughtfully, "I guess you people don't have a culture, so how about you handle the cloakroom."

WILLIAM KILBOURN (1982)

Where is the old Torontonian today? Occasionally a rare specimen is encountered in the panelled confines of the Toronto Club or perhaps at the Hunt Ball. When one of them gives away a bride, or brings a daughter out, or is buried at Timothy Eaton Memorial Church, his picture appears in the press. I understand that one or two are being mounted and stuffed for posterity at the Royal Ontario Museum. But the typical Torontonians today are the New Torontonians. They dominate the city.

PIERRE BERTON, *The New City: A Prejudiced View of Toronto (1961)*

Mangiacake: cake-eater

Early twentieth-century Toronto Italian term for WASPS

In Toronto the Old British Left was generally more gauche than sinister.

SENATOR LAWRENCE ZOLF, QC, Colonel-in-Chief,
the Toronto Nebbish (1983)

Let the Old World, where rank's yet vital,
Part those who have and have not title.
Toronto has no social classes—
Only the Masseys and the masses.

B.K. SANDWELL, on the appointment of Governor General
Vincent Massey (1952)

...there on the edge of the wilderness, beside that cold, empty lake, it has raised itself in 150 years from colonial town to metropolis, absorbed settlers from half the world, yet kept its original *mores* recognizable still....a conservative, indeed a conservationist achievement. What has *not* happened to Toronto is as remarkable as what *has* happened.... The real achievement of Toronto is to have remained itself.

JAN MORRIS Saturday Night *(1984)*

Toronto is the most undemonstrative city I know, and the least inquisitive. The Walkman might be made for it. It swarms with clubs, cliques, and cultural societies, but seems armour-plated against the individual. There are few cities in the world where one can feel, as one walks, or rides the subway, for better or for worse, so all alone.

I caught the eye once of a subway driver, as he rested at his controls for a few moments in the bright lights of the station, waiting for the guard's signal, and never did I see an eye so fathomlessly subdued—not a flicker could I raise in it, not a glint of interest or irritation, before the whistle blew and he disappeared once more into the dark. It takes time, more time than a subway driver has, for the Toronto face, having passed through several stages of suspicion, nervous apprehension, and anxiety to please, to light up in a simple smile.

JAN MORRIS Saturday Night *(1984)*

A DAY
IN THE LIFE OF THE
ELMWOOD

BY GWENDOLYN MacEWEN

Wanda is frying an egg on the two-burner hotplate, which is quicker and easier to use than the aging stove. She always tries to get her breakfast early, before the other ladies start shuffling into the tiny, cramped kitchen off the hallway of the second floor of this sad Victorian building at 18 Elm Street; there are always the irritating little power struggles over who gets to use the front part of the stove first and so on. Then the ladies are not at all ladylike and everybody starts off the day badly.

In the Elmwood Hotel girls' residence they don't refer to one another as women; rather they are all "ladies" who are residing here until their circumstances improve—although there are many who have been here for years, and this is the only place they can call home. When some of them get chummy, then they're the "girls," whether they're 30 or 60, and the "girls" always stick together. There are several such groups of girlfriends, very loyal to one another and suspicious of newcomers and outsiders.

Wanda peers into the cavernous fridge, looking for her blueberry jam. The girls all store their food supplies here, and when it gets too crowded various things like milk and butter are kept on the windowsills of their rooms—except of course in summer, when the building is extremely hot and humid. It's overheated in winter too, like a hospital, and in fact there's no time in the year when the corridors of the Elmwood are cool and fresh. The air always has the stale smell of overcrowding, of loneliness in cramped quarters. Many of the girls sleep three in a room; a few pay a little more for private rooms—if anything can be called private here.

The blueberry jam is gone. Damn. Wanda looks behind the plate of leftover beans, the bits of cheese in Saran Wrap, the open can of sardines—but it's definitely gone. It's that Sonya again; Sonya steals everything she can get her hands on. A couple of times she went beyond petty theft and ended up in jail, but now she sticks to small items, with an occasional stab at the expensive stuff in Eaton's. Wigs, of all things—outrageous, tasteless wigs.

Wanda is mad at Sonya for stealing her jam; she's one of the girls, and they all share or buy or trade things with each other—cigarettes, teabags, coffee. All she had to do was ask. Well, she'll give her hell later; now she spreads her breakfast on the shiny red plastic tablecloth, brushing aside the soggy teabags that somebody forgot to remove, and the jar lids that are used as ashtrays. She wants to get breakfast over with so she can go back to bed and sleep away the morning, for there's nothing else to do. Upstairs on the third floor there are younger women who go out to work every day, who are still making it somehow on the outside, who regard the Elmwood as a temporary residence, not a home. The young ones, for whom life is still an adventure and a challenge, whom life has not yet broken. Wanda is not one of them. She eats her toast and fried egg and waits for the kettle to boil.

Noon: Sharon, who shares the room with Wanda, wakes her up and asks her if she wants a cup of tea and some of her Arrowroot cookies. This has been Sharon's steady diet for some days now; she weighs almost 200 pounds and is trying everything to lose weight. Someone recently introduced her to the religion of Baha'i, and now this is all she talks about. She reads books and pamphlets about the Baha'i faith well into the night, and although she understands little of what she reads, she senses that there is some mystery there, some secret that will save her and make her life more livable and meaningful. She and Wanda are both frequent patients of the mental hospital on Queen Street; both are admitted there once or twice a year, and return to the Elmwood when they get "better." Wanda suffers from manic depression; Sharon is schizophrenic. They've known each other for eight years, both at the hospital and here at the Elmwood. They wonder what they would do if ever it closed down. This is the only place in the city where they feel safe.

Many of the other girls leave the Elmwood from time to time to better their circumstances in rented rooms or flats shared with two or three others—but very often they come back. Here you don't have to admit to being homeless, even though you are; here there are enough of you to cushion the blows of reality, to absorb the shock of the truth: that you are alone, and do not belong to normal society.

Not everyone can get into the Elmwood; it's run by the Young Women's Christian Association and there are very strict rules about visitors, late hours, alcohol, rowdiness and whatnot. But it's known that some of the girls are ex-addicts and even hookers who've had run-ins with the law and are trying, on the surface at least, to go straight. The woman at the front desk downstairs keeps track of everyone coming and going, visitors and friends, and anyone found with alcohol on the premises is automatically out. This is hard on girls like Sharon who enjoy a few beers now and then, and have to go to the local tavern to get them, then disguise their breath when they come back. When they enter, the huge, heavy door downstairs closes with a thud and locks itself with a loud click. Living in the Elmwood can be a kind of voluntary jail sentence, for some at least.

It is safe here, although now Wanda is talking to Sharon about the night two weeks ago when a man was discovered trying to get in the window of one of the rooms. He'd climbed up the rusty stairs outside the building, and if it hadn't been for the clatter of those stairs waking one of the girls, he would have gotten in. As it was, she screamed bloody murder and he was caught. Some girls have been having nightmares about it ever since, and there have been more screams and strange noises in the night. The girls who are in shared rooms are glad now for the extra security of their numbers.

Wanda and Sharon finish their tea and Arrowroot cookies. Sharon decides to go out for a walk, although it is raining. Wanda thinks she might write a letter—but who to?

5 p.m.: Little Daisy is the youngest on the second floor. She is only 28, but she looks more like 14—perhaps because that's the age of her mind. She is Slow, as they say, and she's only recently learned how to take care of herself, more or less. She does piecework in a factory and is making money for the first time in her life. She is very proud of the fact that she can memorize numbers and dates; when she first meets you, she asks you when your birthday is and what was the number of the street where you last lived. When she meets you again,

she rhymes off the whole thing, her face glowing with triumph. Then she sits and says nothing and gazes at you with huge little-girl eyes. She is in love with all of the ladies, and some of them try to warn her that she could be taken advantage of because of that, but she doesn't know what they mean.

Little Daisy thinks its very funny to call the Elmwood an "exclusive club." "Welcome to our exclusive club!" she tells visitors when they come for the first time. "The washroom is right down the hall; it's about 1,000 years old, and you have to wait if you want a bath! We really are very ritzy here, aren't we, ladies?"

Daisy comes into Wanda's room and sits at the end of her bed, saying nothing. She does this every day when she gets home from the factory. Wanda asks her why she doesn't try to get a room upstairs, with the young ladies who also go out to work. Doesn't she find it depressing here with the older ones? No, says Daisy, she likes it here.

After supper, which is a can of stew cooked on the hotplate, Wanda sits on the sofa in the hallway, smoking. One or two other girls are also patients from the Queen Street mental hospital, and are on heavy medication, so the atmosphere is like that in the hospital, where everything moves in slow motion. Cigarettes raised in heavy hands take a long time to reach the lips; eyes are glazed, the attention directed to nothing. Wanda is glad that the day is almost over.

9 p.m.: Wanda goes into Sonya's room to visit and to see her latest wig. This time it's a truly godawful thing, a strawberry blonde creation built into a beehive shape. It looks awful on Sonya, but as usual Wanda says it's lovely. Sonya's losing all her hair, and will soon be bald. She's only in her late forties, and tonight Wanda feels strangely sorry for her; she decides not to get mean about the stolen blueberry jam. Sonya stares at her bizarre reflection in the mirror above the old dresser; the two girls are quiet for some time, then Wanda goes back to her room.

It has stopped raining and the night is clear with a full moon. Sometimes, strange ideas float through Wanda's head, dreamy ideas based on nothing in particular. Tonight she stands at her window looking out over the rusty railings of the balcony, over the rooftops of the city shimmering in the moonlight, and she dreams of another world. It is a world of unspeakable glamour, of society ladies who go around in fabulous clothes and eat gourmet food in the best restaurants.

These ladies all belong to exclusive clubs, and they've all got homes with babies and husbands with real jobs—or maybe they're single with Careers—but they've all got money and they all know where they're going, and somewhere out there in the huge, dark city they're riding around in their big wicked cars, and laughing a lot, and dancing, dancing.

Postscript: Gwendolyn MacEwen's mother lived in the Elmwood in the 1960s. After being gutted by fire, the Elmwood was sold. Totally renovated, it is now a fashionable club for successful women. Annual membership is $1,100.

PEOPLES AND PERSONS:

A Multicultural Mosaic

ST. CLAIR WEST

BY HARRY RASKY

St. Clair Avenue has never left me. Those cold Canadian winter nights over the store listening to the Bay streetcar whish through snow and slush, and those muggy August mornings with heat that actually hurt. The Bay car clanged by and some of me with it.

Later when I was asked which side of the street I was born on, I just answered, "Right on the tracks." It was not far from the truth. St. Clair Avenue West was a wide boulevard with great pretensions, heading nowhere. To the east it disappeared into something quite rich, which I later was to find was the northern limit of the WASP districts of Moore Park and Rosedale. To the west it became mud that ended up in the "Junction" in those early years. The Junction was where the rail lines converged and the slaughterhouse of Canada Packers began. On a hot day the bacon fumes gave the air an unkosher odour. I swear I could taste bacon (God forbid) on my clothes.

The streets on either side of the St. Clair of my Toronto were decorated with names that gave the inhabitants of its lower-middle-class, semidetached grey buildings more than semidetached aspirations. The park was Earlscourt; the public school, Regal Road; the street opposite, Ascot; and the local movie house, my local escape, the Royal George. It was transplanted east-end London and grey Glasgow.

Somehow on St. Clair a band of Jews had decided to set up a merchant fort. The Scots and the English around us were like the attacking Indians in an old-fashioned western. But our block, the 1200 block of St. Clair West, was as Jewish as Tel Aviv in July. How that happened, I don't know. Most of the immigrant Jews had huddled downtown, somewhere around Spadina and College, clustered as if ready for a Canadian pogrom.

The merchants were a mini-nation. You did not have to go far to find a cross-section of Europe in those Jews who shared that block. Every prejudice and pain had come with them. If Israel today is as diverse as the collection of attitudes on my block, it must be a constant argument. Not one of those merchants remains there today. But I can see them in my mind.

Let's start on the corner. The Waller family had no use for any of us. Old man Waller ran a hardware store and gas pump. In those days gasoline was pumped right at curb-side, and what soaked onto the roadway was merely washed down by hose at night. In retrospect, I don't know why Waller didn't blow us all up. Much later, after the Jews had departed, the store was obliterated when the Italians moved in and the Mafia apparently wiped out some inconvenient resident. But in our time, Mr. Waller looked down on the Yiddish-speaking neighbours. He had Palestine plans for himself and his kids, and mingling with us was worse than associating with Gentiles. Somewhere in Israel today the Wallers have taken up residence and have Hebrew names. To us they stayed constant strangers in a strange land. Old man Waller chewed on the stubs of old cigars and the ashes seemed to blend right into his skin. He sat on a camp chair outside his store in the summer, waiting for trucks to stop at the pump. I don't recall him ever speaking. He grunted if you entered his store for a bolt or screw. Ashes flew and he'd be off in his dream of Jerusalem. How could anyone imagine Jerusalem on St. Clair Avenue West?

Next door, with shelves to the ceiling, was the shop of Maylech Zolotovsky (later stylishly changed to Zolt), a Polish Jew with glittering gold teeth that seemed to flash more at the ladies than the men. Maylech was in what was then called "dry goods": skirts, slips, socks, etcetera—a lot of etcetera. I have to laugh when I hear people today say, "You Jews all stick together." Each Jew on the block was his own island. And Maylech Zolt was a kingdom. Waller to the south of him was like an Arab army. And on the other side were the Anisman clan.

In Maylech Zolt's terms, the Anismans did not exist. How

Jewish citizen of Toronto, circa 1910.

could they? They were also in the dry goods line. Competition, competition right next door. Zolt had to stare across the wide avenue, watch the streetcars go by and try to imagine he had no neighbours. Mrs. Anisman had an extra problem. She was a widow with half a dozen kids. She was treated as if she had committed a crime, to live so brazenly without a husband. One of her children was Art, who was one of my childhood friends. Frequently he was chased by my mother with a broom. I never knew exactly why, except that he was half-orphaned and for some reason was blamed for his family state.

Next were the Minks. They were in the millinery line. The Depression was a time when ladies wore hats. Make something of that if you will. I must admit I seldom saw any customers in the store, but regularly those bonnets in the window would change. Veils up and down, pink for Easter, grey for winter. Mrs. Mink was rather puffy cheeked. Her husband worked somewhere downtown in the garment shops and was seldom seen.

The Minks were in hats and the Garaways next door in furs. I always thought there would have been a kind of justice if the Minks were in furs. But what's in a name? My impression is that the fur business was profitable, because the Garaways also had a large car in their garage. Mr. Garaway always seemed secretive and angry. That may have been because we played handball on his garage door.

Every Jewish block needs a socialist. The Levine family next to the Garaways filled the role. Another millinery shop, so you can imagine how they did with the Minks. Who needed a pogrom with all that instant hostility? Young Gilbert Levine went on to become a fiery labour leader.

We were separated from the Levines in my early years by the Ardeys. Now that has always seemed the final irony. The Ardey family sold Christian literature. They were sizzling members of the Church of the Nazarene. Bibles and busts of Christ incongruously decorated their windows. As you can imagine, they did little indigenous business.

We lived at 1281, in what was called "a cottage." That meant there was no basement and the house was made of wood. There was something frail about it. The store had been built over a large chestnut tree root. So stubborn had been the root that when the floor was built, rather than try to cut it out, the workmen merely sloped the floor. This was handy for playing marbles, as the coloured agates could roll with ease while we waited for customers to pass through. To this day I don't recall another store with a sloping floor.

We'll get back to the family Rasky. For the moment let's continue up the street. Our nextdoor neighbour for all of my childhood was a certain Mr. Yung who had a Chinese laundry. He smiled a lot and naturally we never talked. I don't know if Mr. Yung ever spoke English, except to list the price of laundering shirts and sheets. He vanished behind clouds of steam in his back room until summoned by a bell on a blank counter. I always thought there was a strange, hidden hell back there, when he would appear in his apron and the clouds floated over his head. He would smile, deliver a plain brown package and vanish again in the clouds.

Beyond the laundry stood the Church of the Nazarene, site of a former garage. From it blared Christian hymns, organ music and a call to Christ. Not too much business from our side of St. Clair. We always appreciated the Chinese laundry as a kind of no-man's land between the Jews on the block and the church. There was a gentleman's agreement that we would not protest the constant preaching if the church would make no comment about the cries of chickens that used to break the morning street noises. In back of our store we kept a chicken coop of constantly changing chickens, brought in weekly for the ritual slaughter. But roosters never seemed to differentiate between country and town. They crowed as if to wake up the farm that was not there. So the church blared Christ-praising songs and the roosters announced the kosher chickens for sale.

There was a pause in the street beyond the church, an empty lot where once there had been a building destroyed by fire. Personal arson was popular during the Depression years, as businessmen decided to collect the insurance and run. Strangely, no one could recall what had stood there. But for us kids it was a perfect setting for kick-the-can and hide-and-seek and other rituals of growing up in the city.

The stores beyond get vague in memory. Of course there was the dress store of Leslie Feldman's mother. Leslie was part of my gang. And there was Lipshitz, the used furniture dealer. He sat like an Einstein amid the clutter of pots, pans and pianos. He was a growling freethinker. There was Willer's fancy shop near the corner and Magani's Italian grocery on the corner. Later, when Italy entered the war on Germany's side, it broke Mr. Magani's heart that the local Scots and English started their own personal blockade. As if Magani himself were bombing Britain. You really didn't have to leave the block to find a world war.

St. Clair Avenue was so wide that to cross it was almost like entering another village. To be sure there were certain contacts. Snowbell had a jewelry store. It's still there, Clavirmade suits. Lou Litwin of St. Clair Paint and Wallpaper carried paint cans on to a fortune. And we would visit the McQuoid Drug Store for five-cent ice cream cones and to check the temperature at the Ex-Lax thermometer outside. Beyond were the Gentiles, and a Jewish boy wandering around was asking for trouble, or so it seemed.

One block south was MacKay Street. This was the home of the remarkable MacKay Street *shul*, the local synagogue that somehow held our band of diverse Jews together. The *shul* was always a part of my life. I'm told that it was the first home of the Rasky family in Canada.

My family left Russia just after World War I. They had lived in a town near Kiev in the Ukraine, called Desha. They had owned a flour mill. The family name was Poberregesky, which I'm told means "beside the stream." They were modest capitalists, I suppose, in a revolutionary time— capitalist and Jewish. Naturally, they lost all. This was especially difficult for my father because he had been raised to be the family scholar, a nonordained rabbi. Each family allowed one son to be the carrier of the tradition, much as the Irish provide a child to the church. The revolution came and left the family to wander across Europe.

They must have been a strange group of wanderers. My grandmother, the Baba Bayla who had no teeth, my grandfather, a tall, elegant, silent man, my parents and three or four young children. Ads for help were placed in overseas papers. A distant relative from Chicago sent boat fare and the group boarded a boat in Antwerp.

Ellis Island in New York is where the name split in two. My uncle became Pober and my father Rasky.

Our group continued on to Canada because my mother's sister, Aunt Lillie, had married a pedlar, Uncle Ben, who lived in the Junction. So what does a scholar do in a cold, wintry city where he knows no one and not even the language? My father, a short, powerful man with red beard and strong faith, offered himself out as the local religious person. He taught the kids Hebrew and sang. How he sang! He talked to God in the melodies of the suffering of the Jews. He put his family in the back room of the synagogue and there they lived, all of them, safe from the Cossacks and the pogroms and the Gentiles, with no money but lots of time to pray.

Heat was provided by a pot-bellied stove. Since fuel was difficult to come by, the family scrounged around the neighbourhood. My grandmother noted that each morning a young boy toured the neighbourhood tossing papers, *The Mail and Empire*, in nearby doorways. How wonderful to have the paper to start the morning fire. How convenient. Except that the local readers became annoyed at their disappearing papers. A motorcycle policeman was sent to investigate the crime. He caught grandmother red-handed in her black robes. Since my grandmother never had learned a word of English, my oldest sister, Pearl, was sent to the police station to be translator and lawyer. They vanished down MacKay Street in the sidecar of the cop's motorcycle. Somewhere there was a kind judge who understood that the papers had not been stolen for resale, or even for reading. What would the Baba Bayla know about reading *The Mail and Empire*? She never did know how to read. She promised to give up petty crime, and peace returned to MacKay Street.

It was decided that with so many mouths to feed, the most sensible thing was to buy food wholesale. Thus the store on St. Clair was planned to obtain apples by the barrel, tins by the dozen and milk by the gallon. My father was to take on the job of *shoychet*, the ritual butcher of poultry. Slaughter was only allowed by a holy man. Holy and poor and proud—that was my father. The store was our family.

The store set the pattern for all my early years. In all, there were five sons and three daughters. The family plan was quite simple. As soon as a child was able, he would pull parcels in a wagon to the local customers. As he grew, he would mount a bicycle with an oversized carrier and deliver beyond the local scene. Later on we would experiment with second-hand cars as delivery trucks.

On Monday and Tuesday, my father would visit the chicken market down on Baldwin and Spadina, and pick 100 or so chickens he would resell during the week. Wednesday would begin the slaughter, and the chicken plucking would take place in the back shed. On Thursday we would deliver after school and into the night, carrying our kosher parcels to milk boxes on nearby Lauder Avenue and Glenholme and into the hushed luxury of Forest Hill Village. Friday night there was the quick change into our best second-hand clothes for Sabbath eve services at the MacKay Street *shul*. Saturday, the Sabbath, I helped round up the local Jews for the *minyen*, the quorum of 10 men needed for Jewish prayers. I think I got everyone on the block at least once, except for Waller, who seemed to have no use for God, Jewish or otherwise. Palestine, yes, but prayers, no. Sunday was the day of collecting the accounts from those Thursday night deliveries.

Once on a Sunday I was picked up by the police for breaking the Lord's Day Alliance. I don't know with whom the Lord was allied. But in Christian Canada and proper Toronto, I was a criminal for helping collect bills that would pay for the next week's supply of chickens. Indeed, there was never enough profit to do anything but feed the 100 chickens and the 10 Raskys and get us through school. It was no accident that the day my brother Norman, the youngest, had worked his way through dental college, the business disappeared—not sold, just vanished. The store had served its purpose. We had been educated, sent out into the foreign world. The singing on Saturday and the killing of chickens on Wednesday and bicycling up those snowy and sometimes sweaty streets were part of the educational process.

After the collection period on Sunday, there was the question of what to do in Toronto. Fear of the Lord was everywhere. At Earlscourt Park there were tennis courts; no nets could be hung. There were sandboxes and swings; the swings were padlocked. Padlocked! Once, when I found one free and began swinging, a policeman in his bobby hat grabbed my shoulder. His words have never left me: "Nobody swings on Sunday!" Amen.

One summer day we visited the Toronto Islands, the sandbar that was a ferry ride across the harbour. We would swim in the polluted lake, listen to a band concert at Hanlan's Point and chew Cracker Jacks, our one weekly treat. I will never forget the journey home. My mother led the attack. If all eight kids hit the turnstiles simultaneously, the streetcar ticket operator was so confused that at least three got by free. Three times three cents—a saving of almost a dime.

My mother. My mother was a woman of incredible energy. I've often thought that if there were creative juices passed down the line in the family they came from her, despite her lack of any academic skills. But there was a way of expression, a way of sweeping phrases to support or condemn. She was a woman of large emotion. She could cry for two days nonstop, or express joy almost as if in levitation and flight. She embraced us all with varied passion, anger and love. Between childbirths she plucked and cleaned chickens, acted as hostess at the synagogue and tried to find temporary release for us from the pavement existence of St. Clair Avenue West.

We were always tired from our work routine. Even today I can recall the addresses of our customers: Mrs. Cohen, 210 Glenholme; Mr. Wagman, 67 Westmount.... I still dream of that bicycle route. Sometimes we would fall asleep in our classes at Regal Road Public School, only to be startled by Miss MacPherson, our teacher, and begin answering lessons in Yiddish. Miss MacPherson was not amused. We had to collect pictures of the British Royal Family. To this day I have a slight touch of Scottish in my dialect: we were all Presbyterians.

Mr. Foreman, my Hebrew teacher, used to break a dozen rulers a week on our heads and hands to make us learn the five books of Moses as the good Lord had obviously told Mr. Foreman we must. And I can still recite, "*Berayshish boroh Elohim*—In the beginning God created....*"

We slept three in a bed, crowded around a wood stove, and bathed in a washbasin. Our diet was composed largely of left-over chickens and apples bought wholesale by the barrel. I can still recall the lonely, lost feeling of reaching into an apple barrel for the very last piece of fruit, and tumbling into it and crying my eyes out because no one knew where I was. And how many ways can you boil a chicken?

Occasionally there would be unusual treats. Down on Lansdowne Avenue, just across from the cemetery that I always thought was a park, we were invited to a party every Christmas. The family's name was Christian, and they had one lonely, skinny boy. He always struck me as a little sad. My father encouraged us to go because it meant a free meal. We did get the bonus of Christmas crackers; they went bang and there was a supply of candy. Mr. Christian manipulated himself on a board on wheels, a quadriplegic, a basket case from Verdun. It seemed odd to me to see this Christmas host wheel himself about on his platform. But it wasn't until a decade later that I discovered why we were the Christians' guests. They were the neighbourhood's only Negro family. They were being kind to the other minority.

My father had briefly studied Plato and other wisdom. But he remained convinced that no knowledge of any worth existed that could not be found in the Torah and the thousands of books of interpretation that had grown around it across the centuries. His profit and pleasure came in the hours he could steal away to read the works of the learned rabbis. Of course, there was also *Der Forward*, the Jewish paper that always arrived two days late from the Yiddish presses of New York. Even if it was the beginning of war, he would not accept it as fact until he was told first hand by *Der Forward*. Then it was so.

Constantly today we are being told that Toronto has changed, become more worldly. Maybe. There were acts of gallantry then, however, that were marks of a more courtly time.

Take the case of the Baba Bayla. After her husband had coughed his way into his grave and been buried in the distant cemetery of St. Clair Avenue East (West for living, East for dying), she would find her way from the old folks' home on Cecil Street by streetcar alone to the store. She carried a note because, even if she had learned to say the address in English, she might not have been understandable because her teeth had long gone and her voice always seemed filtered through a bowl of borscht. It sounded of beets and cabbage and sour salt. She would sweep into the car and sit beside the conductor in her black, floor-length robes, testing her wig to be sure it had not fallen askew. She kept her dignity always, except for those awkward times when her bladder would not quite hold on cold nights waiting for the car's arrival. Strange puddles would form beside the elegant, doll-like lady in the dark skirts.

The conductors came to know her. She would sit silently, trusting to fate that she would be delivered. Even though we lived between the stops at Elmwood and Greenlaw, frequently the conductor would stop the car midway. The passengers would wait as he escorted Baba across the wide avenue. She would take his arm, as if being accompanied to a dance. She would smile her thanks, and through her gums would come sounds of distant Russia. When was it you last saw an act of such city tenderness?

It was a more personal time. The "copper" on the block would hand test each door as he went by, assuring the occupants of their safety. This was fine, except on Passover night, when we all huddled together for the annual seder to recount the tales of the Jews' escape from Egypt. By tradition the door had to be left open for Elijah, the prophet who was supposed to come and drink the extra glass of wine. Inevitably, when the door was left open, a policeman arrived. He was no Jewish saviour. He scolded us for the inconvenience. When we tried the back door, the cat, which survived off chicken remains, entered looking for some kindness. She was tossed out.

Of course, there was occasional crime. To the south of us were the Italians around Davenport and Dufferin. Later they would take over the entire area. But then they clung to the edge of a church at the bottom of the hill. They were mostly latecomers, and in those years, the '30s, they took on the more menial jobs. They were hard working, but sometimes desperate. There was one young man, who looked remarkably like Victor Mature, who came to deliver parcels two days a week. The arrangement was that he would provide an old car with a rumble seat, borrowed from a brother-in-law. He was apparently newly married and already had a wife pregnant by four or five months, and the $10 he made was his entire income. He spoke no English, but we made do with sign language. He was a worried-looking man. We found out why.

Chickens had been disappearing. There was no way they could wander down St. Clair. It meant that someone had been stealing into the coop after dark and making off with them. My mother decided to lie in wait one night, and under a full Toronto winter moon, broom in hand, she caught the culprit. It was our Italian. What to do? Here he was, a noisy rooster under his heavy coat. Caught in the act. Stealing chickens from our very mouths. *But yet*...who could call the police? He was, after all, a Gentile and thus not trustworthy. *But yet*...he, too, was an immigrant. *But crime*...the curse of the commandments was involved, eye for an eye. *But*...the police were the Cossacks in my father's memory. What did it have to do with them? *But yet*...every loaf of bread counted and food had been stolen. My father seemed to be weighing the words of his prayer books as he decided. He called the Italian mother-in-law.

Oy, did he get it! That woman, not much different from my own grandmother in size, came and pleaded his case. She had no idea that her son-in-law had been stealing. She took the very chicken he had stolen and slapped him across the face with it. I mean, a live chicken across the face must be the greatest insult a man can endure. And then again, across the back of the head. Oy! I can almost feel it now. The chicken let out a cackle. The young Italian thief was in tears. How could he bring such disgrace to the woman he loved, to the child unborn. He was hungry; they had all been hungry. He had been trying to impress his in-laws. After all, what did an immigrant have to offer? The mother-in-law listened. My father listened. My mother, never parting with her broom, listened. And justice was done.

Never would he forget chickens. For each chicken stolen he would personally pluck 40 new ones—about five cents per chicken plucked. As an extra punishment, for one month he would be in charge of cleaning the coop, all those chicken droppings. And then to add insult to insult, there was a suspicion—no proof mind you, but a definite suspicion—that perhaps one chicken's worth of the extras may have been spent on another woman. So along came the pregnant bride on those nightly deliveries. She sat beside him and wept. How could he have? More than a chicken had changed hands. I was sorry to see him go when the war came. Manpower became scarce as Canada dashed off to fight for King and country.

Among the chores assigned to me was delivering chickens to Mount Sinai Hospital. No, not that big, handsome structure that confronts Toronto General and the Sick Children's Hospital on University Avenue. Then it was on Yorkville, now Toronto's most fashionable shopping area. Then it was the darkest, and one of the poorest. The hospital was a brown building crowded with patients and the new crop of Jewish doctors who had managed to fit into the quota system. (Oh yes, there was a system of so many Jews allowed into medical school.) My father had been assigned the contract for kosher chickens. This was, I must add, no big deal. Maybe 25 cents a chicken profit, and they all had to be carefully drawn and koshered. This process involved dipping them in salt for an hour or so, and then giving them a bath. They seldom had a chance to dry.

Twenty chickens were packed into a fruit bushel. I carried them on my hip to the streetcar stop and delivered them on the Bay car. Now this might have been all right except for the Avenue Road Hill. You see, while the street was flat, all that water and salt would merely sit in the bottom of the bushel. But when the streetcar would tilt down the Avenue Road hill, the salt water would begin to flow down the aisle. I tried to read my history text as if I had never seen salt water. My treat was one Chocolate Crisp candy bar. Today one of those bars almost makes me weep salt-water tears. I think of those angry conductors.

My embarrassment was surpassed only on those days when we would run short of chickens and I would be dispatched to the poultry market on Kensington Avenue to bring home about four or five extra live ones. They were wrapped in *The Toronto Star* newspaper. I tried to make it look as if I were carrying opened-ended flower arrangement. But sometimes the chicken would announce its presence, and an angry Englishwoman sitting next to me would stare at me as if my stomach had rumbled. Sometimes a chicken might just decide to relieve itself. Try to look complacent with a wet chicken in your lap some day. And then there was the one that got away. It was a hot night, the windows were open, and for all I know it might still be heading north, following the migration of Jews up Bathurst Street.

Without question, there were a lot of chickens in my life. And no question: the colours of death and life of those thousands of chickens that passed our way worked their way into my thinking. Mine could never be a Wonder Bread world. And so, when later I saw the slaughterhouse colours of Chagall paintings, I suppose they were as natural to me as the life I lived then on St. Clair. And when Chagall told me how he dreamed of flying, I remembered how I used to gallop across the pavements, really trying to fly, to fly away from the cry of the dying chickens, from the life of endless deliveries, to pull myself away from the predictable routine, delivery-collection-delivery, the life and death of the weekly quota of chickens. I could run, jump across the pavements, see those autographed markings paved in '28, '29, '30. Running was easy. Existing was not.

But swimming was free. Every Rasky is a swimmer. Toronto is a city on a lake. In those Depression days the lake and the city were closely bound, before concrete highways built barriers between the people and the water.

Remember the free car? Who was that benevolent soul who arranged that? Several times a week a certain streetcar would make the rounds and gather us up, us semislum kids. What the hell, we were all that way, except for those who were beyond my childhood horizon. Those free cars: across St. Clair, down Dovercourt, across King, swinging around in front of the beaches of Lake Ontario. Huge barrackslike changing rooms, boys on one side, girls on the other, packed with brown-bag sandwiches, always the same, peanut butter and jam. How many hot July sandwiches did I eat? A quick dash into the lake, polluted even then, red bathing suits that looked like assorted long underwear. The whistle blowing, and then a rush like hell to change back again, dash back into the streetcar, and hang the bathing suits out to dry as we passed along Queen and up Ossington to "Hail, hail, the gang's all here." They were rolling singsong sessions. "Pack up your troubles in your old kit bag and smile, smile, smile." So who had a kit bag and what was it anyway?

On Sunday there was Sunnyside. Mostly that meant the pool, sometimes called the tank. It was an Olympic-sized pool that was the migrating place for all the immigrant kids. A nickel would get you entrance, a locker, use of the pool and access to the beach. And on that brown, pebbled strip, social engagements for the week were planned. We would lay our towels down next to young girls who pretended to be sunbathing and strike up a conversation. If things went especially well, an offer would be made to share towels and even Cracker Jacks. And in the event of a real strike, perhaps we might arrange for a walk on the boardwalk later on. The wooden walkway ran the length of Sunnyside. On one side of the street were amusements, naturally padlocked on Sunday, and on the other, the lake. Who could figure that on the other side of the shoreline was something called America?

If the evening was promising, we would stay for the singalong with Jack Sobel at the live radio broadcast arena. A projector announced the words on a huge screen, and the patriotic songs of World War I were intoned by a soprano whose voice had been hibernating all those long, winter nights. "Surely you're proud. Sing it aloud. There'll always be an England." And Scottish sword dancers, little girls who hopped around crossed swords. I never could figure out why they did that for radio, and did a sweet, candy-cheeked girl ever lose a toe? And now, the accordion with a Gypsy melody! And then the streetcar ride home to the hot rooms above the store.

It was extraordinary how exciting was the move from 1281 to 1283 St. Clair Avenue. The Ardeys were giving up. The Bible store next door was an obvious error. Not many crosses could be sold to Willer, Waller and Feldman. Perhaps there had been a quiet hope that a convert would be made somewhere along the line. If anything, it was the reverse. When Mandel delivered that rich cream cheese and that sweet halvah, how could a Christian kid resist even if the neighbours had not accepted Jesus. The Ardeys moved from this corrupting, heathen influence, perhaps to some Bible school closer to heaven.

But with a down payment of $500 borrowed from lawyer Marcus, my father arranged the $3,000 purchase of the building. At last, my own bed. In the early years in the *kaltruum* (the cold room), I could not recall whether I had urinated in the bed, or whether it was my brothers. It was all the same beneath the heavy chicken-feather, homemade comforter. And when one of us caught diptheria, everyone went to the isolation hospital. The entire family was almost wiped out. But we survived. We survived in glory to march up the stairs of the Ardey store. "Onward Jewish soldiers. Onward as to war!" With my mother, slightly hysterical at the mess left behind, shouting, "*Hack mere nisht kine chunik*"—not so much noise—as we entered the Jerusalem next door. Imagine a furnace of our own, a real upstairs!

There was one moment of difficult religious discussion. Upstairs in the hallway leading to the double parlour where I was to sleep in a folding bed was a metal sign hammered into the plaster wall: "Jesus Saves!" Pretty tough stuff for us newcomers. It seemed to me that half the wall came down with the sign. The temple toppled, the reverse side later to be made into a feeding trough for the chickens. Question: Can a chicken eating off a "Jesus Saves" sign be truly kosher? God lived with us in many ways and not on tin.

There never was a hope that my father would accumulate any amount of money. Each customer had a different price. The Cohens paid the full amount, the Wagmans a little less. Old Mrs. Segal, widowed and on relief, made a token payment, but her pride still made her grumble. Wandering Jews with a good religious background were brought home for dinner, their beards pulled apart like half-chewed sandwiches as they enjoyed my mother's constant chicken soup. Eager young rabbis without a pulpit, like David Monson, found a temporary home.

The MacKay Street *shul* could not afford a rabbi. My father never missed a service. How I longed to sleep in on those Saturday mornings when I was required to fill out the traditional number of 10 for *minyen*. During the war they even started me at 12 instead of the compulsory bar-mitzvahed 13. (The Talmud allowed!)

And the voice. Even now I rock back and forth in the memory of that voice of my father. God just moved in with him. How full of longing it was for the storybook Jerusalem, for Jews who were free, free from pressures economic, political, social. Those melodies passed on from generation to generation. My father, Reb Leib (Leib means lion), who never learned to read music, had long ago committed the words to memory, so he could sing with his eyes closed, his face always tilted upwards. Surely God hovered over MacKay Street in personal attendance, now serious, now smiling at a melody that caught his ear. The awful and beautiful Hebrew God was, of course, an old, old man with long whiskers, grown tired from arguing with His people, with naive Abraham, with cunning Isaac, with wrestling Jacob and especially with His Moses. What an arguer! And what's this blasphemous thing about a Son. We were all His sons. The women were behind a separating wall, nudging from the rear, daughters of Zion.

The men would pound their chests to beat out the sins. They would argue over inflection of sound. Who could pray the loudest? And after the prayers, there would be sweet biscuits and shmaltz herring and homemade wine from Niagara grapes, stirred into fire in caskets in our basement. Good fellowship and song: *"Loz mir alle, alle namen trinkin a glazzela vine."* Let us all, let us all drink a glass of wine in honour of the scholar. With herring, yet. Except on Yom Kippur, holiest of holies. The crying for forgiveness. I guess the Gentiles on the block must have figured those Jews had a lot to be forgiven for—killing Christ and all that.

As part of the ritual, twice in the ceremony my father would fall to his knees to pray for the assembled sins of the congregation. Two Rasky brothers would always be given the honour of lifting him up. So we had to stay inside during the long sessions of Hebrew chanting, while other kids tossed filbert nuts in a game on the faded lawn. Once I was missing, I now confess I vanished to the Casino Burlesque Theatre on Queen Street to see three striptease acts—and on the Day of Atonement. I think God is still after me for that one.

When the service was over, there was my father, all the energy delivered to God in prayer and song, and fasting for the *Kol Nidre* prayer and the ritual blowing of the *shofar*. The ordeal over, we walked silently down MacKay and onto Greenlaw toward St. Clair.

"*Nu?*" he asked after a time.

"*Nu*, what?" I answered, still caught up in the majesty and passion of the tones of prayer and the ram's horn piercing my brain with its notes caught in God's arms about us. "So, what?"

"So, how was I?"

So, even with God, maybe especially with God, you've got to have some humour.

"If God had a son, how come he never had a wife?" To the Nazarenes trying to convert us on occasion, we threw the question. "You are too young to understand!" came the answer. Born again? It was so hard the first time, please. Not now, again. Sunday nights, the service from the Church of the Nazarene blared out on loudspeakers. Thank God we had Jack Benny.

Sex was never mentioned in home or school. But we caught a glimpse, a look, if not a feel of female. Sure, there were a couple of Jewish girls on the block. But they were like sisters. And, naturally, sisters were not for feeling. Expeditions were mounted into the dangerous Gentile world beyond the barriers of our fortress isolation. The call of the wild came with the first growth of baby whiskers. Those little breasts, bulging from soft, woollen sweaters. Sometimes in the talk of the street it was called "a handful." How to search and find and finally hold "a handful?"

There were various possibilities. During the summers, the Jews who had found a little money also tried to find a place in the sun. This meant congested summer cottages at Lake Simcoe, 50 miles away, at the resorts known as Belle Ewart and Jackson's Point. We would hitchhike up the long Yonge Street highway, sleep on the hard, brown beach, and chase some of the young Jewish girls. And if there was the opportunity to catch them alone, the answer would always be, "What made you think I was that sort of girl?" "Full moon and empty arms." The dancing was hard on those young aching testicles. Out there was the forbidden fruit.

Beaches in the east end of the city in far-off places beyond what was called the Danforth. The challenge was to get by the signs that spelled out the rule: "Restricted." To pass by without a look of guilt was like stealing green apples. How to look nonchalant when you know your nose might be just a little too long. A skilled observer might just cause that nose to be bloodied. The girls' gum chewing was hard to take, and the conversation—well, was there any? One did get to hold a female body slightly closer, but the "handfuls" were hard to find. How were we to know that Presbyterians, too, had rules, and what was a Presbyterian anyhow?

Sure it was early adventure, wanting to know what was out there. Was it true, as my parents believed, that the world of non-Jews was violent, that penetration outside meant asking for battle? But the mind would not relent, and the young body was travelling under a full wind of desire. Mostly the results were dreary. At the Palais Royal down on the lakefront, it was soldiers first, and what chance did early puberty provide? The Central YMCA held tea dances. The records were scratchy and so were the girls lined against the wall like tattered books in a dark library.

The movie house was the escape. I danced with Fred Astaire. I dared with Paul Muni. I memorized that speech in *Emile Zola* defending Dreyfus, and I *was* Dreyfus, too. And do you remember when Muni and I discovered pasteurization? And Edward G. turned good guy to wipe out the plague or something in *The Magic Bullet*? We did that together, and later when I actually sat and had dinner with Eddy G. in Hollywood, I couldn't tell him. But it was all okay because even then it was rumoured he was really a Jew posing as a gangster—he had a Jewish heart.

It's been said that Jews look after their own. In a way it was true about the organizations that shaped those early years. The Baba Bayla, as I've noted, lived out her last years at the Jewish old folks' home. It was established long before "senior citizens" became a fashionable phrase. And she danced her last dance there, right on her final day.

For teenagers there was something called the AZA, which was part of a youth organization of B'nai B'rith. It meant parading around Dundas and Spadina in uniform: shirts with large letters sewn on. It was a time when Shopsy was called "Shopsowitz," and his delicatessen was in constant competition with a dozen others around, and the garlic from the pastrami followed you down the street.

Camp B'nai B'rith was the summer salvation. Ten days for $10 or so. You just had to be wanting and free of lice. One year we passed the first test, but not the second. Off came the hair, all of it. We were shaved like concentration camp victims. But we got our 10 days at camp. "Oh, what do we do with the drunken counsellor, what do we do with the drunken counsellor, early in the morning." And similar songs around a campfire at Lake Couchiching. There was talk of how one counsellor had actually been to Spain. Had he killed a man? And why? What was a civil war anyhow, and what did it have to do with these Jewish kids, huddled around the site of an old Indian graveyard?

There I learned on August night from my counsellor, Lou Applebaum, about theatre. My first role. It was a dramatic sketch around the writing of the *Moonlight Sonata*. And guess who got to be Beethoven, the first of my many other lives? How at home I was on the camp stage! And even though the music was being played by a record, I knew I had composed it.

There was the constant question of escape. What would be the road out of St. Clair Avenue? None of us was interested in turning the chicken-grocery trade into a supermarket. We were all by nature not merchants. My only real knowledge about the outside world came from the films at the Royal George or the Oakwood cinemas. They were the stuff of dreams. I fashioned imaginary worlds based on the plots. But my fantasies seemed forever unreachable. I would sneak in the exit and sometimes watch a film three times, and dream myself right into the action of the screen.

Sometime during my high school years at Oakwood Collegiate, I discovered a vital fact: that if you were covering an event for the school paper, you were treated somewhat specially. You did not have to wait in line. There was a city-wide paper called the *Canadian High News*, edited by a man named Knowlton Nash. I visited the downtown office and Knowlton issued me a press card. My world changed. I crossed boundaries that seemed till then impenetrable. I also involved myself with the paper's Saturday afternoon radio show on CFRB. My two worlds of fact and fantasy were beginning to take a single shape.

At the University of Toronto, I quickly registered for the *Varsity* paper and became involved in the UC Follies, the annual college variety show. I felt I had arrived, even if it was in the family pickup truck, delivering the parcels of chickens on the way. I was ready for fame and fortune and my first real, outside-the-family job.

Nobody Swings on Sundays *(1980)*

EMIGRANT

He lives now
On a huge new continent,
But he pines away
For a country that
No longer exists.
His letters to history
Are returned unanswered;
He collects them carefully
As evidence of his faith.
In the silence of two continents
He grows thin and old.
"Where is my reward?" he whispers.
At last he falls silent, yearning
For a country that no longer exists.
His children shake their heads
About the old man.
They're doing fine.

WALTER BAUER, *translated by Henry Beissel*

TORONTO CHINESE

BY PHILIP MARCHAND

For decades, Dundas Street between Bay and Spadina existed as a mildly exotic Toronto landmark, like Kensington Market. Chinatown. Every city should have one. Shrimp chow mein, egg rolls, a little colour for the tourists. And residents who seemed nice enough, if not exactly ebullient or handy with the English language. In recent years, however, Toronto's Chinatown has burst through the comfortable boundaries laid down for it, both in actual geography and in our collective idea of what the place is like.

Spurred by a boom in prosperity and in population (there are between 130,000 and 200,000 Torontonians of Chinese descent), Toronto's Chinatown has, like a single-celled organism, divided and reproduced itself. Broadview and Gerrard, and Sheppard and Midland in Scarborough, are now as much Chinatown as Dundas and Spadina. From all these places have emerged shopkeepers, restaurateurs and owners of dry-cleaning establishments, of course, but also a very prosperous and self-confident class, in general, of Toronto residents who grew up speaking Cantonese at home. There are no Chinese Conrad Blacks or Paul Reichmanns—yet—but there are a lot of Chinese dentists and accountants who live in such places as Agincourt with a Jacuzzi in the bathroom and a Trans Am in the garage.

Meanwhile, the old core of Chinatown—Dundas and Spadina—is enjoying a revival, thanks to the influx of 50,000 or so boat people in the late '70s.

Before they came, the area had been becoming a dying

enclave for Chinese who could not speak English. Now a certain vibrancy has returned. And many of these immigrants have already started businesses with a tenacity and a survival instinct that have impressed even the hardworking Chinese from Hong Kong.

It remains true that most of the Chinese in Toronto were either born in Hong Kong or came through there on their way to Canada. Their world has been shaped by traditions and experiences unknown to most of us, but this shaping process has not left them at any very noticeable disadvantage. On the contrary. Their personal histories are often remarkable for the toughness, resilience and dogged intelligence they reveal. Few more so than the history of Eddie Ing's family. Eddie Ing's grandfather came here in 1901, after paying $500 for the privilege. For about 50 years he lived in this country without his family, a pigtailed Chinese labourer who laid tracks for the Canadian Pacific Railway, and when that job was over, sold fish and crabs he caught in the waters off Vancouver door to door for a few pennies each. In World War II he ended up in Toronto, still with no skills, education or even very good English. Here he worked as a cook and housekeeper for a wealthy Toronto lawyer. Through all these years he sent what cash he could spare to his wife and son in Canton Kin in southern China. The family began to prosper as a result. Unfortunately, when the Communists took over in 1949, they threw his son and his daughter-in-law into prison for five years. They were merchants and landowners—enemies of the people. Some of the grandchildren, including Eddie Ing, escaped to Hong Kong, where Eddie married his wife, Nancy, a young woman from his native district in China. Shortly after, in 1954, his grandfather bought a Canadian passport for him for $2,000. His first stop in Canada was Cobourg, Ontario, where a brother, who had arrived earlier in the same way, had arranged a job for him in a Chinese restaurant. Eddie stepped off the bus in Cobourg without a scrap of English—only a piece of paper with the address of the restaurant written on it.

He started work immediately, seven days a week, eighteen hours a day—not even daring to ask what he was getting paid. His first paycheque was for $35, or a little more than 25 cents an hour. Even in 1954 that was rather like starvation wages. A couple of months later, he found his way to Toronto, where he got a job washing dishes in a now defunct restaurant opposite Lichee Gardens. At this time he also heard the news that his wife in Hong Kong had just given birth to a baby daughter, Eileen. Nine months later, his grandfather gave him $1,500 to go into partnership in a new restaurant with three of his grandfather's friends, who also chipped in $1,500 each. They started the 24-hour Cantonese Chop Suey House on what is now Nathan Phillips Square.

Seven months after this venture opened in 1955, they received a notice informing them that their land was being expropriated for the new city hall. Thus ended the Cantonese Chop Suey House. Eddie went to work for another restaurant for $45 a week. This time he had one day a week off. Throughout these years, he kept sending what money he could to his wife and his parents in Hong Kong—about $300 a month in Hong Kong currency ($60 a month Canadian). In 1958, the federal government offered amnesty to illegal immigrants like Eddie Ing and made it possible for them to bring over spouses and children. Eddie went to the immigration people and that year was reunited with his wife, who brought with her the daughter he had never seen.

They lived in a room at 106 Granby Street for $28 a month rent; Eddie eventually landed a job as a cook with the Canadian National Railway (on his days off he worked as a cook for the Noshery on Eglinton Avenue West). His wife worked, initially, in a sewing factory on Spadina Avenue for 55 cents an hour. (Since 1973 she has worked as a postal clerk.) By 1960 they had put $2,000 away for a down payment on a house. Eddie also went to his family association and borrowed another $1,000. Family associations are clubs consisting of people with the same surname. There are as many family associations as surnames, which means that in Toronto there are about 60 of them. They have great social, political and economic influence on the life of Chinatown— performing benevolent works, dispensing credit to members, sometimes determining with their credit and patronage which businesses in Chinatown make it and which do not.

With the $3,000 from his savings and the loan from his family association, Eddie Ing made a deal for a house at 133 Seaton Street, which was selling for $11,000. He and his wife and their two children (a son, Edison, was born in 1960) moved into one room and converted the rest into a boarding house. Their spare cash at the time, Eddie recalls, was something like $10. After their third child—Goldie, another son—was born in 1965, those quarters became too cramped and they bought a second house—the first house was now completely paid for—at 332 Kingswood Road. In this house they treated themselves to three rooms.

In the meantime, Eddie managed to bring his family members to Canada one by one; his mother first and then his father and his two other brothers and two of his four sisters. There was no question about it. You may despise your brother from the bottom of your heart, but you don't forget him. When Nancy Ing came here in 1958 she literally signed a contract with the Ings pledging that she would send at least $30 a month of her own earnings to help support Eddie's father back in China and eventually bring him over. Nancy has not forgotten her own family either. In Chinese society the wife leaves her original family and becomes part of her husband's, but her ancestors are still her ancestors. On one trip to Hong Kong she paid the monks in a Chinese monastery $2,000 to perform the ceremonial rites honouring those ancestors. That, too, is something that is just done. (Chinese homes often have plaques commemorating family ancestors, and observances are paid them on special holidays.)

In 1976 the Ings sold their first house and bought a building on Dundas Street, just west of Spadina. In 1977 they opened the Sun King Cleaners in this building. The business has prospered. Last year they had a celebration to mark its fifth anniversary. Inside there are colour photographs of then alderman Gordon Chong and MP Dan Heap smiling amid a small crowd of people outside the cleaners, while a Chinese dragon prances in the street. There are also photographs of the Ing family, Eddie and Nancy, and Eddie's parents, his brothers and sisters, and the children. (The Ings' daughter is now a supervisor in the public health department of city hall; the elder son takes business courses at the University of Waterloo and the youngest is in Grade 12 at Harbord Collegiate.) "We are very happy here," Mrs. Ing says. "I find as long as you are willing to work you will get everything."

We are talking about people who can live, if necessary, without cars, new furniture, vacations, meat once a day and other North American necessities. Selina Man, a Hong Kong-born woman who now works as a hospital administrator, cites a family with two children living near her house in the Kensington area. Her husband helped them with their income tax, and in the process found that they had saved $6,000 in their first year in Canada—with both parents not making much more than the minimum wage.

True, neither the house they were renting nor the house they have recently bought is something that will be featured in the Homes section of *The Toronto Star*. But it is a house. Many of these immigrants from Hong Kong or China do not feel they have to live in houses suitable for holding exquisite, candlelit dinner parties. They have no urge to "renovate." In fact, Selina comments, "If Chinese buy a house from somebody downtown they don't want to buy it from other Chinese. They know if Chinese owned it, probably nothing has been done to it."

Selina Man's neighbours had an additional problem that makes their year's savings even more remarkable. One night Selina heard shouting from their house, and went over to find the family in tears. The wife's sister, who had sponsored them as immigrants, was threatening to throw them out of their house for holding back on money she was extorting from them (the money she demanded added up to almost $8,000 in their first year). It was only right she should be paid this money, the sister claimed: had she not paid almost as much in bribes to Canadian immigration officials to bring them over? The ruckus ended when the police came. "The family was surprised that the policemen were sympathetic and really wanted to help them," Selina recalls.

Obviously the strong family unit in Chinese culture has its advantages and disadvantages. The ideal of this unit, derived from Confucius, is three generations of a family living under one roof, with the eldest members given most respect—and authority—because they are the closest to the ancestors and accountable to them for the good name of the family. "There's no such philosophy," says You Chang Seetoo, executive director of the Toronto Chinese Community Services Association, "that once a kid reaches a certain age he's no longer a kid and is therefore allowed to be independent."

In the West, the smallest irreducible unit of society is the individual. Until recently, in China, it has always been the family. Governments treated individuals as members of families in matters such as taxation and civil law. People within the family were often not addressed by given names but by what anthropologists call "kinship titles"—in the Chinese language fairly complex titles, such as unmarried paternal aunt, and so on. In the Confucian ideal, harmony prevailed within this family network and in its relations with outsiders; it's an ideal that puts a premium on not letting it all hang out, not getting into confrontations, not putting yourself and your good name on the line with strangers (hence the development of the go-between in business and social matters).

The ideal helps explain why you don't see many Chinese

men getting into push-and-shove with people who hassle them. "We are people of more even temper, we tend not to get into arguments with somebody in the subway or on the street," Bob Chow, editor of the Chinese-language newspaper *Chinese Express*, says. "If somebody speaks to us in a bad way or insults us, a lot of times Chinese people tend to forget it. Once you start any kind of argument, there's no end to it." Historically, Canadian society has massively insulted Chinese immigrants. They have never been quick, however, to demonstrate in front of police headquarters, shout slogans or celebrate Days of Rage. Sidney Poon, a Hong Kong-born lawyer, expresses a quintessentially Chinese view on matters of racial difficulty. "It's very easy in a bad situation to say, 'Oh, I'm discriminated against because I'm black, or I'm Chinese,'" he remarks. "But before you say this, it's better to ask yourself first whether you have behaved properly."

The family ideal has taken quite a beating over the years in Hong Kong because of the huge influence of Western capitalism and Western culture, and in China itself with the coming of Mao. Old men in Hong Kong complain about the lack of respect in younger generations. Discos have sprouted like weeds. Hong Kong television has not reached the pinnacle of frankness represented by such shows as *Dallas*—no Hong Kong J.R. taunts a rival for his sexual impotence—but many Hong Kong operas, aired in Toronto over Channel 47, portray couples who are obviously living in sin, and other non-Confucian situations.

In Canada the deterioration of the ideal is accelerated. Wives of immigrants find jobs in sewing factories on Spadina sooner than their mates find jobs, and make it clear to them that husbands aren't necessarily bossman in the new country, family harmony or no family harmony. Children learn that North Americans easily put up with mouthy kids, and in fact seem to find them—on TV sitcoms at least—positively delightful. Grown-up daughters move in with boyfriends, or obtain divorces with the nonchalance of their liberated North American sisters.

The process horrifies many Toronto Chinese, and not just wizened patriarchs. Hai Chi Ching, a graduate student in electrical engineering at the University of Toronto who has lived here for six years, has taken a good look at the Chinese community in Toronto, and North American society in general, and decided that he'd rather spend the rest of his life in a Chinese society—perhaps as a teacher in mainland China. "If I didn't want to get married, if I wanted to be a loner,

Canada would be ideal because personal independence and privacy are very seriously respected here, and there's a high level of material reward," he says. "But I do want to have a family, and so I think, what country would I choose for my children? I think I would want them to live in a basically Chinese society."

There are many reasons for this preference. One of them is our Brooke Shields ideal—every adolescent girl is a temptress in Calvin Klein jeans. In Hong Kong, Hai explains, "The young women feel less pressure to find a boyfriend at an early age. In a way it's not a healthy phenomenon, but if a girl at the age of 16 or 17 still doesn't have a boyfriend, people will say, 'Oh, she's good, she spends her time on her studies.' And the same with the young man." Hustling chicks is not admired male behaviour. "It's considered impolite to express a lot of sexual interest in a young woman." As for casual love affairs, they are frankly looked down on.

In a serious courtship, the couple discusses serious issues—like how they are going to take care of the man's parents. "If I were to get married, the society assumes I will live with my parents and my wife has to accept this assumption," Hai explains. "The idea that every group of consenting adults can do whatever they want is horrible to me." The most unspeakable act, in his view, is a couple dumping their parents into an old-age home.

The social consensus Canadians lack he considers essential. "It is a very precious part of Chinese culture—and a vulnerable one, because people are physical and they like to do what they want to do," he adds. "I have a feeling you are not sure what this society as a whole is heading toward. Are you heading into a jungle, a group of miscellaneous subcultures without any moral guidelines? Or are you heading as an integrated unit to a happy and healthy society?"

Canadians have developed a fairly hospitable public realm and a fairly cold private realm—the opposite of Chinese society. People on the streets of Toronto are much more friendly, and willing, say, to give directions, than in Hong Kong or China, where it has traditionally been considered asking a lot to call upon a stranger for assistance. And yet, he says, "After a while you begin to discover that the friendship here is less penetrating than Chinese friendship because the privacy barrier will come up. I would be reluctant to say to some Western friends, 'I don't have any money to pay rent, can I come and live with you for awhile?' because they would become embarrassed. They would want to say no, but wouldn't feel they could."

Indeed, Westerners who have befriended Chinese have oftentimes been taken aback by the degree of intimacy this friendship assumes in the eyes of the Chinese, who feel hurt when the Westerners don't reciprocate. This may explain why real friendships between Canadians and Chinese—even second-generation immigrants who live and work among white Canadians—are rare. Cordiality exists, politeness certainly, but, as Selina Man observes, "Very few Canadians are allowed into the sanctuary where the Chinese get together with their families to observe the Chinese holidays or just play mahjong." Recently, she and her Australian-born husband visited a family that has been here for 15 years, and the family's young son burst into tears of fright at the sight of her husband. "They said it was because he had never seen a Caucasian in their home."

The family unit is the force behind much of the famous Chinese work ethic, the drive for success—a drive many Canadians, less highly motivated, are beginning to fear. Children in Chinese families study hard, quite simply, because they don't want to disappoint their parents. Of course, Canadian students are accountable to their parents too. But few of them sweat it—not like Chinese students.

Immigrants and students from Hong Kong know other pressures besides those from the family. They remember Hong Kong, the city that gives new meaning to the term social Darwinism. In Hong Kong the successful are very successful. The top income tax rate is something like 15 percent. Conversely, the deserving poor are out of luck. Welfare, unemployment insurance and social services are minimal or nonexistent. When you're on the streets in Hong Kong you're on the streets. So people work hard. Very hard. "Life in Hong Kong is just 10 times more demanding and competitive," Selina Man observes. Her sister Pauline, a secretary recently arrived from Hong Kong, "just can't believe what her coworkers get away with. People take long lunch hours, long coffee breaks, they leave right on time. There's no sense that you have to outdo the person who was in the job before you, or the person who's going to follow you in the job. She thinks office skills in Toronto are terrible." Her sister can type 96 words a minute, do 160 words a minute shorthand. "In Hong Kong, if you don't have that, you can't work."

As the world knows, determined Hong Kong residents

have created a new industrial power in Asia. Many of those who helped create this power now want to get out with their money and their children before the British lease expires in 1997. (Hong Kong money has already bought up a substantial portion of lower Yonge Street, the Spadina garment industry, old civic landmarks such as the Medical Arts Building on St. George Street, and new civic landmarks such as the Toronto Hilton Harbour Castle.) A favourite entree into Canada for those who want to live here is the student visa. In 1981 – 82, more than 1,000 Hong Kong students enrolled in public secondary schools in the City of Toronto; in 1982 – 83, about 1,400 enrolled; for 1983 – 84 the number decreased to about 1,200 because of increased competition for these students from other countries and because the U of T is planning to raise its tuition fees for visa students over the next few years.

Such a marvellous source of funds has not gone overlooked by our private schools, including those infamous "visa schools," whose enrollment is largely Hong Kong students. Each year, recruiters from these schools fly to Hong Kong. One school, in its brochure, included photographs of the Metropolitan Toronto Library as part of its "facilities." Disinformation flourishes. In fairness to our public and private schools, the temptations to malfeasance are often quite large. Even conscientious recruiters have been faced with Hong Kong parents who want to register a student at their school, pay his year's tuition, fees, everything—on the clear understanding that once the student registers and gets his visa, he'll never bother to show up at the school.

Of bona fide students, almost all study for professions that guarantee high incomes: engineering, computer science, accounting, medicine, commerce and finance. Graduates of these courses often go on to other careers. Alex Yeung, who studied chemical engineering, now, with his family, owns and operates the Cathay Restaurant and Cathay II Tavern and Restaurant. Peter Man, who oversees Chinese-language broadcasts on Channel 47, studied civil engineering. "Very boring stuff," he says, but adds that Hong Kong students don't go to university to find themselves, they go to obtain professional credentials: "Being a doctor is the ultimate."

This attitude explains another trait of students from Hong Kong—their tendency to accept the authority of teachers and professors, even when these teachers and professors, chastened by the '60s, no longer even attempt to exert any classroom authority aside from handing out marks. If these students have questions, instead of interrupting a lecture, they wait until the class is over and then talk to the professor.

Often, students in secondary school and university push their way to high marks in the most dogged ways conceivable. "They get upset if there's nothing to memorize," one teacher in a private high school remarks of his students from Hong Kong. "I mean, they memorize whole sections of textbooks and then write them out for exam questions. Sometimes they don't match the sections with the right questions and the results are just bizarre, like printouts from a computer with a circuit blown somewhere. If you get on a level that's imaginative or graphic or strongly visual, even in math or physics, they start to get lost."

Canadian students tend to see them as Stakhanovite workers of the intellect who have trouble mastering simple English sentences and prefer sticking together. There is an element of truth in the image—Selina Man has a cousin who thought the U of T was great because he didn't have to speak a word of English all year—but it tends to negate the liveliness, humour and genuine concern for social issues most of these students do possess. Periodically, the university community mounts campaigns to "integrate" Hong Kong students more fully into campus life—campaigns that succeed mainly in irritating the Hong Kong students. Armed with politeness, however, they approach their studies as a job that must be done, and therefore a job that must be done well. Where they come from, a job done poorly can have disastrous consequences.

When the job is finished, questions that remained submerged beneath the relentless effort to master the job start to surface. Questions like: can a Chinese person be happy in Toronto? Hai Chi Ching knows a Hong Kong-born Canadian, now in his mid-thirties, with a professional degree and a good income, who is simply drifting. He can't make up his mind to get married. He can't make up his mind to settle in Canada or Hong Kong or mainland China. He has stayed for prolonged periods in all three, and now feels outside the mainstream of society in all of them. "Something here is missing and he's searching for that thing that's missing."

Among the Chinese Canadians that Hai knows, he discerns two basic groups. The first group consists of the young professionals and businessmen who are quite happy to make $75,000 a year and fight crabgrass with their neighbours in the suburbs. "If you ask them what the Chinese Canadian is, or how one should behave, most of them, or all of them, have no idea. They would say, whatever the government wants, we'll do. They want us to pay taxes, we'll pay taxes. They want us to vote, we'll vote." The second group consists of similar professionals and businessmen who are not quite so happy. "They want to have a Chinese style of living and yet they enjoy to a certain extent the political and financial security, and also the larger opportunity, this society offers." Some who try to combine both end up torn apart by the effort. Others turn to politics and organized community groups in an effort to talk the problem down to size.

One such group is the Chinese Canadian National Council, originally formed in response to a notorious *W5* program that strongly suggested there were too many Chinese students in Canadian universities: it's founding president is a 34-year-old Toronto family physician, Dr. Joseph Wong. At a national conference in Vancouver last year, members of the council wrestled with the question of the Chinese-Canadian experience. "We still haven't defined what the Chinese-Canadian culture is. What the Chinese Canadian should know about his background," Wong comments. "We are still in the process of trying to find that answer."

In the meantime, the council lobbies for "a true multicultural society": Chinese-language instruction in public schools during regular school hours, and so on. ("We learned political lobbying is very important," Wong remarks. "We never learned it until we came here." Hong Kong government is not democratic in any way, shape or form. Moreover, the traditional Chinese attitude toward politics in general is that it is a fit occupation for crooks, shysters and con artists. "While you might not trust politicians," former alderman Gordon Chong says, "the Chinese trust them even less.")

Everyone agrees that respect for elders can and should remain a part of the Chinese-Canadian psyche, and also that the less democratic aspects of Chinese culture should probably be discarded. (Automatic deference to authority, for example.) Beyond that, bridging two very different cultures is an extremely tricky venture for most Chinese Canadians. Selina Man, for one, remains dissatisfied with how the community as a whole has managed it—especially when compared with, say, Japanese Canadians. Japanese Canadians have impressed her with their fluency in English, their ability to go out to Canadian society, combined with their awareness of their own society ("not just eating the food and using chopsticks, but they know about their history and art and things like the tea ceremony").

She sees Chinese Canadians as tending either to be ghetto-ized or overly Canadianized. "Either people always talk about the old country or they become so Westernized that there is no trace of it. It's such an impoverished community life. People see Chinatown—what kind of an impression from Chinatown will they get about Chinese people? My husband says they'll think that Chinese people eat a lot, and their kids tend to stay up to all hours of the night." (Sunday nights in Chinatown are particularly lively. It's a favourite time for families to go out to eat—that means, again, grandparents, grandchildren, aunts, uncles, everybody. Hong Kong immigrants in general carry with them, too, a fondness for life on city streets nurtured by the conditions of life in Hong Kong.)

Selina Man believes that the greater cultural awareness of Japanese Canadians stems from the solidity and self-confidence of their original Japanese culture. Almost all of the immigrants to Canada from China, however, come from Hong Kong. (At least since 1967, anyway, when immigration law was completely overhauled and liberalized and when immigration to Canada from China really took off.) Hong Kong is not China: "My husband has quite a few visiting scholars from mainland China, and Chinatown to them is like Disneyland," she says. Hong Kong itself is an anomaly; its population historically has also been drawn from the south of China, particularly the region around Canton, a region noted more for commercial acumen than for scholarly and cultural pursuits, which historically are the specialties of northern China.

Her education in Canada taught her perhaps as much about her native Hong Kong as it did about Canada. When she first arrived at York University in 1971, fresh from 13 years of wearing school uniforms, a girl who felt naked without ankle socks and had never drunk a beer in her life, she felt intense culture shock. That Selina had no close relatives or family here set her apart from most of her fellow Hong Kong students who did, in fact, lodge with family and friends, and therefore had to worry about what these friends and family members thought of them. Selina didn't. And she made use of her freedom. One summer she hitchhiked to Vancouver with a girlfriend from Quebec. Other Hong Kong students were appalled, but Selina blithely wrote to her parents in Hong Kong and mentioned her plans. "They had no concept of what hitchhiking was," she recalls. "They had never seen it. They had never heard horror stories about it. They said, 'Okay, great, take lots of pictures.'"

Perhaps because she mingled freely with other Canadian students, went to visit their families during reading week and holidays, Selina found it possible later to opt for life in Canada with a measure of enthusiasm. "I consciously made the choice I want to be a Canadian," she says. "I think it would be wonderful for all my children, too, to say, 'I'm Canadian.' [She has two sons.] None of my Chinese friends will come out and say, 'I'm Canadian.' I have yet to hear that. And they're all Canadian citizens."

This does not mean she has cut herself off from her native culture or her family. For one thing, her sister is now living with her. "Sometimes my husband asks me, 'Why on earth do you feel you have to support your sister? Why does she have to live with you? Why does she need to be so protected and coddled?' and I say, 'Look, she's living in the house, and if she goes out with somebody my mother wouldn't like, or something happens to her, my mother wouldn't blame her, she would lay the blame on me. I'm her older sister.' And no doubt about it, if my mother comes here, she'll be living with me, although she wouldn't live with me the same way had my husband been Chinese. She wouldn't have the same expectations. She would say, 'Oh, he's not Chinese, he won't understand,' and she wouldn't make the same demands."

Growing up with a heavy weight of family demands, Selina was at first taken aback by the emphasis of Canadian society on individual "self-realization" and other goals touted by sales seminars, therapy groups and management training courses. "I was really surprised to find there was such a thing as personal satisfaction," Selina Man says. Once her mother visited her house in Kensington and began comparing it to the houses of other friends in Toronto. Their houses had sizable backyards, garages, and so on. "I said, 'Mother, why are you so worried about what other people think? I'm happy here.' And she said, 'Happy? Don't mention the word. That's the most selfish word to use. How can you be happy when other people are not happy? When I'm not happy?'" Selina reflects on the incident and then comments, "None of my Chinese friends has used that as a word to describe their goals in life. Happy? What's happy? Money is happy."

Because the family unit is seen as an unbreakable entity, Chinese families sometimes endure strains that cause Canadian wives to invest in do-it-yourself divorce kits. "Chinese men will give more time and sacrifice more of their personal life for business. Wives will accept that," Peter Man says. "I guess they're not so liberated in that respect. They're willing to sacrifice part of their own lives helping their husbands set up their businesses, or if their husbands spend all their time working, they don't complain.''

Again, life in Hong Kong explains much of this work and money-making drive, rather than some innate acquisitiveness. Speaking of Hong Kong businessmen, Sidney Poon remarks, ''They are known for their tendency to make money. But then you can't blame them. They don't know what's going to happen in 15 or 20 years.'' As investors, the businessmen who have come here are not particularly sophisticated or daring. They like low-risk investments, and have a certain affinity for classic standards of wealth such as real estate and gold. Many of the very rich in Hong Kong made their fortunes in real estate, but lately the Hong Kong real estate boom has ended with the political uncertainty, and now gold is a favourite again. ''A lot of the businessmen here are not really businessmen in the Canadian sense,'' Peter Man says. ''A lot of them don't know anything about accounting, double-entry bookkeeping, inventories, tax laws. They just put the money in the till. 'We know how to cook, let's open a restaurant.' That's the way China has been doing business for thousands of years.''

Many businesses in Toronto's Chinatown, like businesses in China, are run on old-fashioned paternalistic lines. The owner provides employment and the employees provide loyalty. Even when business is bad they are kept on. In return, owners expect employees to work for 10 or 20 years. The same long-term approach applies to suppliers. Chinese businessmen are particularly equipped to weather hard times.

Traditionally, Chinatown businesses meant laundries and restaurants. The Chinese restaurant is still, in fact, the small capital venture par excellence for Chinese businessmen. There seems to be no end of them in the city. At some point, however, a saturation point will be reached. Moreover, restaurants are labour intensive and therefore entail high costs, they require a great deal of expertise to run and, as anyone who has worked in a restaurant can testify, they shred your nervous system faster than any other form of business. Naturally, Chinese businessmen are beginning to diversify. The businessmen themselves have become more sophisticated. Those educated in Canada tend to go into manufacturing or food processing as opposed to restaurants.

A curious instance of older-style Chinese entrepreneurship is the growth of businesses owned by former boat people. An unknown, but significant percentage of boat people have never gotten over the trauma of Vietnam, or the subsequent strain in their family life, and have ended up more or less as permanent casualties of their country's "liberation." The more resilient have made Chinatown, west of Spadina, virtually a colony of their own, highlighted by a string of jewelry stores on Dundas between Spadina and Bathurst.

Police worry that some of these merchants may end up victims of some of their fellow "refugees"—extortionists and other criminals who were sprung from jail by the Vietnamese Communists, à la Fidel Castro, and set adrift with the other "antisocial elements"—such as middle-class Vietnamese of Chinese origin. "The majority of them were genuine refugees," Sergeant Barry Hill, head of the Metro Police intelligence unit's Chinese section, says of the boat people. "But I have no doubt there's an ample sprinkling of criminals."

The Chinese in Toronto, regardless of their country of origin, are generally famous for their willingness to abide by the law. It is true, of course, that some of them have also been known to gamble. (Perhaps the only glaring weakness they have demonstrated as a cultural group. Alcohol, for example, has little appeal for most Chinese. In Hong Kong—unlike, say, North Bay—it is no matter of embarrassment for a young male at a party to say he can't handle booze.) But gambling—gambling is a different matter. Many Canadians still imagine that gambling joints, opium-scented fan-tan and mahjong dens, are common in the back alleys of Chinatown. Most of the joints have been closed down by 52 Division, however. The action is now mainly in hotel rooms and private houses.

Serious games are held under the auspices of the Chinese "mafia," primarily the Kung Lok. The dreaded Kung Lok. Most Chinese in Toronto, when asked about the Kung Lok, respond with: Kung Lok? What Kung Lok? Unlike dim sum, it's not something people in Chinatown care to publicize. The organization does exist, however. It is an offshoot of the famous Triads of Hong Kong, the secret societies that grew up in China in the seventeenth century to overthrow the rule of the Manchu Ching dynasty. The Triads, including the Kung Lok, still have the trappings of an elaborate society: blood-curdling oaths, secret handshakes and all the rest of the Hardy Boys Meet the Tong paraphernalia.

The Hong Kong Triads have long controlled the cultivation and initial processing of opium from the Golden Triangle in Southeast Asia. Since the demise of the French Connection in the '70s, they have also taken control of a significant part of its worldwide distribution. The Kung Lok in Toronto, however, according to Sergeant Hill, is not into drugs. The organization—with a core membership of from 50 to 100, loosely controlled by a head man now based in Hong Kong—is concerned mainly with extortion. The extortion is always against Chinese, never against other ethnic groups.

One of the more violent forms of extortion is the terrorizing of visa students, who are beaten and then forced to pay off Kung Lok members for the privilege of not being beaten up again. This money also buys protection from rival factions of the same gang. Moreover, the Kung Lok has recruited about 50 new members in the process and has also forced some young girls and at least one boy into prostitution.

A minor form of extortion consists of a group of Kung Lok members having a meal in a restaurant and then signing the bill as "payment." Respected members of the community are often given the privilege of signing their restaurant bills and then paying later. A Kung Lok signature, however, means: thanks for the meal and, by the way, isn't it nice nobody's thrown a rock through your window lately. If the Kung Lok decides to eat at your restaurant once a week, it can cost you a lot of money. Some restaurant owners don't put up with it. Others do, either because they themselves have used the services of the Kung Lok to collect bad debts, or because they believe if they resist, the Kung Lok will indeed throw rocks through their windows.

This belief is common among the less-educated immigrants from Hong Kong who, like Selina Man's neighbours, have trouble conceptualizing a police force that doesn't take bribes or operate in concert with gangsters. Extortion victims in Toronto have been warned by the Kung Lok that if they don't cooperate, something will happen to their relatives in Hong Kong—at the hands of the Hong Kong police. The threat is usually hollow—but not unbelievable. Even if these immigrants were convinced Toronto cops were clean, they still would hesitate to approach them—most believe simply that the purpose of Sergeant Hill's Chinese section is to protect whites from Chinese criminals.

The police talk to a victim if they've heard about his victimization and have then sought him out; otherwise, the crime goes unreported. This does not make for wholesale arrests and convictions of Kung Lok members. (In Sergeant Hill's years in the Chinese section, it has secured the conviction of seven extortionists. Twelve to 15 Kung Lok members are currently before the courts on charges of extortion or assault.) Now Kung Lok leaders are starting to go into legitimate businesses. They have served their apprenticeship as street toughs and acquired a little seed capital—as well as the kind of reputation that makes it hard for other companies to turn down their business. The Kung Lok are already notorious for their involvement in agencies booking talent from Hong Kong for local concerts.

Their influence will probably persist as long as immigration from Hong Kong continues. Their chief prey is the unsophisticated, uneducated Hong Kong immigrant, however, and that is not the kind we'll be seeing much of in the future. The kind we'll be seeing in the future is the kind with money, and lots of it. The kind that has already had a noticeable effect on us.

Rhoda Ironside, a saleswoman with Dot Realty, says of Hong Kong investors, "They're very aware of the market and they don't buy just anything. They buy the best." And they buy all over the city, in Mississauga and the suburbs, as well as such places as Harbourside condominiums, a particular favourite of Hong Kong investors because waterfront property here is about half the price it is in Hong Kong.

Toronto is not like Vancouver, of course, where Hong Kong real estate investment is a long-established reality. As yet, Hong Kong investors have not made any bigger splash here than, say, West German investors. But give them time. The closer we get to 1997, the more attractive Toronto will be to people from Hong Kong who have the means to cultivate their fortunes elsewhere. Their influence on the commercial and business life of Toronto can only grow. To be sure, their cultural effect will lag far behind. As a people they do not like to attract attention, make waves, "express themselves." They will simply continue to go about their business, be exemplary citizens, train their children to be exemplary citizens, and prosper quietly.

Toronto Life *(1983)*

TORONTO SWALLOWED ME

Toronto swallowed me,
like water fish.
But I counted on time and its help.
Some things are more important in life
than life itself.
A tiny spark burnt Rome,
but my spark burns within me, incognito.

Jean Lumb, one of Toronto's leading citizens, shown with Prime Minister Diefenbaker and other dignitaries on the occasion of a change in Canada's immigration policy which made it easier for Toronto's Chinese people to be reunited with their families.

I was at ease with people,
with my face in the mirror,
but I was not at ease with my dreams.
At night I was trapped in the past
without appropriate warning.

I used to arrive at night
at Swift's slaughter-house
in a shabby street car
driven by a conductor
who was always sleepy.
His face was half-Irish and half-Scotch,
his colourless eyes were without distinction.
The neighborhood was choked with the slaughter-house smell.
My working hours were hopeless,
from eleven at night till five in the morning.
Then I would take off my apron full of blood
and my factory overalls soaked with the smell
of dead animals.

Life was so mechanical,
so programmed: stuffing,
washing, sleeping, eating.
For one year I had neither mornings
nor evenings.

Luckily
I escaped from the Swift trap
as Houdini escaped from the sausage skin.
But my Houdini was Mrs. Jaworski
of Concord Avenue.

How little we know ourselves.
How foolish we all are, blaming people
for their imperfections.

At eleven o'clock the guard
would take my name and lock the factory gate.

First, Swift's novelty amused me.
I killed animals with the same skill
as I destroyed enemies at war.
But later, despair overtook me,
muscles manifested their displeasure.

After one year I left the slaughter-house,
my mind stronger but my lungs in poor shape.
                    WACLAW IWANIUK

TORONTO ITALIAN: NEW WORLD LANGUAGE

BY NORMAN HARTLEY

Toronto's 400,000 Italian Canadians are proudly independent. They hate to borrow money—but they have no such hangups about borrowing words.

Any Canadian who has become the *boiffrendi* or *ghellaffrendi* of a young Italian and has sat on the *cesterfilde* in the *dainirummo* or the *frontirummo* of the friend's home wondering how he will manage linguistically with the rest of the family is likely to discover he can have an interesting conversation with the *sisteralo* or *broderalo* about his life in *aiscuola*.

For 25 years, Italian immigrants have been demonstrating their common-sense attitude to language problems by borrowing words they needed. Most often it began at work, where early immigrants, who came mainly from the rural south of Italy, had little or no formal education and no contact with city life and industrial jobs. They simply didn't have the words so they listened and borrowed and added a few Italian-sounding endings and the result is a way of speech that enables Italian workers to deal with the *bosso* on the *giobba* whether they are a *lebura* or a *foremenni* or whether they drive a *buldoza* or a *crena* or lay *bricchi* on *pisiguorco* (piece-work).

Now their children are at university—and are starting the process of unlearning this new mixed language, or at least learning how to say the same things in standard Italian.

There are between 1,500 and 2,000 Italian-Canadian students at the University of Toronto, most of them enrolled in the department of Italian studies.

For many, one of their early courses is one that teaches them the difference between Italo-Canadian Italian and pure Italian and gives them practice in using the language without all its English borrowings.

The course was made possible by a study done by Domenico Pietropaolo and his wife Laura Springolo, who both teach in the department. Mr. Pietropaolo made a collection of more than 1,000 "loan words" while he was working at the Centro Organizzativo Italiano, a grassroots community organization helping working-class Italians. Now he and his wife teach the course and wean Italo-Canadian students away from the language they grew up with.

At the end of it, they won't talk about taking a *bucco* off the *bucciselfi* to read in the *bacchi-iarda* or the *fronti-iarda* or the *basamento*.

Nor will they talk about starting the day with a *brecchifesti* of *becon* or *amma* with a slice of *ciso*, and when they go to the drive-in, they won't discuss whether to put *grevi* or *checciappa* (ketchup) on their *frencifrai*—always assuming, of course, that they don't order a bag of *pappacorna* or *pinozze* (peanuts).

When they go shopping, they won't call at the *drogghistoro* or the *sciustoro* (shoe store) to buy *buzzi* (boots) or the *becheri* to buy a *lofo* and when they drive they won't talk about *fare un raitti* (make a right hand turn) or *fare un leffiti* at the end of the *stritto* or the *aiguei* (highway).

It may be hard to stop eating *aisi crimmi* or wearing *bluginsi* or putting *erpinsi* in their hair or *mecappa* on their faces.

It may be hard at times to remember not to say *sori* (sorry) or *ariappa* (hurry up) or *caman* (come on) or that the telephone line is *bisi* and to stop calling the building in Nathan Phillips Square *sitiolla*.

But it will put the students in the mainstream of Italian speech and Mr. Pietropaolo says they don't mind relearning the new vocabulary, even though old habits sometimes die hard.

But there is one word that may outlast the others. There is no standard Italian for that shoppers' wonderland at Bathurst and Bloor, and so future generations of Italian-Canadian doctors and lawyers may still talk about taking a trip to *Onesteddi* on Saturday afternoon.

The Globe and Mail *(1974)*

NOSTALGIA

The sunlight dashes in from the lake
in large armfuls, stretches itself on
the room; some clouds are putting the lid
on the western light.

It was so brief, and I am thinking still of
summer; the snow rags the streets, a little bit of
wind wraps the cold bones of the maple.

and now it is waist-high grass in
Michael's orchard, the slender cypress on the hill
beside Bruno's house, the light taking small
steps over the Tuscan hillsides, pines,
and the green lizards basking beside the cathedral.

I am obsessed with warmth, is it not common,
even here friends are a premium; I would think
they'd run head first into the love of friends,
they suffer everything else.

The lake is warming its hands, but fails; more snowflakes
ditto in from a low cloud, the light draws itself
in on the farthest sky.

Italia, far beyond that, always, Italia
and the rooms of warmth, the landscape searing
its edges at noon.

Under a few cold lilies, my father dreams
cicadas in Vallemaio. I am sure of it.
He left me that, and a poem that is only a

dream of cicadas; the brown glove widens
on the dry december earth.
I am a little marvellous, with the sunken
heart of exiles.

PIER GIORGIO DI CICCO

FAREWELL
TO LITTLE ITALY

BY MARQ DE VILLIERS

When DelZotto, the industrialist, and Bondino, the opera singer, met for the first time backstage after the performance, they found themselves talking about...pigs...about seedlings...about milking and how the earth smelled when it was tilled. Now, Elvio DelZotto was born in Canada and his normal milieu is the plush corporate headquarters of DelZotto Enterprises, and if we can begin to understand why he and Bondino slipped back so easily into the dialect of the province of Udine and found themselves obsessed with the land of their origins, we can get some clues to the patterns now making up the Italian mosaic—the urgent search for roots, for identity, the decay of ancient rivalries and loyalties, the collapse of old value systems, the creation of a new self-confident elite, the groping for a culture that is neither Italian nor yet old-style Canadian. Picture the scene after the opera at the Friuli Club (which many say has the best kitchen in town), at Islington and Steeles. There's a group of them. DelZotto himself, steersman of an industrial empire, and Bondino, urbane, witty, performer and raconteur. There are lawyers, developers, manipulators of men, money and machinery, most of them equally at home in boardroom and caucus. Bondino starts the evening with stories of the opera, but soon the talk is less and less in Italian and more and more in Friuli, the language of Udine. The whole conversation takes them back to the farm, to the land, their common bond.

Many from Italy's industrial heartland arrive in Toronto expecting to a deal with a people cut off from their heritage, southerners of peasant stock. To their surprise, they find instead a confident establishment: urbane, significantly rich, as international in outlook as the Milanese themselves. But these people are *from the wrong regions*, say the visitors from Milan. Why, they're from the south or from Udine, "the north's south." And at once their value systems begin to collapse.

Canadian Italians watch this process with some satisfaction. It is one of the constants of present-day immigration patterns: Italians and Italian Canadians are not the same people; it is often a bruising shock to newcomers to discover that the home-country hierarchy of origins doesn't mean the same thing in Canada, that most of the money is southern money, that money buys style and that Canada hopelessly blurs ancient dividing lines. It is hard on the professional classes from the north and hardest of all on the Milanese upper crust, the few of them that come, because they expect to make the same quick impact here as Diane and Egon von Furstenberg made in New York or generations of languid aristos made in Paris, only to find that no one here really cares.

Not that home-country distinctions have altogether disappeared, but their significance has changed. DelZotto insists that his and Bondino's regression to the state of mind of their forefathers has nothing to do with clannishness of the old-fashioned sort. It has more to do with the global obsession with roots and the fact that the Italians here, Metro Toronto's second largest ethnic group, have recently been freed from the grinding need to succeed and are free for the first time to ask the elegant question: Who am I?

It's only in the last few years that we've had this return to roots by those who had broken away, and that the Italian community in Toronto has been unified enough to undertake projects that cut across old rivalries. As lawyer and developer Rudolph Bratty puts it, "The community was very divided in the past, kept apart by language, culture, even physical appearance. Villa Colombo, a unique old-age home at Lawrence and Dufferin, built above a recreational centre for the whole community, was the first universal project. And it was a hard sell, because traditionally it is the family's role to look after the aged. But the project worked." Anthony Fusco, the cartage-firm owner who as much as anyone is responsible for bringing about the new spirit, says profound changes have taken place deep within the community. "Traditionally we were a passive people, in the sense of accepting economic and government pressures. Our lives were to an extent predestined. Individualism in the sense of taking responsibility was not strong. This tendency had deep, historic, cultural roots. And we came to Canada as labourers, desperately needing economic security. Homes, mortgages, security—these were the preoccupations. No time or inclination to be involved in the collectivity. The fact that there are now universal projects such as Villa Colombo shows that we're coming out into the larger community. The first floor of the project duplicates a typical street scene in a town in southern Italy. With the young people downstairs, the old people upstairs, we're trying to duplicate life as it should be, where the family unit is important."

Fusco, a heavy-set, articulate, softspoken man in his fifties, passionately believes in the Italians' Canadian destiny. "We're going to have a significant influence on Canadian culture. I believe culture is not just beer gardens and folklore, it's a value system based on a lifestyle. We are now in a position to choose—to select good things from both cultures and to create a third, a new culture greater than both.

"The English heritage teaches us many things: it has public discipline, privacy, respect for the individual. These are all things the Italians can learn. And the Italian culture can offer this marvellous thing, the family structure, the basic attitude toward sharing. We can restore to Canada some basic things that have been lost here."

Tony Fusco has been strongly influenced by the idea of communes. He senses that an immigrant community is similar in some ways to the dropout communes; it is trying to preserve, futilely, a lifestyle in isolation. "We have to drop back in, reshaping society with our ideas—the same process that happens on a smaller scale in our community in the intermediate steps, such as persuading parents that a girl who goes out on a date doesn't automatically lose her virginity, while at the same time persuading the young to accept some limitations on their conduct." His dream is the 17-acre community and recreation centre on Lawrence Avenue, the largest project of its kind on the continent. It includes a library, art gallery, visual arts centre, sports complex and community referral centre. "But even if we draw the whole Italian community, even if we manage to overcome all the old regionalisms, even then it will not be enough. Unless we can get the larger society involved, we will have failed."

Almost all leaders among Italian Canadians are fiercely multicultural; they reject the melting pot. They feel they have the ideas—and the numerical power—to do so. Father Benito Framarin, a parish priest and polemical newspaper editor who arrived in Toronto in 1973 from Aosta, a few miles from the Swiss border, says: "We want integration, not assimilation," and it's apparent he speaks for most of the community. These people don't want to disappear, they want to contribute.

There are now half a million Italian Canadians in the Metro Toronto area. The main currents of their immigration history are familiar: the first arrivals showed up in the 1880s, though most settled in Montreal. Many in the first wave went back home after a few years, as did Tony Fusco's grandfather.

The first important immigration flow happened in the late 1920s and early '30s, when there was general poverty and a good deal of starvation in the Italian south. Rural people arrived here, peasants with little or no education, no English and no discernible advantage except a willingness to work hard. It's their children (despite a proportion of them who fell victim to cultural dislocation and failed to enter the Canadian mainstream) who are now the leaders of the community.

In the late 1940s and '50s it seemed half of Italy wanted to come to Toronto. Indeed, in some cases, whole villages packed up and left, and still maintain themselves here. The children of this group will be the community's next leaders; they are now making their way through college and university. The last of the immigrant waves is still coming; it is both smaller and different in character—the first group to come for political rather than economic reasons. As other immigrant groups did before them, they have settled in lower Ward 6 and along College Street near Grace, Clinton and Manning, an area that became the centre of what the Anglo majority called Little Italy.

In retrospect, it's clear the Anglo parent culture was bemused by this influx of alien and exotic outsiders. Bemused, a touch hostile, and yet not totally rejecting. Toronto was for other reasons beginning its transformation from English colonial outpost to cosmopolis, and at least one of the results was a pleased curiosity about "ethnics."

Naturally, there was hostility, and there is still some. Most early immigrants recall incidents of genuine abuse. But considering the size of the invasion and the relatively closed nature of the Anglo society, the Italians were, when all is said and done, received pretty well. Few of them now feel the need to be defensive; where they were once ashamed that their fathers couldn't speak English, they now boast of it; where they were once ashamed of eating spaghetti, they now proselytize Italian food. The Toronto newspapers were full of clumsy but good-intentioned attempts to understand this new culture. Their stories were little more than travelogues, emphasizing the colour, the warmth, the exotic, the peasant, the food, the tastes, the sounds, the smells, but edging the larger consciousness closer to acceptance nonetheless.

Stereotypes still exist. Even now the daily press may run the odd piece referring to Johnny Lombardi of radio station CHIN as "the unofficial mayor of Little Italy." Or it will refer to the College-Clinton intersection as "the bustling heart of Toronto's Little Italy," whereas, in fact, this heart has long since bustled off north and west.

Old news clippings yield three primary stories about Italians: *The immigrant worker works hard and finds a new life; the Mafia, violence, crime; unemployment and the Workman's Compensation Board.* Labourer saves and buys own home apparently made good copy; a lawyer who parlayed a professional income into a considerable fortune, such as Rudy Bratty, apparently was too mundane to mention. So it was in this way that the size and scope and sheer complexity of the Italian presence was consistently underrated.

The Mafia is the preeminent example of stereotyping: the Cosa Nostra or the Honourable Society or the Syndicate—it depended on which reporter you were reading. *The Godfather* has a lot to answer for. As Bratty puts it, "I'm not saying our community was persecuted or faced prejudices like the Jews or the blacks, but there are some things we have had to put up with. This thing about the crime syndicates—it's a prejudice we've all had to live with." There's a lot of arcane nonsense written about codes of silence and oaths of vengeance in the Italian community; the plain truth is that organized crime exists but that few Italians would recognize even the names of its perpetrators. It is irritating that such simple truths as this still have to be stated.

Yet there are some problems. In Italy, as Father Benito, the priest and editor, puts it, "blood is not water. The family takes precedence over all." Things are accomplished in Italy's south by networks of obligations, which makes possible what Father Benito calls "the petty mafia, the bustarelle, the envelope [that is, the bribe], the petty corruptions" that are universal facts of life in certain regions. "These customs erode slowly."

Dan Iannuzzi, founder and former publisher of Toronto's fourth daily, the *Corriere Canadese*, is the grandson of a glass blower from Calabria who arrived here in 1886—one of Toronto's earliest Italian immigrants. A man with an impeccable international style, Iannuzzi has tracked Little Italy's exodus with his network of secret agents, the carrier boys of *Corriere*. These boys now patrol Downsview as they once patrolled Clinton Street. In fact, there exist today suburban Mississauga schools facing the same problem as inner-city schools—children who have only a rudimentary command of the English language. And the changes are economic as much as geographic. It's true that Workman's Compensation Board proceedings are still often in Italian, but the community at large has made its way into the Acquisitive Society— wet bars, rec rooms, 40-foot cruisers, holidays in Acapulco and the other ornaments of *la dolce vita*. The talk in the boardrooms and offices of the Italian elite is an echo of the mood of Victorian England. The office décor is haute Milanese (all chrome and curved space and cunning plastics, as is much of the design around the city). The panelling may not be of British oak, but the mood is the same: a sense of infinite possibility. The Italians speak of Canada with a mixture of awe and possessiveness; they speak of the future in a way Anglos haven't done since the last politician said the twentieth century belongs to Canada and was laughed off the podium. Canada is the land of opportunity for those who would seize opportunities.

Joe Zentil can come here from Italy at 17, penniless and without a trade; he can turn himself into a plumber and from a plumber into a millionaire property manager—and there are hundreds more in the community like him. The Ruscica family, the Orlando family, Cam Milani, who gave $100,000 in a recent telethon—the success stores are legion. It may be true, as Fusco says, that this drive for affluence is produced by a "mania for security. Many of us remember when there was literally nothing to eat and people were dying of starvation.... Where your average Anglo company president is satisfied with his $300,000 a year, the Italian in the same circumstances parlays it into $3 million."

The patterns of immigration are reinforcing the transformation of the community to middle-class status and higher. The avalanche of Italians wanting to come ended in the late 1960s, not entirely because Canada was limiting admission but also because things were looking better at home. Immigrants are now middle-class, professional people, often with substantial resources, mostly from the industrial north—Turin, Milan, Bologna. Many are coming here because they're afraid of the Communist influence in Italian politics; naturally, they're bringing with them cultural baggage that doesn't always stow neatly into a Canadian space. Strains are set up within the community—not all Toronto Italians are anti-leftist by any means.

This is probably the most serious division within the community, transcending most of the older rivalries. But the National Congress of Italian Canadians, the largest of the local umbrella groups, has come out for total autonomy from the Italian political process. Father Benito's early training in movie criticism under director Franco Zeffirelli seems to be standing him in good stead in Canada. He wrote in his parish paper *Il Samaritan*: "Our ideas and culture are Italian, but they are also different. Immigration to Canada has taught us something, and we are no longer Italians." In this sense, immigration is a rite of passage to a new culture.

The church itself is becoming less interested in ritual and more in political process. The main thrust of *Il Samaritan*'s polemics is to give its parishioners a more political sense of Canada. "We want religion, not just piety. We want understanding, not blind adherence." They are directed to explore what it means to be Canadian. "We also," says Father Benito, "have a sense of what it must mean to be Quebeckers, because we, too, have gone through all this—these rivalries, these divisions. But we are convinced—all of us, I believe—that we are better off in Confederation and that a multicultural concept can work and will. We will make it work."

Still, it's important not to underestimate the old spirit of Little Italy. On Sundays near College or St. Clair the elderly men still enthusiastically take part in the *passeggio*: they walk, talk, gossip, ogle. And many come down from Downsview to do it, because the gregarious life of villagers doesn't adapt easily to shopping-plaza lifestyles. Many still come down to St. Francis' Church, at the corner of Grace Street and Mansfield Avenue, when one of the religious processions is held. The peasant culture is richly present and alive: the food, the faces, the more than 60 regional clubs and associations, the cafés and bars, the peacocking young men, the family gatherings, the first communions, the 600-strong, eight-course-dinner weddings. In that sense, it's hardly any distance at all from Clinton Street to the austere elegance of

DelZotto's corporate headquarters in Downsview or to the authoritative decor of Pal's Café on Yorkville. Nor, on the other hand, is it far from Clinton to the restless, spoiled, alienated youths whose peasant parents, determined to give them everything, ended up giving them nothing but a distaste for the old and an inability to cope with the new. Both of these are part of the Italian-Canadian Dream.

Toronto has already changed in response to the Italian presence, and not just in adopting chicken cacciatore and a more relaxed attitude toward the sensual pleasures. It's not sufficient to say, as many have, that "Toronto was built on the back of Italian labour." It's more than that. Toronto grew partly because Italians restored to it a sense of the future, of its own possibilities. Along with pasta and pesto they brought a confidence, a reintroduction of a phrase long in disuse: "I can do it." At the same time the Italians are changing, from the Little Italy represented by Johnny Lombardi (which was gregarious, community-oriented, folkloric, devoted to ward politics, and whose symbol was the annual Island picnic) to the new style represented by Dan Iannuzzi (which is outgoing, urban, efficient). As the community begins to act for the first time as a community, it becomes less and less passive. Out of all this Tony Fusco's dream of a third culture may be emerging.

Dan Iannuzzi, who relinquished his hand in the day-to-day operations of *Corriere Canadese* to become a television mogul, wants to plug into Eurovision, buy satellite time, show movies never shown here. He's full of the possibilities, enormously pleased by the fecundity of his ideas. He twirls a glass, one of Pal's specials, heavy as stone. Everything at Pal's is appropriate. The pepper and salt grinders are straight out of Eurodomus '76, the fashionable Milanese design show. Chrome and steel and deep blues and blood reds—the pedigree is international chic. The hubcaps of a Rolls glide by outside (Pal's is below grade, and lunchers can watch the richly dimpled knees of Yorkville stroll by). There is a style to everything here, a haughty, grandbourgeois Milanese style. . . Iannuzzi breaks off as he spies a waiter, summons him with a tiny imperious flick, a gesture so quick, so subtle, so. . .*stylish*. . .that I recognize it at once; the last time I saw it used was at the Ristorante Cavour in Milan, by a brittle old man who'd arrived in a Lamborghini with his skinny mistress. The waiters there clustered round him, shooing away tourists as if they were so many snapping turtles: *si, signor; prego, signor; grazie, signor*. . . But at Pal's it was just a flicker, a hint of bloodline, then it was gone. Dan Iannuzzi is not Milanese, though he's at home in Milan. He's not really Italian, though he's at home in Italy, too. What he is is living proof of the viability of Tony Fusco's dream. The fact is, he's a Canadian, at home in Toronto.

Toronto Life *(1979)*

TORONTO - BUDAPEST: FUSED PERSONALITY

The deepest regions of my soul don't seem to accept that I split my life and my self into two, in 1956.

In my dream, my mother talks to me in a Canadian-accented English, she is thirty-two years old, I am forty-five. She asks me to show her the city where I live now (or I ask her to take me around my birthplace), so we go for a long stroll.

In the middle of the city, instead of Yonge Street, the river Danube (Duna) flows majestically, separating the capital into two distinct parts, the hilly Budanto on the West, and the flat Toropest on the East. She shows me Ròzsadomb (Rosehill), I show her Rosedale in exchange. We like very much our (each other's) city. The two sides are connected by nine gorgeous bridges called (going from South to North) the Front-bridge, the King-bridge, the Queen-bridge, the College-Carlton-bridge, the Bloor-bridge, the St. Clair-bridge and the Eglinton-bridge; the Margit-sziget (Center-island) is connected with both banks by the Lawrence-bridge on its South-end, and the Wilson-bridge on its North-end. My mother is especially proud of the recently built Highway 401 which wasn't there yet when I left. She loves the view from the top of Gellert-mountain from where she can clearly see Lake Ontario, the O'Keefe Center and the New City Hall. I prefer the view from the top of the CN Tower: the old Parliament, built in Gothic style, and the baroque Basilica (great Cathedral) are an unforgettable sight.

We go home where my father watches TV, in 1938. The Prime Minister of Hungary, János Trudeau, talks about repatriating the Constitution from Russia. I say farewell to my parents because I have to go homes to my two wives, Ibolya (Violet) in Sándor-utca, and Janine, on Austin-Terrace. I play with my two baby daughters, Aniko in 1956 and Natalie in 1972. We are (one big) two small happy families who don't know about each other, except me.

After dinners, as usual, I go to my favourite coffee-house, the meeting-place of poets, writers, artists and musicians. On the Gallery, around a huge round table sit Karinthy, Atwood, Kosztolányi, Callaghan, Weöres, Purdy, Bartók, Gould, Kodály, Schafer, Szász, Kurelek, Kerényi, Frye and many others. The conversation is profound and witty, I am glad to belong to this tightly knit élite-group of creative people. We read (sing, show) our latest works to one another.

*The Caribana Parade every summer is
one of Toronto's most colourful events.
In this photograph taken on August
4th, 1979, 3,000 participants danced
down University Avenue to
Harbourfront. In the 1980s the parade
is bigger still, and its organizers claim
that it brings in more business to
Toronto than the festivities
surrounding the Grey Cup.*

Then I leave them to find a quiet table where, sipping my espresso coffee and chain-smoking my cigarettes, I wrote a poem for the excellent literary magazine called Search for Identity. *I write down the title in Hungarian, but I realize that my English readership won't understand it, so I cross it out and write it down again in English, but now I think about my oldest childhood friends who won't be able to read it. My right hand holding the pen freezes in mid-air while I ponder the problem, but the pain in my right shoulder wakes me up. I look around in the dawning bedroom and try to sneak back into my soft and warm dream, but it has already faded away, now hard and cold objects surround me.*

ROBERT ZEND

TO THIS COLD PLACE

BY MAGGIE SIGGINS

I t's 11 o'clock on a Saturday night at a house on Christie Street. There's not a soul in the small basement except for an impatient disc jockey. A lone red light bulb pulsates to the beat of the Mighty Maytones, casting a devilish glow on the pink concrete walls. The $8,000 stereo system makes most disco equipment look like a child's record player. There are two turntables—so as not to miss a beat between records—a BA 5000 amplifier with 300 watts RMS per channel and two Altec Lansing 15-inch woofer-type speakers, which in English means the music is unbelievably loud. Your ears go dead immediately, as if perpetually popping in a soaring supersonic jet. The disc jockey has more than 2,000 reggae and calypso records, but requests are refused—they're considered an erosion of his power. There are a few lonely chairs along the wall for anyone crazy enough to want to sit down over the next eight hours. The smell of curried goat permeates everything.

One o'clock in the morning. There must be 60 people packed in the room. Most are well over 30, few are a lighter colour than mahogany. The throbbing music washes over them like molasses as they gyrate to the reggae beat. Though it's freezing outside, sweat pours off the crowd. The smell of curried goat is lost as the room's temperature hits 85 degrees Fahrenheit.

Florence Campbell has come this evening with her friend Lucy Byrant. Both are domestics, both have been in Canada about two years. Florence, a large woman pushing 40, is dressed in a peachy pink, one-piece, polyester pantsuit with elephant trousers. She proudly displays, on a rather large bosom, the most valuable possession she owns: a huge, chunky necklace ("Genu-ine gold, missus!"). On her feet sit sensible black oxfords ("Dancin' what's we here for; not struttin'!"). Bryon Brown, her partner, wears a brown fedora, sunglasses, a checkered brown, white and blue cotton jacket, a pink nylon shirt, black baggy pants and white shoes. There's no chatting between these two; they can't hear each other.

Three o'clock. There are 100 guests now. It's unbelievable that all could be dancing in this small cave. Lucy, the sharpest of women in skintight blue satin pants and revealing red bolero, sways to the soft beat of the Majestics, pelvis to pelvis with the latest arrival: a college student studying accounting. At one side of the room, a half-dozen men line up for their turn at the microphone. It seems as if the singer will never give it up as he croons on and on, "Reggae! Reggae! Reggae! Dig it! Dig it! Dig it! Manohmanohman!" in countertime. The curried goat and roti are served, but the music never falters.

Six o'clock. Florence and Lucy are putting on their knee-high boots. Both agree they've had a marvellous time. Says Lucy, "Florence, when I in the party, you see, I feel like I's in Jamaica. It was real good. You did see that handsome guy that was talking to me? I feel so good. He mes-sage me, and me mes-sage he."

"He looks a nice boy."

"Yeesss man! He gave me some good word, you know. He all right."

"My God, Lucy, look the snow afall. It lick me on my face!"

"We in Canada now, brother!"

It's difficult for someone who's not West Indian to understand how pervasive and important music is to the Jamaican. From the baby at the breast to the stooped and grey farmer, it's as essential to the daily diet as milk and white rum. It reveals political messages, advice on marriage, the philosophy of Rastafarianism. The toothless old cane-cutter and the tall young woman selling yams at the market, the slick and affluent lawyer and the enthusiastic college student—all have the same impeccable taste and the same ability to distinguish the phony from the sentimental, the wise from the didactic, the electrified from the original (they like both). Calypso and ska, soul and reggae have been such pervasive and influential forces on the world's music that they're unqualified achievements for the entire culture—all four million citizens of Jamaica, not just an educated few.

When Third World and Jimmy Cliff give a concert at Massey Hall, they draw a full house—the majority of the audience young, white Anglo-Saxons, who must surely, even if not consciously, recognize the contributions the Jamaicans are making. Many other Anglos in the society do not. As one of the newest and poorest groups of immigrants in Toronto, Jamaicans live in virtual exile, appreciating little of their adopted country's culture, just as they themselves are seldom appreciated. At a cocktail party, a high-class journalist and wealthy advertising executive joke about the Jamaicans, throwing out condescending and disparaging terms they wouldn't dream of using to describe English, American or German newcomers.

There was a scent of fear at that party on Christie Street. "When will the police come?" whispered the guests. It wasn't so much that the music was louder than most Torontonians over 40 had heard in their lives—the house was bought because it has a church on one side and a wide lane on the other. And it wasn't a drug bust that was feared; no Rastas were invited because the host didn't want the smell of *ganja* hanging heavy over the place. No, what was illegal was the selling of liquor. The Scotch sold for a dollar a drink, which meant an $18 bottle yielded a $22 profit. The host that night pocketed about $800. In Jamaica it's customary for a fellow who has, say, smashed up his car and finds himself uninsured to throw a bash and collect some needed cash. It's illegal to sell liquor without a licence in that country, too, but the police there seem to have better things to do with their time and the parties are conducted on front lawns with little interference. Just weeks before the Christie Street affair, black activist Dudley Laws had been charged with a minor breach of the liquor act ("failing to remove signs of liquor") during the annual dinner of the Universal African Improvement Organization at the Hourglass Hall. Eleven minutes after the permit expired at 9:30 p.m, the police discovered two empty glasses and two empty beer bottles. No wonder the host on Christie Street was too busy watching his front door to relax.

A Trinidadian-born psychiatrist living in Toronto thinks that the lack of the sun's vitamin D during the winter makes us uptight and cranky. It's this sudden deprivation that makes a Jamaican's first winter here often seem like a nightmare about being locked in a meat freezer. Leisure hours on the island are spent in the outdoors, chatting with the neighbours on the stoop, playing dominoes and drinking white rum in an open-air bar, flirting in the marketplace.

In Toronto the encumbrances sometimes seem unbearable. The bone-chilling cold that forces you to spend months indoors; the heavy clothes that restrict movement; the landscape so ugly and stark in November compared with the lushness of the island in the sun even in the rainy season; the coldness of your neighbours. Delmena Byran learned about life in Toronto the day after she arrived. "I went out on the street and saw the people them coming. I went up as in Jamaica, smiling and saying, 'Hi! How are you?' to them. But they all turned their face away."

These are small matters. Every group of immigrants has to learn to adapt to the manners and customs of the adopted country. The Jamaicans, however, face something far more devastating than the Italians or Greeks or even Chinese—the ugliness and totality of racism.

More than 90 percent of all Jamaicans are descendants of African slaves brought to work the plantations of Spanish and English overlords. Although Chinese, East Indians and whites are mostly found in the middle and upper classes of the island, large numbers of blacks are found there as well. Jamaica is not a colour-conscious society. It's an unsettling experience, then, to come to Canada and, for example, realize that people who have been waiting a much shorter time than you are being served first; when finally there's no other excuse and the clerk must help you, he is so arrogant and disdainful that you almost faint with mortification.

In 1978, Professor Frances Henry of York University published what is probably the only comprehensive study of attitudes toward race in Toronto. After interviewing 617 white Torontonians, she found 51 percent were racist to some degree. Sixteen percent would be considered extremely racist and 35 percent inclined toward racism. What is as interesting as the numbers is the prevalent logic behind these attitudes. A majority were certain that not only is the black race genetically inferior to the white, but also that God decreed it should be this way. How do you reason with that?

Even before Kent Thomson, a Jamaican technician, moved to his new house in Toronto, police were there investigating a complaint that he was causing a disturbance. Thereafter, they were at his door practically every time he turned on the radio. City inspectors arrived because of a tip that garbage was piled up in his backyard. They found only fallen leaves. The Children's Aid Society was told his kids were neglected. The Toronto Humane Society even appeared one day to check on his dog, which was chained in the backyard. He finally became so harassed that the ethnic relations unit of Metro police stepped in and discovered all the complaints had come from one neighbour, a Danish immigrant, so fundamentally racist that he stopped only under threat of a lawsuit or of charges being laid.

Predictably, Henry's study indicated that the racist is more apt to have an authoritarian mind. Most blacks learn to live with everyday bigotry, but it's different story when those in positions of power are deep-rooted racists.

Evadine Williams is a a tall, elegant woman of 35, the mother of four children. She's the daughter of a well-to-do Jamaican physician and lived the life of landed gentry before migrating to Canada three years ago with her husband, a dentist. On a warm day last September, she was shopping at a suburban department store for last-minute supplies for school. Her 11-year-old daughter pleaded with her to buy a special binder. Mrs. Williams considered it too expensive and said no. She made her purchases and gathered her family into the car. Suddenly two uniformed security guards approached and said she must return with them to the store. Unknown to her, her daughter had taken the $5 binder and had it with her in the back seat of the car. The security guards led Mrs. Williams to a small room in the store and proceeded to lambaste her with obscene racist remarks ("black sow" was among their favourites). Once they pushed her against the wall so hard that she bruised her arm.

Finally the police arrived and she was charged with possession of stolen goods under $50. Her lawyer thought the charge would be quickly dismissed, but in the middle of the proceedings the judge declared a mistrial. The seemingly minor offence is now before the Ontario Supreme Court.

Security guards are trouble enough, but the major bone of contention among West Indians is Metro Toronto's police force. There are few blacks in this city who don't have a horror story about the police. An accomplished architect who immigrated to Canada from Jamaica in 1962 says that he was never bothered by the police when he drove a Pinto, but he was continually stopped after he bought himself an expensive BMW. Most of the time the police simply asked for his driver's licence and insurance, but sometimes they came right to the point: Where had he gotten the money to buy such a car? "In their eyes I obviously had to be a pimp to be able to afford such an expensive vehicle."

Even the most moderate spokesmen in the black community complain bitterly about police brutality. Wilson Head, a York University professor and chairman of the national Black Coalition of Canada, says, "I thought with the pressure on the police after the Albert Johnson case, they would have behaved differently. We get just as many complaints of police beatings now as we did before. They haven't slowed down one bit. The police complain about the number of attacks on them recently. I think they started this—they set the tone."

David Martin, a Toronto lawyer with a large clientele of Jamaicans (including Albert Johnson before he died), can recite a list of offences with which black Jamaicans are customarily charged: causing a disturbance, resisting arrest, assaulting police. He has very blunt advice for blacks who have been charged with a serious crime, such as armed robbery, and are acquitted: Get out of town. "I say to them, 'Look, you've been acquitted of a serious criminal offence when the police believed you were guilty. There are a large number of unsolved robberies in the occurrence reports of the Metro police department and it is our experience that you will be charged with a further offence.' Most don't leave until they've been charged again. Ultimately they throw up their hands and say, 'I can't deal with this for the rest of my life, taking time off work to go to court, worrying about it.' And then they leave."

Professor Henry's report drew a correlation between education and racism; predictably, the lower the education of an individual, the more racist he is apt to be. Charles Bens, former executive director of the nongovernmental Bureau of Municipal Research, Toronto, found that in 1979 only 1.2 percent of Metro's police force had a university degree. Most had not completed high school. Applying these statistics to Henry's findings, one might assume that a considerable proportion of the police force could be considered racist to some degree. While social scientists, including Henry herself, insist that the police force is too small a sample to apply her formula fairly, racism in an authority-oriented institution such as the police is obviously something to be deeply concerned about.

A computer has been made available to the police complaints bureau to keep tabs on complaints against police involving racism. But Bromley Armstrong, formerly of the Ontario Human Rights Commission, says he knows of at least one police officer with as many as 14 such complaints against him and still the force doesn't fire him. The police brass have, of course, the powerful Police Association to deal with; this is the policemen's union, and its existence makes firings more difficult.

To be fair, the police are trying to grapple with the problem. Constables Keith Wiltshire and Karl Oliver, both West Indian immigrants, have more profound and sympathetic insights into the black community than most social workers or academics. They work for the force's ethnic relations unit and it's their job to help in the investigation of crimes or complaints that have racist overtones—anything from mediating neighbours' disputes to investigating a beating where racist remarks were made. One of their most important functions is to lecture on the dangers of racism to police recruits. They claim the department has come a long way in the past few years.

Wiltshire and Oliver constantly encounter another face of racism: using one's black skin to account for all one's troubles. The person who does this heaps more abuse on the white police officer who is giving him a speeding ticket than he ever would have in Jamaica; or he complains to the Human Rights Commission about discrimination in the workplace after he was late five days in a row. Using race as a scapegoat is almost as insidious as using race to belittle the scapegoat.

A Brink's guard has been shot point-blank and killed by a group of criminals who get away with a large amount of cash. In the first few minutes while the police scramble to organize the hunt, a radio dispatcher warns the officers to be on the lookout for "four heavily armed Rastas." After witnesses came forward moments later, the description is changed to "four white men with Italian accents." It's a typical example of how Rastafarians have become *the* symbol in police jargon for crimes of violence. It's a little like labelling all white rapists as Presbyterians.

Many cultures have their bogeymen, like the Mafia in Italy or the Teddy boys of Britain. But few are as mysterious or misrepresented as the Rasta brethren. The popular picture is clear—the dreadlock spikes hidden under the multicoloured tam, the obvious devotion of the "miraculous wisdom weed," the hint of sexual prowess, the affinity for the reggae beat. Few political-religious groups, not even the Hasidim of

New York City or the Doukhobors of British Columbia, have been so isolated in society.

The PPC autobody shop, located off Dufferin Street, is a cooperative owned by six Rastas. They've been in business for three years and and have a reputation for doing high-quality work at reasonable rates. They, like all Rastas in this city, say they are continually harassed by the police. Their shop is searched time and time again, often by the same police officers; they are stopped on their way home from work; they are questioned in their homes while eating dinner. They've been called "nigger," threatened that they'll be forced out of business in six months and told that all Rastas should be deported.

The pretext is that Rastas are thought to carry large amounts of marijuana all the time. And while there's no question that they enjoy the "natural *ganja*"—they won't touch the "manufactured white rum"—they actually use about the same amount as your average Grade 12 student. It's simply a case of the harassment of individuals who refuse to conform to what the authoritarian mind thinks is the norm. It's a straightforward case of religious persecution.

The movement was born in the early part of the century in the mountains of Jamaica as a passionate reaction to the colonial mentality that still grips the island. Instead of participating in the political process, Rastas, like many religious groups in history, developed a counterculture with its own ethic, philosophy and self-expression (thus the birth of reggae). They consider blacks as people in exile. Central to their philosophy is the formation of a nation in Africa—the ultimate independence for blacks.

At the heart of the Rasta way of life is the belief that "man is God and God is man." They have rejected all notions of afterlife and, therefore, all connection with the established churches. Says Seymour Lane, a cabinetmaker and the most religious of men, "We don't business with religion! A colonial thing that! When we hear the bell ring at Sunday morning time for church, we think it the same slave bell."

The Rasta personal philosophy includes many virtues that our society holds dear: self-improvement, cleanliness, independence, excellence in one's craft. In Toronto, Rastafarians work in a variety of jobs, but they're also developing their own businesses as carpenters, handymen, mechanics. Ironically, as skilled tradesmen become as rare as slums in Cabbagetown, the Rastas could become the most sought after entrepreneurs in the city.

The trouble is there are so many phony Rastas everywhere. The genuine Rastas are pacifist, the others far from it. Jamaicans sing about them: "Some of them plant seed/And smoke the weed/But they're really wolf/In sheep's clothing." With little appreciation of the brethren's philosophy, they work hard at looking like a Rasta for a variety of reasons: an overt rebellion against authority, an excuse to smoke lots of *ganja*, even to gain a disguise to rob a bank.

For some time the Children's Aid Society of Metropolitan Toronto had been alarmed at the growing number of West Indian teenagers and children coming under the agency's care because conflict in the home had gotten out of control. In July, 1979, more than 11 percent of the total number of children under 16 in CAS care were black. (Although these include all "Negro" children, the large majority are West Indian in origin.) By October, 1980, that figure had jumped to 14 percent. To put this into perspective, in most years the number of children of all immigrant groups combined represents 19 percent. Given the deep love Jamaicans hold for children generally, no other statistic could illustrate the severe culture shock, the alienation from society that so many Jamaicans experience.

There's a common scenario:

Leaving the three kids with grandmother in Jamaica, the mother comes to Toronto as a domestic on a work permit. Depending on the luck of the draw, she'll end up with a family who will overwork and underpay her—might even sexually abuse her—or she'll settle with decent people who care about her. Every spare cent of her small salary is sent home for the care of the children. She denies herself the winter coat she's wanted, the new curtains for her bedroom. After several years she obtains landed immigrant status and an Ontario Housing Corporation apartment and sends for her oldest child. Even though she hasn't seen him for long periods, she has very set ideas on how he should act. She expects a lot. Nothing could be more shocking for a boy of 14 than being wrenched from his beloved grandmother and his friends and the open-air freedom of Jamaica to the confining space of a two-bedroom apartment in outer North York. The school is also unlike anything he's known. He's been taught since babyhood to be seen and not heard in the presence of adults, especially teachers; to be cooperative; to be neat and tidy, above all else. He finds himself in a class where the bright kids volunteer the answers, where getting a perfect spelling score is considered of far more value than helping the teacher wash the blackboards, where creativity is admired over order.

While he doesn't adapt to school very well, he quickly picks up the teenage lifestyle. He wants an allowance, stays out after school without telling his mother where he's gone, doesn't understand why she can't afford the $40 designer jeans he wants. And naturally he makes friends with young Jamaican immigrants who have the same problems as he. They began to congregate—liming it's called—outside the pinball parlour in the plaza near his mother's high-rise. His first run-in with the police is minor: an old woman complains that the boys were crowding the sidewalk. The second contact is more serious: he is seen with a kid who was later arrested for dope dealing.

By this time his mother is frantic, threatening to send him back to Jamaica, restricting his newfound freedom more and more. One night he stays out to the small hours of the morning and won't say where he was. An uncle is called in who beats him and, horror of horrors, he strikes back. A neighbour, hearing the commotion, calls the police. They contact the Children's Aid and it's decided that he would be better off in a foster home. The mother is devastated but, terrified of authority of any kind, agrees.

There has been severe criticism from the West Indian community that CAS workers interfere too much, that they don't understand that corporal punishment has long been an established method of raising children in the islands, that the separation does more harm than good. CAS officials have a simple answer. They are required by the Ontario Child Welfare Act to step in to prevent child abuse. They would be considered negligent if they ignored these situations.

In the areas of Toronto where the West Indian community is concentrated (there is no one ghetto)—Bloor and Ossington, Oakwood and Vaughan, the Jane strip to Finch—gangs of black kids can be found at any time of day, lounging about, smoking a joint, listening to reggae on somebody's radio, chatting. They have dropped out of school, aren't very welcome at home, aren't plugged into any social services. They exist almost entirely outside the mainstream of society.

If they do go to school, they're often streamed into vocational courses that prepare them for nonexistent jobs. If they develop a simple skill, many employers will hire the white kid instead. And the West Indian immigrant population is too new in this city to have developed the economic base—the shops, factories, restaurants—that absorbs the difficult young of the Italian, Greek and other ethnic groups.

If there is trouble in the black community, it will have been nurtured in these gangs. As the American experience has shown, hopelessness breeds contempt and vindictiveness.

In *Storm of Fortune*, Austin Clark's novel depicting the life of the West Indian immigrant in this city, Boysie Cumberbatch has just lucked into a job as a church caretaker. An apartment comes with the position. He shares his joy at this great fortune with his good friend Henry White. Henry brings up a serious matter: Boysie's wife, Dots, must not be let in on the bonanza. Says Henry, "If you haven't already tell Dots that an apartment exists, well this ain't the time to give her that information."

"God!" responds Boysie.

"Think of the parties, man! And the women! You will be free."

"Jesus!"

"There's nothing like goddamn freedom for a man. A man have to be free. The word 'man' sometimes means freedom. And you is a man who should be free."

"Christ."

Male chauvinism in Jamaica is as common and as accepted as ingesting large quantities of White Lightning rum every night at the local bar. To be born a man is to be born a superior being. For many Jamaican men, experience with the opposite sex in Canada is something akin to running into a brick wall at full speed.

He waits impatiently in Kingston for several years while his woman works in Canada as a domestic. When she finally is in a position to sponsor him, he finds a person different from the one he knew. She has a job as a machinist making $4 an hour and, man, does she flaunt her newfound independence.

They must get married in this new country! He must dress differently! He must find a job that pays good overtime! Their first major quarrel occurs when she refuses to switch the channel from *Let's Make a Deal* to the John Wayne movie he wants to watch.

He writes to his cronies back home that his job in a chemical factory pays wages to match their daydreams. But in his pride he omits to tell them how unbelievably expensive it is to live in this city. Often it seems to him that he is worse off than he was in Jamaica. The soothing television commercials of the finance companies seem to be the answer. But after nine months of backbreaking payments, he discovers that he has hardly decreased the principal of his $5,000 loan. The expensive Buick he bought with the loan cost so much to get repaired—and it always seemed to be breaking down—that it sits dead in the parking lot. His wife had managed to scrape together a small down payment for a suburban condominium, but in two years the maintenance charges and interest rates soared so high that they lost the home and her small nest egg with it. Their quarrels turn into bitter fights.

He finds some relief from these nagging problems by talking them over with his friends, a closely knit group of Jamaican immigrants, most of whom he has known all his life. They are his only solace, his only source of enjoyment. Although he talks proudly about the white Canadians he meets at work, neither he nor any of his friends has ever invited one to their homes. They'd all feel too strange, he says.

Nobody seems to know for sure how many Jamaican immigrants live in Toronto. In the years between 1974 and 1979, 41,000 landed immigrants from Jamaica arrived here and that doesn't include those with work permits—most of the nannies, for example—and those here illegally. A figure of 130,000 seems reasonable, and the number is growing quickly.

They arrived here in three distinct waves. In the 1950s and early '60s, when our restrictive immigration policy excluded about 90 percent of the Third World population, Britain welcomed Commonwealth peoples. All a Jamaican needed to immigrate to Britain was his air fare. Many lived there a few years, often developing a skilled trade, and then came to Canada on a British passport. The second wave of West Indian immigrants came after a 1967 change in Canadian immigration policy that allowed certain skilled people into the country. The early 1970s saw a great influx of carpenters, woodworkers and skilled factory hands to Canada, primarily Toronto. Then, about four years ago, Michael Manley's experiment in democratic socialism began to enrage the middle and professional classes to such an extent that they emigrated by the thousands. Toronto got its fair share of doctors and lawyers.

The rigid class structure of Jamaica is pervasive. There's an often-told story about the black history professor who invited a guest to his home for dinner. He told his gatekeeper that he was expecting the guest at 6 o'clock and to watch out for him. Two hours went by before he went again to the gatekeeper. "Have you seen nothing of Mr. Jones?" he asked. "Not a sight," replied the gatekeeper. "I see a black man hangin' round but I run he away." "But that was my guest!" cried the professor. "Why did you do that? I'm black, too." "You not black," responded the gatekeeper, "you a professor."

Jamaica may have become independent in 1962, but it has managed to hold firm to its stratified society with layers of distinct social classes. Until a few years ago, very few could afford to send their children to a secondary school, which nicely kept everyone in his place. Health care for the rural farmer was appalling and such social benefits as unemployment insurance were almost nonexistent. (Last year unemployment reached 30 percent in Kingston.)

Hugh Marshall was born privileged. His parents were well-off, which meant he went to an excellent high school and, like most Jamaicans of his class, was sent overseas for his college education. He went to Ryerson in Toronto (his sister attended medical school in Scotland). Although he had every intention of going back to Jamaica, he was offered a good job here and has been with an architectural firm for 15 years.

He says he suffered a tremendous cultural shock when he came to Toronto. "In Jamaica, people are immediately identifiable by the way they dress and speak. I knew who I was and I could look at anybody and know exactly who they were—their job, their lifestyle. Here everybody looks alike. When you get on the subway you know nothing about the people around you. That was traumatic for me. In Jamaica the first question a new acquaintance is asked is, 'What high school did you go to?' Right away you know everything about that person."

Upper-class Jamaicans have brought remnants of this class system with them like so much excess baggage. Marshall is president of the Toronto chapter of the Kingston College Old Boy Association, which boasts more than 100 members, including 20 physicians, who get together at cocktail parties and dinners to raise money for their old college.

There is a saying among upper-class Jamaicans, "Your name only appears in the newspaper twice: when you're born and when you die." This is more than just shunning the glare of publicity, more than not allowing your daughter to enter the Miss Jamaica contest. It's a studied silence from this city's educated West Indians. There are few organizations that provide support systems—raising money for old-age homes and cultural centres or helping new arrivals. The Harriet Tubman Youth Centre, one of the few facilities for Jamaican young people, conducted a drive a year ago to attract volunteers to the Big Brothers. It got one response.

Says a social worker in the Jane-Finch area: "The educated Jamaican immigrant in this city had better smarten up pretty soon. If these problems aren't solved, there's going to be trouble, especially among the young. And no matter what colour the middle class think they are, they will be tarred with the same bad reputation as the rest of us."

Friday, October 3, 9 p.m. The CBC Radio news has just announced the results of the Jamaican election held the day before. Florence Campbell rushes to the phone. "Lucy, me here. Missa Seaga win!"

"Thank the Lord. Freedom! Freedom!"

"And the people them going to the supermarket now. Everybody face is pleasin', no grumblin' any more. Just please, thank you, excuse me. No more rudeness there."

"But we have to pray for them leaders because the country's really in a bad state now. We can't expect it to come back overnight."

"But thank God Seaga win."

There was as much rejoicing in parts of Toronto as there was in the parishes all over the island when voters last fall rejected Michael Manley's eight-year experiment in socialism. Here was a small ray of hope that now maybe economic conditions would improve. Maybe soon they could go home.

Ask a Jamaican where he lives and he doesn't answer Parkdale or the Beaches—he says St. Elizabeth Parish. Ask him when he is going home and he doesn't say at supper-time on the subway—he says a few months from now when he has saved the air fare. His friends are Jamaican, his retirement dream is of the island. Except for the game shows and westerns on television, most Jamaicans have little appreciation for Canada as a country. It's just a place to work. They see a simple truth: If you could make enough money to support your family properly in Jamaica, why on earth would you leave that beautiful place to come to this cold country?

Many other immigrants who have longed for the home country have taken the $2,000 cure (returned only to find it wasn't what they expected and come back here); Jamaicans seem unable to sever the tie with their native land. Ask any Jamaican, no matter what age or occupation, if he plans to return to his birthplace and he looks at you as if you were crazy for even posing the question. Maybe in the end they won't go home. Maybe their children will establish deep roots here like other immigrants and laugh at their parents' homesickness. Maybe we'll learn that a black driving an expensive automobile doesn't mean he pimps as a profession. It seems a shame that the Jamaican lives in perpetual exile here. The Canadian mosaic could be enhanced by the exuberant, vivid new colour.

Toronto Life (1980)

AN INVISIBLE
WOMAN

BY BHARATI MUKHERJEE

*I cannot describe the agony and the betrayal
one feels, hearing oneself spoken of by one's own
country as being somehow exotic to its nature*

The oldest paradox of prejudice is that it renders its victims simultaneously invisible and overexposed. I have not met an Indian in Canada who has not suffered the humiliations of being overlooked (in jobs, in queues, in deserved recognition) and from being singled out (in hotels, department stores, on the streets and at customs). It happened to me so regularly in Canada that I now feel relief, just entering Macy's in Albany, New York, knowing that I won't be followed out by a security guard. In America, I can stay in hotels and *not* be hauled out of elevators or stopped as I enter my room. It's perhaps a small privilege in the life of a North American housewife—not to be taken automatically for a shoplifter or a whore—but it's one that my years in Canada, and especially my two years in Toronto, have made me grateful for. I know objections will be raised; I know Canadians all too well. Which of us has *not* been harassed at customs? On a summer's night, which of us *can* walk down Yonge Street without carloads of stoned youths shouting out insults? We have all stood patiently in bakery lines, had people step in front of us, we've all waved our plastic numbers and wailed, "But I was next—"

If we are interested in drawing minute distinctions, we can disregard or explain away nearly anything. ("Where did it happen? Oh, *Rosedale*. Well, no *wonder....*" Or, "Were you wearing a sari? No? Well, no wonder...." Or, "Oh, *we* wouldn't do such a thing. He must have been French or something. . . .'') And I know the pious denials of hotel clerks. In a Toronto hotel I was harassed by two house detectives who demanded to see my room key before allowing me to go upstairs to join my family—harassed me in front of an elevator-load of leering, elbow-nudging women. When I complained, I extracted only a ''Some of my best friends are Pakis'' from the night manager, as he fervently denied that what I had just experienced was in fact a racial incident.

And I know the sanctimonious denials of customs officers, even as they delight in making people like me dance on the head of a bureaucratic pin. On a return from New York to Toronto I was told, after being forced to declare a $1 valuation on a promotional leaflet handed out by a bookstore, that even a book of matches had to be declared. (''I didn't ask if you *bought* anything. Did you hear me ask about purchases? Did you? I'll ask you again in very clear English. *Are you bringing anything into the country?*'')

Do not think that I enjoy writing this of Canada. I remain a Canadian citizen, though I have returned to live and work in the United States and also for a time to my native India. This is the testament of a woman who came, like most immigrants, confident of her ability to do good work, in answer to a stated need.

I am less shocked, less outraged and shaken to my core, by a pursesnatching in New York City in which I lost all of my dowry-gold—everything I'd been given by my mother in marriage—than I was by a simple question asked of me in the summer of 1978 by three high school boys on the Rosedale subway station platform in Toronto. Their question was, ''Why don't you go back to Africa?''

It hurt because of its calculation, its calm, ignorant satisfaction, its bland assumption of the right to break into my privacy. In New York, I was violated because of my suspected affluence (a Gucci purse) and my obviously foreign, heedless nondefensiveness. Calcutta equipped me to survive theft or even assault; it did not equip me to accept proof of my unworthiness. (Friends say, ''Rosedale? Well. . .'' or, ''Teenagers, well. . .'' and I don't dispute them. But I owe it to my friends, and I have many friends in Canada, to dig deeper.)

Thanks to Canadian rhetoric on the highest level, I have learned several things about myself that I never suspected. The first is that I have no country of origin. In polite company, I am an ''East Indian'' (the opposite, presumably, of a ''West Indian''). The East Indies, in my school days, were Dutch possessions, later to become Indonesia. In impolite company I'm a "Paki" (a British slur unknown in America, I'm happy to say). For an Indian of my generation, to be called a "Paki" is about as appealing as it is for an Israeli to be called a Syrian. In an official green paper on immigration and populations I learn that I'm something called a "visible minority" from a "non-traditional area of immigration" who calls into question the "absorptive capacity" of Canada. And that big question (to which my contribution is really not invited) is, "What kind of society do we really want?"

A spectre is haunting Canada: the perfidious "new" (meaning "dark" and thus, self-fulfillingly, "nonassimilatable") immigrant, coming to snatch up jobs, welfare cheques, subway space, cheap apartments and blue-eyed women.

America trusts confrontation; its rough sense of justice derives from slugging it out. It tolerates contradictions that seem, in retrospect, monstrous. Perhaps it trusts to the constitution and the knowledge that somehow, someday, that document will resolve all difficulties. This is not the British style, not the Canadian style, in which conflict is viewed as evidence of political failure. In Canada, Parliament's sacred duty is the preservation of order; its mandate, at least in recent years, is to anticipate disorder. I can appreciate that, and if I were a white mainstream Canadian I'd probably endorse it wholeheartedly. Toronto really is a marvellous, beautiful city, as I tell all my American friends. Good God, if ever there was a city I should have been happy in, it was Toronto. But when you are part of the Toronto underbelly, invisible and nakedly obvious, you can't afford a white man's delusions.

While preparing to write this account, I interviewed dozens of people, mostly of Indian or Pakistani origin, in many parts of Canada. I read until I grew sick—of the assaults, the recommendations, the testimonies. I attended meetings, I talked to grandparents and to high-schoolers. I walked with the police down the troubled streets of east-end Toronto; I pursued some of the more lurid stories of the past year in Toronto. I turned down collaboration on some other stories; I did not feel Canadian enough to appear on a TV program celebrating the accomplishments of new Canadians; nor did I wish to take part in a TV show that set out to ascribe suicides among Indo-Canadian women solely to community pressures to have male children. Friends who supported this research will probably not find their observations in this

Children of 15 different nationalities at
York St. Public School at York and
Richmond Street West,
photographed circa 1926.

piece; they will find, instead, that I turned it all inside out.

To a greater or lesser extent those friends and I share a common history. We came in the mid-1960s for professional reasons. We saw scope and promise, and we were slow to acknowledge the gathering clouds. Some of us have reacted positively, working with the local or provincial governments, serving as consultants, as organizers, as impresarios of understanding. Others have taken hockey sticks on vigilante patrols to protect their people. Many, including myself, have left, unable to keep our twin halves together.

Saturday Night *(1981)*

WHILE IN THE CITY

While in the city
I have no delusion, no passions.
All I see is the darkness of office hours
against the dark tunics of the walls.
Empty and chilly streets with two million dwellers
in two million dreams.
Some waking not even at dawn.
After all,
no one died twice, ever.

While in the city
I hear the Lake's voice
responding to my foreign tongue.
Yet the Lake is not foreign,
it speaks all languages
and all are mine.
It speaks with understanding,
with affection,
with some sort of silent diplomacy
in its voice,
that we may communicate
about everything and nothing,
in all languages and none.
By the deep shadow of the Lake.
By the sleepless conscience.
WACLAW IWANIUK

A CITY
AFTER MY OWN HEART

BY JOSEF ŠKVORECKÝ

*The Toronto skyline is more beautiful to me than the familiar,
silhouette of Prague Castle, although there is probably no objective
difference. There is beauty everywhere on earth, but there is more of it
where one feels that sense of ease which comes from no longer having to
put off one's dreams until some improbable future....*
The Engineer of Human Souls *(1984)*

My first night in this coun-
try was one of the most blissful I have experienced in my life.
I shall never forget the feeling of security, of an utter absence
of that central European nightmare called doorbell-ringing-
at-4-a.m. Prague was only some eight hours away: the funeral of Jan Palach, the student who immolated himself in
protest against the Soviet invasion of Czechoslovakia, was
only a couple of weeks away, and here I was in Toronto.

After a period of utter hopelessness, my wife and I began
comforting ourselves with the great little pleasures of life in
Toronto. We rented a furnished apartment. It was as simple
as that. What is so strange about it? Well, the vast Atlantic
divides the people of Canada from less drastic but nevertheless very bothersome central European experiences. At the
time my wife and I were married in Prague in 1958, I lived in
a sublet room and she lived in a one-bedroom apartment with
her mother and younger sister (no bathroom, toilets shared
with three other apartments on the outside corridor). So she
moved in with me—not because I could not afford to pay the
rent for an apartment, but because there were no apartments
to be had. There were waiting lists at the housing office. You
joined them and you were evaluated. You got points: for
having children or tuberculosis, for living in a wet souterrain,
and so on. Most points you got if you managed to bribe the
housing commissioner. These gentlemen were the most frequently replaced of functionaries; invariably, after amassing

a sizable fortune from bribes, they failed to please some customer and were found out.

But I bribed too little, so we continued living in our sublet room. The whole suite consisted of one room, a kitchen and a bathroom. The bathroom was accessible only through the kitchen, where the landlady spent her days; consequently we were not allowed to use either the kitchen or the bathroom (the toilet was fortunately separate). We ate cold food and once a week we went to the public baths, which meant waiting in line for a couple of hours. And there was no laundry room; my mother-in-law did our washing for us in the classical manner, the only remnant of which in this country seems to be the washboard used by some of the tradition-minded Dixieland bands. This is how the more fortunate young couples lived in Prague.

During the first weeks of our stay in Toronto, my wife did all the laundry in the bathtub. We didn't trust the door on the first floor with the sign "Laundry." No doubt also, in a building of that size, there would be waiting lists of tenants with appointments to use the laundry in three weeks' time. But our European experience proved false. One day, by chance, my wife glanced into the laundry room and discovered that it was lined with automatic machines, similar to those which had been in the two or three public laundromats in Prague. Armed with her scanty knowledge of English, she entered the laundry room and started asking for the overseer. For that is how it was in the public laundromats in Prague: in each of them a bulky lady took your money first and then your dirty linen and started the washer. You were not allowed even to touch the machine. It was a good precaution, since no vending or otherwise automatic machine survived two weeks in Prague. People always tried to fool them with buttons or homemade coins.

Well, my countrymen are enterprising people. The popular belief in this country is that in a socialist society there is no private enterprise. In fact, it thrives there more than in Canada, with no bankruptcies and only an occasional jail sentence.

A delicatessen shop, for instance, might get 50 kilos of Italian salad (a popular item in Prague) each day from the central supply station. The manager gives orders to the shopgirls. These clever kids buy 10 kilos of cheap carrots, boil them at home, cut them up and mix them with the 50 kilos of salad. The alchemy produces 60 kilos, but the store is only charged for 50. What remains is divided according to the old pirate laws. The customers notice nothing: and if they do, they attribute the low quality to a new restriction in the state food regulations.

This is teamwork, but there are also individual entrepreneurs. Once, during a world hockey championship, my TV broke down. I called the municipal repair shop. A girl's voice said: "Okay. You live in the Brevnov district of Prague. Let me see. . .our man will come the second week of June."

This was in March. "But I want to see the championship!" I wailed.

"I can't help you. We have to work according to our plan and Brevnov comes for treatment in June."

"But I have to see. . . ."

"Unless," said the girl, "unless you speak to our repairman personally. Shall I tell him to call you back?"

In five minutes I had a call from the man. He started in the official way: June was the month assigned for Brevnov, he couldn't make it earlier. Unless, of course, I would like him to come after hours.

The same day, five minutes after five, the man was in my apartment. He repaired my set with spare parts he had stolen in the municipal shop, and consequently was able to charge me less than the shop would have charged me for the same man's services had he come during his working hours and in June. After that I became his frequent customer.

Not that Canadian entrepreneurs were that much less efficient. When the 1968 wave of Czechoslovak immigrants was given refuge in Canada, all kinds of salesmen, kindly concerned about our welfare, descended on us. I got off relatively unharmed. A young man came to my door, offering to deliver five books a week for only $5 a month.

"Books?" I asked, amazed.

"Yes," said the man. "Books. You know what they are? Things to read."

"But five a week? And what kind of books?"

"Excellent books," he assured me.

"But can I choose them?"

"Sure you can. Here's a list!"

He produced the list and my English vocabulary was enriched: what he meant were magazines. I hardly knew their names: *Field & Stream, Argosy, Mademoiselle.* One was called *Modern Screen* and I selected that first, thinking it was a film magazine. As a result of that subscription I would now be an expert on the love relations of Jacqueline, had I time to read *Modern Screen.* I also get *Field & Stream,* although I hate killing animals for sport, and *Mademoiselle*, although I have no daughter.

Recently I had a phone call: a female voice speaking in Czech. It belonged to an old lady who had been permitted to visit her daughter, now the wife of a Toronto WASP. "Are you sure that nobody is listening to what I say?" said the lady.

After five years in Canada I have lost some of my central European sensitivities. "Well, there is my wife sitting on the chesterfield," said I.

"I don't mean *that*! You *know* what I mean!" she interrupted. Then I knew what she meant.

"Oh no!" said I. "There is no bugging of private citizens' phones in Canada."

"Are you absolutely *sure*?" inquired the lady. "Because I don't know—I just dialed the number a friend of yours in Prague had given me, and instead of you there was this woman who said: 'What number are you calling?' I got so scared that, instead of hanging up, I told her your number—I hope I didn't do anything stupid—and then this woman gave me *this* number, and it was *right*! What does all that *mean*?"

I instructed the frightened lady in the mysteries of the Bell information service, but I am not sure that she was totally convinced. During the remainder of her stay she only wrote me notes, sealed with wax containing the impression of the Queen obtained from a dime.

I hope you believe me when I say that this lady had good reasons for her anxiety. A Toronto businessman to whom I told this story did not believe me. He had just returned from Prague, where he had been selling Canadian products to the Czech government. "It's not so dreadful there as you people make out," he said, by "you people" meaning us reactionary exiled socialists. "I didn't see anyone sad in the streets. The restaurants are full of pleasant-looking beer drinkers; people promenade in bright clothes on St. Wenceslas Square. Everything is apparently in order again." He was right, of course. He only overlooked one detail. Thirty kilometres east of Prague, that is some 20 miles, there is a small town called Lysa nad Labem. Two miles from that small town there is a military camp called Mlada. In this camp there is a Soviet tank division, an inconspicuous reminder to the independent Czechoslovak government that, should they decide something not to the liking of the power that commands those tanks, the division might do some slight manoeuvring in the direction of Prague.

I don't see any Yank divisions in the vicinity of Kitchener, and in spite of all that's going on now in the U.S. I am not worried about seeing one in the future. And that's one of the things I like about sweet Sister Canada and her Big Brother, with all his distasteful shortcomings.

But shall I tell you about a particular thing of beauty that is a joy to me forever? It is the students' directory of the University of Toronto. Why? The Einsteinian montage of the first and last names listed there. The beautiful contrast of the hopelessly non-English names these students inherited from immigrant parents, driven out of their old countries by hunger, racial discrimination or some sort of political saviour—and of the hopelessly English first names the students were given by their homesick and hardworking progenitors.

I have made up the following names but they could belong to my students: Linda N. Ujihara, Marshall J. Postnikoff, Jeanette Fuentes, Alister M. Kuzma, George Makebe, Pearl Marie Stribrny. When I browse through the pages of the directory, I am reminded of the old jazz bands, which later, in the era of swing, were the first to break the race barrier and displayed similar Whitmanesque poetry: Art Rollini, Irving Fazola, Bix Beiderbecke, Leon Rappolo, Gene Krupa, Joe Venuti, Max Kaminsky.... To us, Czech students of an "inferior" Slavic race who were trying to imitate the swinging sounds these very "inferior" musical wizards were making, their names were a manifesto. And so are my students at U of T. In these incongruously named children a dream is being realized. It has not yet obtained its final shape. Let us hope it will be as beautiful as the deep woods, the golden wheatfields and the Polar light up north over this young continent.

Adapted from "A Country After My Own Heart," Maclean's *(1974)*

TAKING POWER IN
THE SEVENTIES AND
WHAT HAPPENED AFTER

$\mathbf{B}$ack in the 1930s and '40s, our family used to have a vast gathering of the clan every New Year's Day. My cousins and I would crowd around the radio for the civic election broadcast and work out bets with nearby assorted uncles on the contests for aldermen and controllers and mayor—Sam McBride or Ralph Day or Jimmy Simpson the labour man, etcetera, etcetera, but never, of course, on Nathan Phillips, who was inevitably being returned as alderman in Ward 4 as he had been every year since 1923.

On the first of these occasions that I remember, my great-grandfather, a tall, ferocious-looking figure who had been an alderman way back in the 1880s, proposed a toast to the Little New Year, and then my grandmother, his heir apparent as our tribal chieftain, was told, to her chagrin, that she had unintentionally voted Communist: she used to get excited in the polling booth and, losing her *Evening Telegram* slate of candidates, she would look over the ballot for likely names. The other time it happened was about 1943 and she lit on Stewart Smith (Uncle Roy was a Stewart); when she discovered that once again she had helped to elect a Communist to the board of control, she uttered the strongest oath I had ever heard pass her lips: "Oh, *jolly* boys, *jolly* boys!"

My first direct experience of city hall (apart from the handshake from Mayor Bob Saunders when four of us as college students were given a civic send-off on a jeep trip to

*Mayors, controllers, aldermen, old and new, photographed at a
celebration of Toronto's 150th birthday, March 6, 1984.
Can you find Mayors Lamport, Givens, Sewell, Crombie,
Beavis and Eggleton? Mayor Leslie Saunders, 86, Grand
Master of the Orange Lodge, first elected to public office in
1923, is half-hidden between Fred Beavis and Mary Temple.
Front and centre is sometime M.L.A. and Alderman Joe
Salzberg, one of the most astute and astringent critics of
government in Toronto and Ontario for over fifty years. The
author is kneeling in the second row beside David Rotenberg and
above Elizabeth Eayrs and Alice Somerville. June Marks is
kneeling second from the right and William Archer is standing
at the far left. For a full account of the rogues gallery, call the
City Clerk or the author (964-8739).*

South America) dates from the time in 1963 that Eric Arthur asked me to join the city advisory committee, which was planning locations for art in the new city hall. During its construction we marched about the place in our hard hats and after due consideration chose places that would add points of drama and colour—as the architect Viljo Revell had intended—to his austere and magnificent building.

We had not really prepared ourselves for the reception we got from city council. The councillors seemed scarcely to have changed their behavior from what I remembered or had been told of their antics during my childhood. Even some of the names were the same. Although our committee had worked hard to produce its report, and it included a few rather impressive members—Roland Michener, the ex-Speaker of the House of Commons, for example—the councillors who received our deputation (it must have been a meeting of the board of control) behaved in a manner reminiscent of the Mad Hatter's Tea Party. They were suspicious of any proposal to spend money on art, and they seemed more interested in squabbling among themselves than in paying much attention to us or our suggestions for carrying out the architect's plans. We were eventually dismissed, and nothing at all was done about art inside city hall.

The best municipal reporter in those days was Ron Haggart, and before he left the scene he wrote what must still be the definitive article on the antics of the politicians we had been meeting with and their predecessors. Here is a part of it:

The buffoonery of Toronto's city hall has usually been of a harmless, and indeed ingratiating, quality. When a woman councillor refused to go to a Chicago convention on shade trees with a bachelor alderman because, she said, he kept winking and calling her "Junie Baby," Toronto remained unrepresented on the subject of shade trees. The chief result of the incident was that Controller June Marks and Alderman Michael Grayson were assured of longevity in office. When the erudite economist Amazasp Aroutunian was Russian ambassador to Canada, he never forgave Mayor Nathan Phillips who, unable to pronounce his name, referred to him in public as Mr. Rootin'-Tootin', but Toronto rewarded Nate Phillips with an unequaled record of reelection to its city council. Mayor William Dennison thought out loud that the prime minister of Guyana came from Ghana but was re-elected anyway.

Nathan Phillips, while mayor of the city, went one lunch

hour to a meeting of the businessmen in the area of Yonge and St. Clair, where he told them how everyone at city hall admired the work of the Bay-Bloor Businessman's Association, correcting himself only when a kindly listener tugged at his sleeve. He then hurried down to the regular Tuesday afternoon meeting of the metropolitan council, where he proposed that henceforth their sessions should begin at 2:30 p.m. instead of two, since so many of the members had vital engagements to attend during the luncheon hour. Although his own city council continued to meet at 2 p.m., the metropolitan council continued its 2:30 habit for many years, a lasting memorial to the importance of the banquet circuit in the lives of Toronto mayors.

Before Nathan Phillips completed his term, the record of longevity in office was held by Controller Donald MacGregor, who died in 1942 after 25 years on the city council. Can anyone doubt that the events of 1925, early in MacGregor's career, won his place forever in the hearts and minds of Toronto voters? MacGregor was a controller in that year, which in Toronto means a member of the council elected city-wide, as distinct from aldermen, who are elected by wards. He waited one afternoon outside a meeting of the property committee, knowing that Alderman Sam McBride would soon leave and walk through the empty council chamber to the parks committee, which was meeting in the room beyond.

"You dirty yellow dog!" MacGregor shouted at McBride as he chased him into the council chamber, pinned him against a heavy oaken railing and chopped him in the cheek with a hearty punch. Alderman McBride grabbed the railing and slid to his knees, while Controller MacGregor continued to hit him from above, inflicting six separate and discernible cuts and bruises on McBride's head and neck. A doctor later testified that it was MacGregor's Masonic ring, more than his prowess, that made his blows so effective.

All this was incredible conduct, coming from Controller MacGregor, a soft-faced music teacher and a bachelor. A few days before, he had stood in the Toronto City Council and proposed that a group of perfectly competent typists and clerks be fired because they were aliens; the jobs should go to the daughters of the deserving men already on the city payroll (who, almost without doubt, would be Shriners, Masons, Orangemen or, at the very least, Moose, Elk or Antediluvian Buffalo).

Alderman McBride had been no less irrelevant: he let slip the secret that Controller MacGregor, who called himself a doctor of music, had obtained his degree from a mail-order American university that he had never visited. Toronto voters didn't much care who was the dirtier yellow dog. They took both men to their hearts and MacGregor, as we have seen, stayed in office for 25 years, and McBride was elected five more times as a controller and three times as mayor.

As these men's careers were fading, an alderman, and later controller, named David Balfour was coming into prominence. He served during the 1940s and '50s, being assured of almost automatic reelection because Toronto at that time had an unwritten but universally respected rule that there must always be one Roman Catholic among the four members of the board of control. As a controller, Balfour is remembered for his espousal of only one cause: the great, and annual, license-plate debate. At that time, the mayor's limousine always bore the license number 5000 and the four controllers had license numbers 5001, 5002, 5003 and 5004. They were awarded according to each controller's standing in the previous election. This as a tradition Controller Balfour wished to upset, after he had been there a while, and he argued that license plate 5001 should not go to the controller with the most votes, a distinction he never achieved, but to the controller with the greatest seniority, a distinction he held for some time. No one can really remember much else he did, and he even lost that debate.

Controller Balfour had gone by the time the City of Toronto and a dozen of its suburbs were federated into a metropolitan government in the 1950s; Metro council under Chairman Gardiner, who ran things more like a construction company than a government, was building waterworks, roads, sewers and a solid system of regional government with vigour and efficiency. But somehow only the other politicians' names were changed. Albert Cranham arrived as an alderman from the east end and suggested that the city mayor's chain of office (donated by a hardware store, a distillery and other long-established merchants) failed to afford sufficient dignity to the office. Alderman Cranham wanted to decorate the mayor with a three-cornered hat and a robe, "perhaps with a touch of ermine." This, and his urgent demand for passes to get aldermen past fire barriers (some hapless constable hadn't recognized him), should have ensured the alderman a seat forever, but they gave him a job at city hall instead, a job that they then abolished when Cranham retired.

The debate on fluoridation was perhaps a low-water mark,

even for Toronto. Mayor Jack Holley of Weston simply could not understand how the campaign to fluoridate the water supply could be led by dentists, who presumably would lose the certainty of future business. "I have never heard of any organization in favour of doing away with business," the mayor of Weston told the Metropolitan council one day. "To my way of thinking there is a nigger in the woodpile somewhere." No one seemed to notice, really, and the reeve of Etobicoke, Ozzie Waffle, used the same expression a little later the same day, until Alderman Philip Givens suggested that a government in the focus of so much attention should not express itself in such questionable terms.

Nathan Phillips, after his Rootin'-Tootin' remark was carried in newspapers around the world, rather fancied himself as the master of the intended malapropism; it was part of his image his voters loved so well, that he was just an ordinary guy thrown in with all those political wolves, a rather generous assessment of a politician who survived longer at city hall than any other. A sweet little old lady alderman named May Birchard complained one day that she had been trying to speak but the mayor wouldn't recognize her. "I've been holding up my hand for 20 minutes," she said.

"Well, go ahead," the mayor replied from the dignity of his carved throne chair, "leave the room."

Another woman alderman, Mary Temple, was under the impression that the council was still discussing the problem of 262 abandoned trash containers spread around the downtown area, and she rose to speak.

"Oh," said the mayor with pained innocence, "are you still on the can?"

While many, if not all, of Nathan Phillips' misapplications were intended to be humourous, no one has really ever been sure about the wild, weaving and swooping language of Allan Lamport, who has been alderman, controller, mayor, transit commissioner and finally controller again, an almost permanent fixture in civic life. Did Lamport, for example, really mean it when he was reporting to his board of control colleagues on his appearance before a royal commission on civic organization, triumphantly asserting, "Why, I even went so far as to be fair!"

Lamportisms are a hobby among many students of Toronto government, although most of them are some years old, which may indicate, as Lamport himself once said, "You can't lead a dead horse to water." The late Frank Tumpane, a columnist for the Toronto *Telegram*, was an enthusiastic student of Lamport; Tumpane once told me that Lamport was a firm believer in forthrightness among public men. "In politics," Lamport told Tumpane, "you need more of the kind of men who will crawl out from behind the woodwork."

My own collection includes:

Lamport on the difficulties of getting governmental decisions: "It's like pushing a car uphill with a rope."

Lamport on political infighting: "If anyone's gonna stab me in the back I wanna be there."

Lamport on the need to terminate an expensive project: "Let's not just discontinue it, let's stop it."

Lamport in opposition to building a Centennial concert hall in a city already well supplied with auditoriums: "We have these theatre seats coming out of our ears."

Primarily because of Lamport's opposition, Toronto did not officially name its 1967 Centennial project until 1968, although no one in Toronto really found that remarkable. The government, after all, had come within an inch of having a brand-new and world-renowned city hall—and no furniture to put in it. The council was deadlocked for months over which of two companies should get the contract. It was not the first time: in 1954 the city opened its first subway and came with a whisker of having no subway cars to put in it.

The failure to name a Centennial project in Centennial year did not arise from any lack of advance preparation. The project had been surveyed to death, almost literally, and even some of those who were skeptical of building a concert hall agreed to finance the surveys required. Even Alderman Fred Beavis went that far when he told city council on one occasion, "I happen to represent these here lunch-pail constituents who don't speak too well of the King's English. These lunch-pail people, I want to get something for them, too, but for the time being I'm going to go along with this here survey."

When a vacancy occurred through a death on Toronto's board of control, the councillors gave Beavis the promotion. In due course, which means in 1968, he voted against naming the St. Lawrence Centre for the Arts as Toronto's 1967 Centennial project. "It seems we've got these here theatre seats coming out of our ears," said the newly created Controller Beavis, and fellow Controller Lamport didn't flinch at all, apparently believing that anyone who votes the right way is entitled to swipe his material.

The idiosyncrasies of Toronto politicians have always seemed to me, however embarrassing, to be harmless enough, frequently providing better television on the local news than the same old retread situation comedies, and hardly a distraction at all from the indisputable fact that the city and the suburbs loosely federated into Metropolitan Toronto are honestly, competently and progressively governed. Civic politics in Toronto lacks the ideological warfare of Winnipeg and the blatant self-interest occasionally uncovered in Edmonton.

Some years ago, I wrote down a sentence spoken by a kindly old Toronto alderman named Frank Clifton who was trying to prevent the Sunday laws being liberalized to include stock-car racing. The way I happened to put it down in my notebook made it, I thought at the time, rather a lovely piece of blank verse:

> *I always done the best I could*
> *to leave things just the way*
> *they were.*

But it's not true, really. It doesn't apply to the city, or to its government, or to the look and the feel of Toronto today. Although it may apply, just a bit, to the politicians of Toronto themselves.

By the beginning of 1968, when Ron Haggart wrote those words, the buffoonery of city politicians was assuming a more sinister aspect. And things were not being left just the way they were.

Toronto was riding the biggest building boom in its history. Old neighbourhoods were being obliterated, and our stock of older houses was being demolished at the rate of several dozen a week. Under the banner of "progress" or "slum clearance," city politicians were falling over themselves to cooperate with developers in the process. Eager for the increased tax base to be had, they forgot that all the extra revenue and more would be needed for the welfare and police and community services necessary because of the social problems they were creating.

A prime example of all this was happening in St. James Town just across the Rosedale ravine from where we lived. Here is something I wrote about what it did to one family that had had its roots in St. James Town for a long time:

Consider the Farrells, an extended family who used to live in an old house on the west side of Bleecker Street between Wellesley and Howard. The Farrells had been there for two or three generations, like many of their 4,000 neighbours in

St. James Town. In 1960, that sort of non-middle-class area was called a slum. It contained hundreds of family houses. They were old, and a bit rundown and dirty for Toronto, though not by the standards of Europe or the American east coast.

With bonuses for "good development" and with the very best planning advice, city council succeeded in destroying that "slum" as thoroughly as if they had dropped a Nagasaki bomb on it. It was replaced with windy concrete canyons and sunless prophylactic greensward and a dozen 25-storey monuments for people to live in—though not, it turned out, the same people.

The Farrells' house on the west side of Bleecker Street was torn down in 1964. None of the family lives in the area now. Nobody has lived on that site since. The developer was even unwilling to build luxury apartments nearby until he could get his zoning increased, which city council dutifully did, adding, at Alderman Beavis' suggestion, an extra bonus for "good planning" by counting roadway as "open space." (Nearby residents painted the road green one night and named it Fred Beavis Memorial Park.)

The slum dwellers of St. James Town have meanwhile been removed from their undesirable lifestyle, and scattered to the far reaches of Metro and beyond, to places like the village of Oak Ridges, for example, that lovely festival of free enterprise on Yonge Street 20 miles north of the city limits.

The Farrells were luckier than most. They managed to find a house just inside Metro—in Rexdale—almost as big as the one they lived in before, and with no cockroaches. Separated from their neighbours and the community they had always known, they determined at least to survive as a family. First problem: Grandfather Farrell let the side down. Though in excellent health and with a nice little room to himself, but no neighbours to talk to or watch from the verandah, grandfather promptly died.

On the brighter side, the oldest girl married into a North York split level on a 100-foot lot, and she has two children now, though she might be in Vancouver for all she sees of the family. Grandma Farrell is fine and has more time around the house than ever (she doesn't get to church much any more because the relevant new liturgy and the relevant new minister and the relevant new coffee hour are not quite what she is used to). The second boy is fine too—working on a farm. He dropped out of collegiate the first year they moved. And thanks to his memories of the week he spent boarding at the

*"... well, you can't join on
here ... this is where you started from
two weeks ago.... you'll have to go
somewhere else..."*

Toronto Island Nature School, when he was an inner-city kid, sought out a rural commune to join. If he had stayed in St. James Town he would likely have been streamed into a dead-end commercial course and job along with some of his buddies from Rose Avenue Public School. But against these minor triumphs of upwards or sideways mobility, we must set the debit side.

The youngest son has joined a gang that specializes in terrorizing suburban shopping plazas. The feeble-minded sister who used to live at home is now committed to Queen Street (at $100 per day, courtesy of the taxpayers). For great-aunt, since there was no room for her in the new house, it was off to the expansive cement orchards of Applewood Acres 20 miles away, where she lives out of sight and out of mind in the closest available old people's home, again at public expense.

Father is at home full time on welfare now, instead of taking the downtown restaurant jobs he used to find out of Bleecker Street, and mother no longer has the Rosedale jobs she used to walk to, although she still manages to work illicitly, by commuting downtown to a part-time cleaning job. The oldest boy kept his steady job at the other end of the Danforth, which he used to reach by the Bloor streetcar; kept it, that is, until his old car was wrecked in one of his 30-mile daily round trips and he was fired for not getting there on time by public transit.

There's lots more to say about the Farrells. Their former social worker, for example, now lives in the apartment building on whose site 50 St. James Town houses used to stand. But the picture is clear enough. What was destroyed in St. James Town was not just a community and its physical fabric of houses and backyards and trees, but the possibility of growing another one there remotely like it.

It all seemed so inevitable. Another decade of this sort of thing and there would be no more old houses nor old communities left in the centre of Toronto. This prospect was a particularly bitter one for me because I had been giving public lectures about preserving old buildings and streetscapes, and at York University I had been lobbying for the establishment of a faculty of environmental studies which could help change attitudes toward urban planning.

Though I was not really aware of it at the time, by the end of the 1960s a lot of other people felt the same way I did. Perhaps a futile gesture in favour of what we believed in would be more satisfactory than watching helplessly from the sidelines. You could at least shake your fist at the juggernaut of progress as it rolled by. You might even try standing in front of it. But I had long ago made my decision to be a writer and an academic rather than a politician.

During the 1958 federal elections, I ran a campaign called "Non-Liberals for Pearson" (against Mr. Diefenbaker's vision). I later chaired a policy group of academics at the request of the Ontario Opposition leader, John Wintermeyer, which was supposed to provide him with a program for government. His caucus did not entirely welcome us or even understand what we were talking about, but it would have made little difference in the next provincial election even if it had. I was now an expert at spitting into the wind.

After Mr. Pearson's thinkers' conference at Kingston, in which I was involved, he asked me to run for his party in 1962. I opted instead for a part in the creation of York University, and for the study of Pearson's political career that I was planning to write. When I did join the Liberal party and worked in the 1963 federal campaign, I noticed that it was the artists and intellectuals I recruited from the Kingston conference—none of them party members so far as I knew—who were my most effective poll captains. When Mr. Pearson announced in 1967 his intention to retire, I decided to run as a delegate to the leadership convention in support of the potential candidacy of the new minister of justice, Pierre Trudeau. I had met him when we were both wandering about eastern Europe in 1948, and had later admired his writing in *Cité Libre*.

Once again I backed away from becoming a full-time politician. I knew I was good at election organizing by now, and even at speech-making for causes I believed in, but ineffective in debate. I did not regret, then or later, the decision to avoid a parliamentary career. But I still had political yearnings. A dose of Anglican church politics, a heavy involvement in the Couchiching conferences on public affairs and such jobs as chairing the national committee to fight the cancellation of the CBC's *This Hour Has Seven Days* only whetted my appetite.

The one kind of politics I was no good at, and found distasteful, was academic politics. The York experience had been exhausting and discouraging, and for this and other reasons I went into therapy. The university also gave me two years' leave to work on a book for another employer.

As the 1969 city election approached, David Crombie and Gerald Robinson of the new Civic Action Party (CIVAC) asked me if I would be their candidate for mayor. I was sorely tempted, but I also knew that the chances of beating an entrenched incumbent were next to nil and that my own grasp of bread-and-butter city issues was very weak. Being pitched straight into a mayoralty campaign would be the wrong way to learn. My old fantasy about working downtown in the heart of the city persisted, however. Charles Caccia, the one city council member I admired and agreed with, whom I had nominated for MP at the wild Davenport Liberal riding circus in the Coliseum during the Trudeaumania of '68, urged me to run for alderman now, and see about trying for mayor in 1972.

The Municipal Liberal Party had just been formed and was fielding candidates in every ward. Here was a group with a comprehensive program and an experienced set of campaign workers. My friend Jane Jacobs helped me and our mayoralty candidate Stephen Clarkson to get the party to publicly oppose more expressway building and gross urban development. I obtained our party's nomination as a candidate in Ward 10, where I lived, the area of Toronto between Bloor Street East and the city limits, Yonge Street and the Don Valley, and began walking the streets and subway platforms looking for voters.

That fall there were other stirrings of resistance to business as usual at city hall. When city council tried to have a vast new concrete obscenity constructed right below Wychwood Park, the residents of the park, led by Marshall McLuhan, Colin Vaughan and Douglas Ambridge (one of the city's last old-fashioned tycoons still in eruption), came down to city hall to protest. They almost succeeded, and because of their strong arguments and solid opposition, even though they never persuaded city council, the whole development was later condemned by the chairman of the Ontario Municipal Board, the crusty and outspoken James Aloysius Kennedy.

Mr. Kennedy did something even more important. He threw out a city application for new ward boundaries which was nothing more than a neat piece of gerrymandering devised to suit incumbents. And instead he forced on Toronto a pattern of homogenous wards, so that the affluent north ends of the old elongated ward salamanders could no longer submerge the interests of the south-end working people. Under the new system also, as the city had requested, there would be no board of control, but instead an executive chosen from among the 11 aldermen who received the larger number of votes in each of the 11 new wards. These 11 senior aldermen would go to Metro council as well, while their 11 junior colleagues would be members of city council only. Such a drastic change in the rules caused a fair bit of scrambling and bargaining among the incumbents to ensure that they would not be running against one another in the same ward.

As the 1969 city elections approached, no one could be sure of the old verities or the same old results any more.

Besides the new rules, there were other unsettling factors. The largely middle-class Confederation of Residents' and Ratepayers' Associations (CORRA) was now keeping track of which councillors voted against homeowners' interests in favour of accommodating developers. In addition to the two new municipal parties, CIVAC and the Municipal Liberals, a number of NDP candidates and some independent community organizers also took aim at city hall's old guard. They were given the cautious blessing of CORRA in most cases. Another important factor in the election was a major series of op-ed articles by James Lorimer run throughout 1969 by *The Globe and Mail*. The *Globe* also opted editorially for the idea of sweeping but coherent change by supporting all the Municipal Liberal candidates, even though few of them had any municipal experience. The op-ed articles, unlike the editorial endorsement, clearly had an impact on the electorate's attitude to the old guard at city hall. Here is an excerpt from one of them describing a 1969 campaign event:

Incredible. That has always been my reaction to city politicians ever since I encountered them for the first time two or three years ago. There is no other word for it; they are incredible.

Last Monday's election meeting organized by the Don Vale Residents' Association was for all the aldermanic candidates running in the new Ward 7, but it turned out to be Oscar Sigsworth Night. It was the first time Don Vale residents have encountered Mr. Sigsworth, at present alderman for the old Ward 1, which lies east of the Don River and outside their area.

What made last Monday's meeting a special occasion was that it illustrated very well what an "old guard" city politician is, and what happens when such politicians and people active in citizens' groups confront each other.

"Old guard" is not a very precise term, but one thing it does mean, everyone is agreed, is a consistent willingness to support developers over the objections of local residents on controversial rezoning and redevelopment proposals. On the nine votes of this kind at city hall which have been tabulated by CORRA, Mr. Sigsworth has the best record of all from the point of view of developers, the worst from the point of view of citizens' groups. He ties with Controller Fred Beavis, with eight votes against ratepayers' associations, none in favour. There is no doubt that Mr. Sigsworth belongs in the "old guard" category.

None of the other candidates running in Ward 7 has been on city council, so none can properly be called "old guard." There are two types of aldermanic hopefuls in the ward. The first is candidates who have been active in the ward's political problems of the last few years. John Sewell, running as an independent, has worked full-time in the ward for three years for the Trefann Court Residents' Association and for a number of other citizens' groups. Karl Jaffary, running on the NDP ticket, was president of the Don Vale Residents' Association in 1967 – 68, when the organization was beating off the city's first plan for the area, which involved substantial expropriation.

The other group of candidates are a few newcomers, people who have had little or no involvement in dealing with urban renewal, expropriation and redevelopment. Last Monday's meeting came to life only when Mr. Sigsworth arrived a few minutes late. It didn't take him long to get to his explanation of why he is running in the new Ward 7.

He noted that the block ward boundaries split the old Ward 1, where he and Controller Fred Beavis were elected in 1966. "I had to make a decision whether I would take one half of Ward 1 or the other, in view of the fact that the ward was split. The people there have been very good to me," Mr. Sigsworth said, "so I decided that I would make a choice, along with Controller Fred Beavis, who is my running mate and fellow alderman. And we decided that we would each take half of the ward, for better or for worse. I took this half, Fred Beavis took the other, and we're going to see how it turns out."

I took this half, Fred Beavis took the other: Mr. Sigsworth made it quite clear that he considered Don Vale as territory to be divided up among the sitting aldermen at city hall.

Candidates were asked about election expenses and sources of campaign funds. The budgets quoted by the other candidates ranged from $500 to $3,000, though Mr. Sam Rotenberg, a local businessman, refused to estimate his expenses. All said they were relying on small contributions, with no money coming from developers, except for Mr. Rotenberg, who said he has received $100 in contributions and that his wife is paying the rest of his expenses.

Mr. Sigsworth also detailed his financial situation. "I've received $5,000," he said, "and I expect to contribute $2,000 myself. A great deal of my money has come from people in the contracting business because I am associated with the contracting field. And it is my conviction that they believe in good government and they are willing to contribute to it, just as they are willing to contribute to the United Appeal."

A great deal of my money has come from people in the contracting business: Mr. Sigsworth was making no bones about the fact that his money was coming mostly from contractors and developers, and he made a point of saying that he has personal connections to this field. In fact he works in public relations for a large ready-mix concrete firm.

Just to remove any possible source of confusion, the close similarity between contractors and developers was pointed out to Mr. Sigsworth. His amiable reply: "I wouldn't be surprised if one or two developers contributed to my campaign, right."

People at the meeting then zeroed in on Mr. Sigsworth's voting record at city hall, and noted his score on the CORRA tabulations: eight votes for developers, none for their rate-payer opposition.

"I suggest to you," said Mr. Sigsworth, "that the people who were opposed to those applications were a small percentage, even a fractional percentage, of the citizens of Toronto."

"But these people," protested his questioner, "were representing the people in their areas."

"I think you elect people to make decisions," replied Mr. Sigsworth. "I don't think you elect people to be Charlie McCarthys for the public afterwards."

Charlie McCarthys for the public? That is evidently what Mr. Sigsworth calls aldermen who pay serious attention to the views of citizens' groups on city council.

Another questioner went after Mr. Sigsworth on his record on the Don Mount urban renewal scheme, which is located in his old ward.

Mr. Sigsworth responded by listing some of the good works that he has achieved for the people of Ward 1. "I just happen to have built a $7-million public housing project at Blake Street, I just happen to be responsible for a $1.5-million senior citizens' home on Logan. If that isn't being concerned with the people, I don't know what is."

I just happen to have built? The Blake Street project is an Ontario Housing development; the senior citizens' housing on Logan was put up by Woodgreen Community Centre.

Mr. Sigsworth was not the only candidate at last Monday's meeting who was questioned by Don Vale residents. The other candidates were also asked their views on the Don Vale plan, on decision-making power for citizens and citizens' groups, on the airport, on amalgamation and on party politics.

Mr. Doran, an independent, arrived too late to answer more than one or two questions. Mr. Rolfe, also calling himself an independent, generally limited himself to agreeing with what someone else said. Mr. Loney, the Liberal candidate, expressed his good intentions and concern for the people of the ward. Mr. Rotenberg went off on a number of sidetracks.

Mr. Jaffary criticized the kind of aldermen Don Vale has had in the past: "The people we've been voting for in the past have been utterly unresponsive to anything we wanted." He proposed a ward citizens' council, hedged a bit when asked if he would always take his instructions from this council, but stated firmly: "Any time that a representative body of people come from this ward and says, "This is what we want," then that's what I'm doing."

Mr. Sewell said that he felt aldermen should be directly involved in helping to start and working with citizens' groups. "This is probably the most effective way of finding out what that community happens to want," he said. "My function as an alderman would be to make sure that the people of this community got together and expressed their opinions, and told me what to say as alderman, so that I would be a mouthpiece for them."

The last question asked at the meeting was directed to Mr. Sigsworth, and was concerned with how much attention he was prepared to give the views of organized groups of people in his ward.

"If you're asking," replied Mr. Sigsworth, "am I receptive to people, the answer's yes. Yes. I listen to people, for sure."

It was a fitting end for Oscar Sigsworth Night in Don Vale.

On December 2, 1969, civic election day throughout the province, the citizens of Toronto went to the polls in the middle of a blizzard and did an astonishing thing. They defeated Alderman Oscar Sigsworth and no fewer than six of his old guard colleagues. Since three other sitting aldermen had also left, one to retirement, another for a plum city job and a third for the House of Commons, it meant that there were only 12 of the previous council of 23 returned, along with Mayor Dennison, who had defeated his two challengers, Controller Margeret Campbell and Stephen Clarkson.

The motley ranks of the new council contained some talent. For the first time an opposition group formed, but not one strong enough to effect any basic change in direction. The NDP elected three aldermen: Karl Jaffary, the Don Vale lawyer who defeated Sigsworth; Reid Scott, who had already been both an MLA and an MP; and Archie Chisholm, a union man from Parkdale. The Civic Action Party produced a quick-witted political science lecturer, David Crombie, and a cautious, well-meaning young accountant named Art Eggleton—"an albino liberal," one critic dubbed him. But as a force, CIVAC had been pretty much coopted by the newest of the old guard: Aldermen Tony O'Donohue and David Rotenberg (who was really to run the city for Mayor Dennison), who had both joined CIVAC and found it useful in getting elected as "reformers" to the new city executive. Another alderman, Ying Hope, also joined CIVAC, though it was not quite clear when, prompting Stephen Lewis to comment that he wished *he* had a party like that, which could run four candidates and elect five.

Two of the most voluble members of the new council were essentially loners: the veteran William Archer, whose mastery of the civic machinery enabled him to pull off a few major coups, such as the Yonge Street Mall, but who usually stuck to the status quo and to brilliant tinkering with details; and John Sewell, whose ideas and tactics, more than anyone's, focussed the real opposition on council. The only member of the Municipal Liberal party to get elected was me.

Over the next three years at City Hall, the hard-core opposition became Jaffary, Sewell and myself, though when Sewell and I went to the extreme of voting against the whole civic budget for 1970, Jaffary disassociated himself from such radical folly. Chisholm usually voted with us, and though David Crombie played the role of conciliator and man of reason, he too was in opposition on the many occasions when he could get no response from the executive. Scott, Eggleton and Hope also opposed the government more often than not.

Sewell, Jaffary, Crombie and I published a newsletter every two weeks called *City Hall*, a biased account of what we thought every alderman was doing and why. Though our own opposition within council could do little in itself, all sorts of outside groups—in a spectrum from the bluest of tory ratepayers to the hippie aficionados of the black flag of anarchy—gave regular vent to their unhappiness about what council was up to. Citizens' action or discussion groups sprang up like mushrooms. In neighbourhoods where there were no residents' groups, some of us did our best to help organize them. CORRA, the city-wide ratepayers' coalition, religiously kept track of how everyone on council voted, and this information was now more widely circulated. To many people it seemed that for once you *could* fight city hall. And that it was worth doing even if you usually lost.

The loudest protest group was SSSOCCC—Stop Spadina Save Our City Coordinating Committee—led by Alan Powell, a sociologist from the University of Toronto (which subsequently did not renew his contract). SSSOCCC directed itself primarily at Metro council, which was proceeding with the construction of the first dumper expressway (the Spadina), to aim directly at the core of the city from outside. SSSOCCC tried all kinds of urban guerrilla theatre, though members also got the prudent advice: "Always stand in front of the *second* bulldozer."

On Earth Day, 1970, the SSSOCCC people, along with Father Dan Heap, who worked in a box factory, and his wife, Alice, June Rowlands of the Association of Women Electors, Reverend Arch McCurdy of the United Church, columnist Dick Beddoes, a *Star* photographer and Alderman John Sewell and me, trespassed onto a clearing where the Spadina (officially named the William R. Allen) expressway was due to run. We dug holes for the little trees we had brought with us, and as the sun rose above the horizon planted them. Father Heap sprinkled some holy water and blessed the place and declared it to be a park. A Metro crew cleared out the trees soon enough, but we got a fair bit of press notice. It helped that that morning at the city executive meeting, Mayor Dennison denounced me as an anarchist for something I had said about a taxpayers' strike. He had not heard about the William R. Allen Park yet, but his timing, from our point of view, could not have been better.

To involve more cautious and respectable folk in the expressway battle, we formed the Spadina Review Corporation. This body raised money with art auctions, concerts and festivals, and engaged J.J. Robinette to argue our case against Metro Toronto at the Ontario Municipal Board. There Chairman Kennedy wrote a strong minority opinion as to why Metropolitan Toronto should not be allowed to build such an expressway but was outvoted by his two colleagues sitting on the case. It took another public campaign, in which Marshall McLuhan was again heavily involved, to make a last ditch appeal to the provincial cabinet. Our *deus ex machina*, Premier William Davis, announced the cancellation of the expressway in June of 1971.

The biggest and most complex battle—against the blockbusting developers—was meanwhile being carried on in city council by John Sewell, Karl Jaffary and David Crombie. The Public Works Committee afforded a forum, however, in which simpler examples of ordinary taxpayers getting overridden by city hall could be debated. Marshall McLuhan once more sounded the alarm when the city prepared to widen a street that cut right through the middle of St. Michael's College and past his office. I got to set up a debate on the issue at the works committee, then to vote on it and finally to write it up for the *Globe*. Here is an abridged version of the *Globe* article, called "Moreness Versus Chicken Talk: Lamport and McLuhan at City Hall":

"A moral victory! A moral victory! We lost!" cried Pogo triumphantly the day after that U.S. presidential election when Adlai Stevenson went down for the last time.

What St. Michael's College lost last week in Toronto City Council was its attempt to stop the city from widening the street that cuts through the heart of its peaceful retreat from the traffic roar of Queen's Park Crescent and Bay Street. Council decided to reject the compromise proposed by the college, and instead, with much self-congratulation upon its own spirit of compromise, agreed to widen St. Joseph Street to 28 feet instead of the original 30 feet proposed by the works commissioner, who himself had rejected his staff's request for 44 feet and the removal of a row of big trees.

And yet Pogo was right—this time, anyway. The moral victory lay in the process itself, and in the political education it produced, rather than in the end result. The message was not that council generously surrendered two feet of roadway for grass, but that a lot of people got involved in city politics. And the initiates stuck with it for the next battle.

Once again, a citizens' group demonstrated that if it is doggedly persistent, firmly united and courteous in its approach to council; if it consists of a nice mix of radicals and conservatives, young and old, rich and poor; if it is thoroughly representative of its constituency; if it is willing to put up a lot of its members' time and money; if it has done more thorough research on the problem than the city has; if it is prepared to be gratuitously patronized and talked down to by members of council; if it is willing to repeat its own case over and over again for aldermen who do not bother to attend committee meetings where the matter is being examined; if it is willing to face with equanimity any alderman who gets his facts mixed up while accusing the group of bad faith when any of its members mix theirs; and if the group is willing to be told that it should stop letting "its tail" (in this case the faculty and students) "wag the dog" (i.e., the administra-ion)—if a citizen's group is willing to go through all this, then the present council will likely respond.

Of course it does help if your citizens' group contains, like this one, a couple of presidents, the chief abutting property owners and institutions, the city's largest institution and has the support of the city's majority church.

The metaphor of tail-wagging can be extended to city hall. In the dog's body politic, the citizens of Toronto (like St. Michael's faculty and students) are the tail; the aldermen and the commissioners are the dog; and they must not let them-selves be wagged. If it objects, the tail can get itself another dog in three years' time. In theory, at least. We shall test this out in practice when the next triennial name recognition contest comes along in the 1972 civic elections.

Meanwhile, city hall will listen to some of the people some of the time—provided you don't expect city hall to give people what they ask for rather than what aldermen know is good for them.

One delightful benefit of the St. Joseph Street affair was the surreal episode of a debate in Public Works Committee between Allan Lamport and Marshall McLuhan—both of them at the top of their form—a marvellous nonmeeting of minds. Mr. McLuhan talked against the cult of "moreness," while Alderman Lamport, in the name of progress, led several of his famous dead horses to water.

Mr. Lamport is an ornament and oracle of city hall for many reasons—one in that he is some sort of cousin to Dublin's Leopold Bloom and that his use of language can resemble *Finnegan's Wake* on occasion. He has a delightful way of unconsciously coining new words with double meanings (e.g., "mis-cheevious") or inventing names to suit his view of character (e.g., "Alderman Newell" or "Alderman Fuel" for Alderman Sewell). Mr. McLuhan and Mr. Lamport have one patron in common: James Joyce.

Here are some more of Mr. McLuhan's remarks, along with those of aldermen and other deputation members, to the Public Works Committee:

Mr. McLuhan: Moreness is not conducive to sanity or dialogue. The university is a place of dialogue, encounter, awareness. The present program of moreness may make the next dialogue impossible. There is disadvantage in dialogue with a large truck. I cannot converse with a jackhammer. Even economists see that the cult of moreness is finished. The GNP is no longer the test of health. By the time economists can see something, you may be past the point of no return. They are the last to see anything. They are drunk with figures. Moreness is the alcoholic's dream of a cure. The cure is at the bottom of the next bottle.

Alderman Lamport: Couldn't we get back to the subject?

Mr. McLuhan: Yes, the subject is the campus and what you are doing to it. The subject is moreness. You want moreness.

Alderman Bruce: Who does McLuhan represent? Himself?

Voice from deputation: Us—St. Michael's College.

Alderman June Marks: May I ask our commissioner what ways there are to improve pedestrian safety if we widen the street?

Mr. McLuhan (*sotto voce*): A tunnel of love.

Mrs. Marks to the deputation: Are you aware that the contract is already let?

Voice from deputation: Yes.

Mrs. Marks to the president of St. Michael's College: Did you consult your ward alderman [i.e., Alderman Marks]?

The President of St. Michael's, Father Kelly: I felt it was enough to consult the Public Works Department.

Mrs. Marks: To encourage dialogue on something is excellent but this is only sociological talk. Solitude is nice, but you go to cottages for that. Traffic congestion, not better flow, will hurt solitude.

Mr. Lamport: The widening will do a lot of good in the area and I'm surprised at the furor. Father Kelly's been most fair, and we have to rely on the more dignified type in the community like yourself, Father, to be objective. But it would only be something created by pressure if we don't widen the street.

Alderman William Archer: You got Sunday sports by pressure, Lampy.

Mr. Lamport: That wasn't done by small minds. The city

cannot progress if every little satisfactory improvement is due for a fight by a local group. You can't stop making automobiles. They create employment. This city's become great by people who have strong minds. Let's not talk chicken talk.

Mr. McLuhan: Every bureaucracy in the world is breaking down, including yours and the university's, through speed-up—the factor for breakdown is the efficiency of speed. Anything that speeds up an environment around another environment destroys the environment it surrounds.

Altogether, there were about 20 hours of this, at seven meetings of council and committees. For parts of it, at least, I regret there isn't a city hall Hansard.

I spent five hours in the British House of Commons a week ago Monday. It was all very dry, clear and rational, sometimes brilliant but ultimately predictable, abstract and boring. But for good nonfiction drama, for the element of surprise, for the wisdom and truth of the absurd, for sheer delight and a rare kind of uncommon sense, and for lending to "aery nothing a local habitation and a name," give me Toronto City Council every time.

St. Michael's College was good for a lot of our workers in the 1972 civic elections. And "every little satisfactory" street widening, as Lamport put it, proved a wonderfully useful way to get people organized.

The next case to hit the local news was a proposed throat-widening at the corner of Church and Wellesley. This would improve traffic flow, and probably attract more cars. It would also take away a precious bit of sidewalk in an area with no other public space, and practically pitch people out into the street as they emerged from the corner door of Novack's Drug Store. The local alderman, June Marks, intervened as I was giving a television interview outside the works committee room, and we had a little live impromptu drama. I was accused of interfering in "her" ward. (Civic feudalism must be defended.) Now Alderman Marks and a number of other city hall veterans were very good about responding to my requests for local favours in "my" ward; they were normally courteous and in the case of people like Alderman Bill Archer, who knew a lot more than I did, very patient about teaching me the techniques for getting things done at city hall. So I felt a bit of a heel for prolonging the battle with Alderman Marks, but her intervention did afford a golden opportunity to cast her as the neighbourhood villain and help us with our plans for getting a council majority in

*" . . . no . . . as a matter of fact, this is
a new locker design we're evaluating for
the city hall superintendent's
staff. . . ."*

the 1972 elections.

A resident of the Church-Wellesley area, Millie Green-span, phoned me up after the broadcast and asked what she could do. I knew Norman Depoe lived nearby so I suggested that we draft an open letter for him to sign, which we would circulate in the neighbourhood, using the Greenspan house for a base. The Greenspans lived next door to a couple named Allan and Sue Sparrow, who also got involved. The letter started off: "Do you want your throat widened?" Anyone who lived, worked or went to school in the area was invited to a meeting at Jarvis Collegiate. To our astonishment, several hundred people turned up. The North Jarvis Community Association was founded on the spot, and there were more than 30 volunteers for its executive. Alderman Marks was furious. She made the mistake of prefacing her remarks to the meeting with the words: "Most of you here are innocent, but . . ." and then accusing troublemakers of invading her ward. Norman Depoe as first president was later succeeded by Allan Sparrow, who was elected junior alderman there in 1974, after Dan Heap had defeated June Marks, the senior alderman, in 1972.

Next to giving people the works committee, city property afforded me my best material for *City Hall* magazine. Here are two examples:

GRANTS FOR TOMMY THE ELEPHANT & THE EASTER BUNNY

Last Thursday the City of Toronto officially received a request for funds from an elephant—with some assistance from McNabb Public Relations, the Garden Brothers Circus and the East Scarborough Kinsmen. The elephant's letter read in part: "Dolly, who has left Riverdale Zoo to hit the big time, warmly appreciated the honour and pleasure you have given in allowing her to pay her annual visit to city hall. She confesses, however, that fame has caught up with her, and she has had to ask Tommy to take her part this year. She respectfully requests therefore that the courtesies extended to her be awarded this year to Tommy and his friends.

"She points out that Tommy is handsome, that he is the only gentleman elephant in circus show business on this continent, and although large with glorious tusks, is as gentle as a fastidious lady elephant could wish."

The city property commissioner duly recommended that Tommy the Elephant and his friends be allowed to use the city's public address system and Nathan Phillips Square, to erect a platform there, and be given a grant to cover the standard fee of $60. The city property committee also approved six other requests for free use of the square. But the sponsors of one event, a rally and musical entertainment to protest the Vietnam War, would have to pay. Unlike the other applicants—which included the Air Cadet League of Canada, the Civic Employees War Veterans Association, the Daffodil Day and Beautify Toronto parades and the sponsors of Toronto Police Week—the peace rally was deemed to have a political purpose and should therefore not get the Square free.

Alderman Horace Brown argued that this group's claim was at least as valid as that of the others. But Executive Aldermen Rotenberg and O'Donohue said we have a clear policy that political groups should pay the fee, and if we didn't stick to it, O'Donohue added, there would be people "blaring forth their theories 24 hours a day." Brown replied that in one session alone last year council had allowed half a dozen obviously political groups to disturb the peace of the square without charge.

I asked why Rotenberg and O'Donohue began by picking on a group like the Vietnam Committee, which was apparently making only one request this year. If we disliked certain political views strongly enough, such as those of a Nazi group, we should come out and say so, and deny them any use of the square at all. All the groups using the square among the current batch of applicants were political in a basic sense, in that they were promoting some views or other of human community. Obviously they were distinguishable from a purely commercial group using the square to make money for itself (although I am not sure about Tommy's owners, the Garden Brothers Circus). But it was not really possible to divide the goats from the sheep, or elephants, by labelling one applicant "political" and the others "charitable" or "religious" or "civic."

Alderman Brown's motion to let the peace rally in free, along with Tommy the Elephant, the veterans, the air cadets, the beautifiers et al., was lost on a tie vote. So these groups will be guests of the taxpayer, and the peaceniks will have to pay.

Tommy wasn't the only animal to get a city grant last week. Council supported the East Toronto Community Association's Fifth Annual Easter Parade on the Beaches Boardwalk. "We plan a variety of activities," said their request, "ending with the Easter Bunny landing by helicopter." Council in its wisdom decided that the Easter Bunny was just fine and determined that "such organization be deemed as one engaged in work for the general advantage of the inhabitants of the city; that funds therefore be provided from the grants account; and that the appropriate civic officials be authorized to do whatever is necessary to give effect thereto."

BEAUTY CONTESTS, YES! WOMEN'S LIB, NO!

Last Thursday the city property committee again debated the question of which groups were "political" and therefore should be charged for the use of Nathan Phillips Square. Alderman Brown moved to delete the old $60 fee in all cases, and Alderman Beavis moved to levy a charge equal to the labor cost ($40 on weekdays and $75 at other times) in all cases. Both motions lost. Then Alderman Hope made a motion to "reaffirm the present policy," which, as we have discovered from hours of wrangling over the political content of peace demonstrations, police benefits, Daffodil Days, the Arabs, the air cadets, the Jaycees, the Ukrainian Liberationists, the Kinsmen's elephants, etcetera, etcetera, is no policy at all.

So it was open season on all of them when their requests got to city council. This took up about half of all the time we spent on the 100 or so items of business before us—some involving vast amounts of money or major changes in the character of the city. The long debate was interrupted by a scuffle between the guards and three women's libbers in ancient bathing costumes who managed to get on to the council floor bearing a sign that told aldermen their thinking was out of date and became the first protest group to be dragged from the chamber this term.

Mayor Dennison made a long speech defending our present policy—which was presumably beauty contests, yes!, women's lib, no!, but it was never entirely clear what he was talking about. He made such enigmatic remarks as "We've made the square as free as we dare" and "We should keep to something acceptable to the ordinary person coming on the square." He refused to be trapped by Jaffary into stating whether "as a very, very ordinary person" he would enjoy a beauty contest more than a women's lib festival. Our motion to charge the beauty contest the same fee as the women's liberation rally was defeated.

But sometimes Dennison did let himself be drawn into debate. Once a CCF member of the legislature, he had long since been coopted into city hall's old guard. His views were simple: demolition of the old, development of the new meant jobs and prosperity for Toronto. Any deviation from this article of faith was incomprehensible. But a few of his opponents were in a position to bargain with the powers at city hall and their developer-allies.

Holy Trinity Church, for example, where some of the urban reformers such as Crombie used to meet before the 1969 election, was right in the path of the proposed Eaton-Fairview Centre. But our congregation refused to be bought off and it also ruled out the suggestion that the church be moved to another site. The Holy Trinity development committee was even taken around seven downtown buildings by the president of Fairview Corporation and asked if it would accept one of these in a trade for the church. One of the buildings shown, to their astonishment, was Massey Hall. So in the end, Fairview was forced to build an L-shaped new Eaton's store around the church and to negotiate for whatever else it needed in building the Eaton Centre. Like a number of journalists at the time, the *Star* columnist Alexander Ross was as sympathetic to the church's cause as Mayor Dennison was hostile. "Yowling Babies, Jelly Sandwiches, Holy Trinity: The Eaton Centre Debate" is something he wrote near the end of the struggle:

It would have horrified Mayor Dennison if he could have seen it—offended his sense of order, freaked him out completely. For here were these 100-odd parishioners of the Church of the Holy Trinity—a group that, by an accident of history and church attendance, holds an effective veto over a $200-million downtown development scheme—debating this immensely important issue and, at the same time munching peanut butter and jelly sandwiches as little kids tumbled and rough-housed by the altar.

People who held the power of life and death for the Eaton's-Fairview project in their hands wandered in and out of the church's kitchen, helping themselves to chili and chicken soup. As Douglas Gibson, the downtown lawyer who is chairman of the church's development committee, gravely expounded a point, two children sprawled on a sofa at the west end of the nave got into a hairpulling match. Infants yowled and mothers retired discreetly behind the pulpit to nurse them.

"Now sit, or go outside," a mother scolded her noisy kid, "or I'm going to be *really* cross." By Trinity standards, that's pretty strict. Trinity parents usually like their kids to express themselves.

The mayor complained about Trinity's congregation in a luncheon speech only last week. These people, Dennison complained, were holding up Progress because they insisted on haggling about the amount of sunlight that would fall on Trinity Square after the redevelopment is completed. You got the feeling the mayor felt their position was almost impertinent. Who are these people, after all, to be inconveniencing two such fine, public-spirited corporations as Eaton's and Fairview?

Well, it's easy to understand Bill Dennison's consternation. The people of Holy Trinity are mostly not Bill Dennison's kind of people. They tend to be the sort of citizens who fly ecology flags on the front porches of their houses, and sign anti-Vietnam War petitions, and send their kids to free schools, and support the California lettuce-pickers, and put on blue jeans to shop at Kensington Market on Saturday mornings, and let their kids paint creative graffiti on their kitchen walls, and play guitars and use the word "community" a lot.

About 100 people usually turn up for worship on Sunday mornings—a lovely communion service at which people feed each other hunks of homemade bread as the consecrated host and, to a guitar accompaniment, sing hymns that sound as though they were written by Pete Seeger. Before the communion, people turn to each other, murmur, "Peace," and then wander about hugging and kissing each other and offering startled visitors a vigorous welcome for a good six or seven minutes, until the person in charge of the day's service can cajole them back their places and into the rhythm of the mass.

The beautiful old church no longer has pews arranged in neat rows facing the altar. People sit or stand in a circle now. Part of the nave yesterday held an Artario exhibit of plastic pop-art objects; people milled and wandered around the cavernous church like traders on the floor of the stock exchange. A while ago part of the nave was set aside for a few months as an emergency shelter for American deserters and draft dodgers seeking asylum in Toronto.

Yesterday's gathering resembled the meeting of a rebellious union local. The church's seven-member development committee, which has spent months haggling with Fairview, presented a proposal that embodies a tricky formula to guarantee that the city park to be built south of the church as part of the Fairview development will enjoy sunlight at least part of the time.

The solution the committee recommended to the vestry

meant less sunlight than the congregation demanded at its meeting last August. And, as the meeting wore on, the congregation separated into hawks and doves: those who wanted to play ball with Fairview and those who wanted to hold out for an even better offer. "We found Fairview to be sincere, honest and open," said Gibson. "They dealt with us as equals. If the developments go through, we're going to be neighbours for a long time. Situations will come up, as this development progresses, where we'll want to ask them for compromises. I don't believe in taking the fullest advantage I can in a business deal. Who wants to sell at the top? Is that what life's about? We've got to live together. . . ." So spoke Doug Gibson, a dove, who invited the congregation to treat Fairview in a spirit of Christian charity.

Dan Heap, vestry member, worker priest, spoke for the hawks: "Our obligation to the people who live and work in downtown Toronto far overrides our obligation to give Eaton's an 11 percent return on investment, instead of just 10 percent."

Architect Gerald Robinson, in white denim and clog sandals, pointed out that, under Gibson's compromise, there'd be no sunlight at all in the square during the lunch hours of Indian summer.

It went on for almost four hours. At the end of it, after the vestry voted narrowly to accept the development committee's proposal—thus clearing the way for the big project to go ahead—you could feel some bitterness in the air. Jim Fisk, Trinity's business-suited minister, herded hawks and doves into a circle, where they joined hands and embraced. "Come on in!" cried Fisk. "Let's feel our alienation for one another, as well as our closeness."

"Let us go forth in peace," intoned Fisk, and hawks and doves together, hands joined, swaying slightly, eyes closed, chanted their response: "In the name of the Lord."

Holy Trinity's resistance meant there would be a pleasant small-scale oasis in the midst of the glass and concrete giants, and, as it turned out, more sunlight than expected in the new city park there. One other bargain struck was that the church would be given two nineteenth-century houses—the old rectory and the Reverend Dr. Henry Scadding's residence—if it could raise the money to move them a few feet out of the path of Eaton's new store. Twelve years later, in 1983, after further negotiations, a three-way land exchange between the city, Holy Trinity and the developer enlarged the public park to the south of the church and required that the developer build several hundred units of socially valuable housing nearby.

The church's determination to stay put turned out to be a considerable public service. But perhaps the most crucial change in the proposed Eaton development came from the decision of the developers themselves. The original concept of the Eaton-Fairview Centre would have put a Berlin Wall between city hall on one side and Yonge Street on the other. It was simply a suburban shopping plaza dumped down into the heart of the city. However, one of the ultimate owners of Fairview, Phyllis Bronfman Lambert, who had already persuaded her family to have Mies van der Rohe as architect for the Seagram building in New York, now saw to it that one of Canada's best architects, Eberhard Zeidler, was engaged to design the cathedral-like galleria connecting Eaton's and Simpsons department stores. And so Toronto's mercantile heartland was given an attractive focus, with the excitement and elegance that it sorely needed.

As election year arrived, our side could celebrate a few small victories, such as extra sunlight for Trinity Square, and even the odd big one, such as the cancellation of the Spadina expressway. But the great developments that were destroying Toronto kept coming on inexorably—Quebec-Gothic, Windlass, Lionstar and the rest, their names sounding in our ears a bit like those of the battles of some old imperial war.

One executive alderman asked me with puzzled pity why we were trying to hold back the inevitable. The centre of Toronto simply could not be a place for old houses and old buildings; there would be none of them left standing in the Parliament-Bloor-Spadina-Waterfront core in 10 years time; the laws of economics made it all inevitable. And to many people it seemed he was right, though not necessarily because of the laws of economics. Here is one of Marshall McLuhan's probes on the subject published at that time, which he called "Hijacking a City":

The ready possibility of extending the hijacking procedure to cities appears in the following news items in *The Toronto Star*: "The head of the company that owns Toronto's Yorkdale shopping centre yesterday revealed a secret used by commercial developers to get their projects approved by local governments. The secret: Start with a 'totally unreasonable' plan that is oblivious of the people involved, against motherhood and so forth. After that, the politicians can score their points and whittle it down—and it goes through."

". . . they're gaining on us"
Mayor Crombie and Executive
Aldermen Scott, Smith, Eggleton and
Kilbourn fight off
the developers in 1975.

The most spectacular and successful, but unseen, hijack has been the takeover of the North American city by the commercial developers. Like the hijacker in the airplane, the only concern of the developer is a private destination, without any assumption of the responsibility for the flying, or governing, of the airplane or city.

Similarly, the passengers, or residents, are not consulted on where or why they are going. They are expected to fly along, whether they want to go or not. They are asked to watch the in-flight movie, take a few cocktails and enjoy the trip. The crew, or governors, are under strict instructions to obey the hijacker without resistance, and certainly without causing trouble.

The only limitations are on range and speed due to fuel capacity, or the tolerance of the electorate, which requires an occasional stop for refueling—the election of a new government—but then the aircraft takes off and continues to its selected destination. Neither passenger nor city resident has the choice of alighting—neither could survive the 30,000-foot drop to the hard reality of the earth.

It would take the hijacking of 5,000 Boeing 747s to equal the simple hijack of a single small city, destination unknown. Both hijackers impose their preferences on service environments designed for others—and hijack can be applied to any environment: the air, a business, a culture or the nation itself.

Hijacking a business is easier in proportion to the size of the business, as witness the Pennsylvania Central, where $7 billion of assets were hijacked by the bookkeepers to non-transportation uses. The bigger the operation, the less the shareholders know about the flight plan. Hijackers don't presume to have expertise. They allow the plane, or the business, or the country that they take over to be operated by those normally in charge. The hijacker does not interfere with the operation, but with the flight plan. He decides where to land.

McLuhan's metaphor may appear questionable now, but at the time it seemed all too real. Our side could really not do anything more at this stage but publish the facts as we understood them, and make plans to win a majority on city council in the 1972 election. So we went on writing up the comic side of city hall and playing urban guerrilla—if only to keep up our spirits. But such tactics did seem to be contagious. Ward newspapers and a citizens' forum were founded, and many new ratepayers' groups sprang up. There were always people out standing in front of trees threatened by road widenings; there were sit-ins to save houses scheduled for demolition and campaigns to turn surplus firehalls into day-care centres instead of parking lots; a movement to stop the TTC's plans for phasing out all its streetcars; and a book, *The Open Gate*, to plead for Union Station, which the railways planned to destroy to make room for the proposed Metro Centre. My particular job was to rouse the new professional classes and the old Torontonians who lived north of Bloor Street, and remind them that our side's radical commitment to conservation in the face of progress was at the heart of Toronto's heritage.

To prepare for the 1972 elections a group of about a dozen of us met regularly in the offices of the Toronto Labour Council. We had in mind a very loose coalition to defeat the old guard majority, a ward-by-ward strategy to gain control of city council. We called ourselves CO 72. It was crucial that no more than two of our community candidates run for the two aldermanic seats in each ward, but also that there be at least one candidate, wherever one or both incumbents had a prodeveloper voting record. We would start with a base of our own incumbents on city council: Jaffary and Chisholm of the NDP, Sewell and myself. Crombie and the other two CIVAC aldermen sympathetic to many of our goals, Eggleton and Hope, were not with us but not against us either. We would not try for the mayoralty because Toronto has a weak-mayor system—that is, in council the mayor counts for only one out of 23 votes. To succeed Dennison for mayor, however, two of the executive aldermen, Rotenberg and O'Donohue, were running against each other. Crombie believed, as our group did not, that there was a good chance for a candidate from our side in a three-way race for the mayoralty. At the time some of us were angered by Crombie's unilateral decision to run, since it risked losing us one sure vote and his strong personal presence on council. We also feared that it would divert workers and election funds away from the necessary ward campaigns into his own city-wide one. As it turned out, we were wrong and Crombie was right. While our ward campaigns were more or less linked to his throughout, and this did cost us some workers and funds, the focus and public interest generated by his compelling attack on Rotenberg and O'Donohue did our common cause far more good than harm.

Retiring Mayor Dennison gave us a nice boost too when he compared CO 72 to rabbits in a swamp. "You see thousands of tracks and you think the place is infested with rabbits," he said "but actually there are only two or three of them running around all over the place making tracks." We published a yellow button with the picture of a speeding rabbit on it. The enormous demand for them made rabbit buttons a useful campaign device. The front-runner for mayor, Tony O'Donohue, whom almost everyone expected to win, also gave us a boost by opening his campaign in a park. The demonstrators on hand to mourn the old guard's pitiful parks acquisition policies took most of the television and press coverage away from O'Donohue's announcement. He looked surprised and somewhat confused by what was happening.

Election day produced a welcome victory. Our leading candidates won record majorities. My own vote total was over 20,000, a figure not surpassed in any of the 11 wards before or since. Crombie's underdog campaign for mayor had caught fire in the last three weeks and he came steaming in ahead of O'Donohue, with Rotenberg running a poor third. These two former executive aldermen, along with the five old guard councillors who either retired or were defeated, were thus no longer members of council. The aldermanic candidates from CO 72, including CORRA executives Elizabeth Eayrs and Colin Vaughan, won 10 of the 22 aldermanic seats on council. The antediluvian old guard was reduced to two: Fred Beavis, the friend of the lunch-pail voter, and Joe Piccinini, gloriously orotund in girth and speech. They had four new allies on council, and all six usually voted with two veteran independents, Paul Pickett and William Archer, whose presence partly compensated for the intellectual leadership the old guard had lost with Rotenberg's demise. Between these eight on the right and the 10 of us on the left, the balance of power was held by a group of five moderate reformers in the centre: Mayor Crombie himself; his CIVAC colleagues Eggleton and Hope; Reid Scott, the former New Democratic MP; and another newcomer, David Smith, who later became a federal Liberal cabinet minister. The 23-member council was thus free to pursue whatever goals the moderates and the 10 CO 72 aldermen were committed to, or, if the mayor and his moderate reform allies could persuade the eight-man opposition to vote with them, to go in another direction. The line between the CO 72 reformers and the moderates in the centre usually shifted according to the issues and the occasion, and was never entirely clear. Nevertheless, this three-way balance on council was to be maintained, with a few retirements and defeats and some new recruits in all three groups for the next decade. In 1984 it looked as if it would prevail well into the future.

Three successive mayors—Crombie, John Sewell and Arthur Eggleton—differed from one another greatly in personal character and their style of government. But the substance of what they could and did accomplish was related to the fact that neither the radical reformers nor the old guard remnant ever quite achieved a majority. The balance was always held by a group in the middle who were generally sympathetic to the goals of the reform movement of the late 1960s.

What were these goals, besides a determination to wrest power from the old guard? And were they achieved? The reformers' central objective was to slow down and redirect Toronto's massive redevelopment. Unchecked growth in the body politic was seen not as "progress" or civic well-being, but rather as a form of cancer. The first step was temporary but drastic. In 1973 a bylaw was passed to prevent the construction of any building more than 45 feet high or with an area greater than 40,000 square feet. This check to unbridled demolition and development gave Mayor Crombie's administration a chance to work out a revised plan for the city, one that has been expanded and refined in the period since.

The height and area limits were of course later removed; the density allowed to a developer in most parts of the city became as generous as before, but the restrictions were now related more subtly to the zone for which a building was proposed. And developers could acquire bonuses in the form of increased density if they preserved historic structures or built housing. Within the urban core, density could also be transferred from one site to another, as could the open space required by the city. In addition, the city became a demolition control area, thus preventing the demolition of a residential building until there has been an opportunity for interested parties to negotiate its preservation.

The result has been that developers have begun to find new uses for many of Toronto's best remaining buildings: from the old factories and firehalls to a huge art deco warehouse on the waterfront, they are being turned into apartments, offices, theatres, nurseries, shops and restaurants. The once shabby gentility of our Victorian and Edwardian and Georgian heritage has been polished up for the twenty-first century. New structures sprout amid the scrubbed pink and cream brick of the old. Such refurbishing is not always in the best taste, often downright vulgar—a sure sign of vitality, no matter how grating to the nerves of architectural historians and aesthetes.

What could not be expected during the mid-1970s recession was that private enterprise would move to increase the stock of moderately priced rental housing that Toronto so desperately needed. So Cityhome, a public housing company, was created to buy up old buildings and construct new. One of its first undertakings, of great significance for the next phase of Toronto's development, involved two dozen rundown old mansions on the chestnut-lined west side of Sherbourne Street. The developer-owner, with a permit obtained earlier, had actually begun demolition one morning in 1973 when about 100 people appeared on the scene. While a sympathetic policeman looked the other way, we ripped down the hoardings and so prevented work from proceeding. This illegal action gave Mayor Crombie time to bargain for funds from the housing authorities of the provincial and federal governments. Eventually architects Jack Diamond and Barton Myers produced a plan for the city that would retain the old houses and behind them build small apartments with courtyards. The whole development is at present home for more than 900 residents, a greater number than the two towers surrounded by grass that had originally been planned for the site. And in contrast to earlier public housing, the Sherbourne development contains people from a variety of income levels: no one but the housing manager knows which tenants receive rental assistance and which do not. One of the oldest restored houses in the group was once the residence of Enoch Turner, Toronto's pioneer educator. It is almost the twin of the home of Chief Justice Campbell, which was hauled across the city at enormous expense by the Law Society of Upper Canada; but the interior appointments of the Turner house, unlike those of the Campbell house, remain basically intact.

In the process of creating the Sherbourne complex, city planners and architects and housing company officials learned how to bend or change rules and practices that had been accepted as gospel. That experience enabled them to innovate in other parts of the city. Instead of blasting sites to rubble and then building isolated circles of single-class ranch-style clones uncontaminated by community or commerce, they have mixed all types of people and buildings and functions into small city blocks. To do so, the planners actually moved their offices from city hall into the neighbourhoods they were supposed to be serving. And, incredibly, some private developers began imitating their approach. When the prestigious luxury of Hazelton Lanes was unveiled, the new apartments were nestled in behind the rows of little old Yorkville houses; shops and restaurants and courtyards were crammed underneath living quarters.

Even on such bleak sites as the former industrial lands south of Front Street, variety and a human scale have prevailed. The heart of Toronto is a little less like a bomb site or a parking lot now. Amid the clearings and the giant buildings, there is new growth. The torn fabric of the city is being stitched together by bits of invisible mending. The microsurgery of our urban ecologists is freeing the body politic to heal itself.

Other consequences of Toronto's new politics are also still with us. The unique Island community is still there, and, in spite of the regional government's resolve to wipe it out, still squatting on Metro parkland. Expressways once destined to plunge into the heart of the city have been stopped. The electric streetcar, a Toronto invention, far from being phased out, has been revived in the form of a brand-new model. The warm glow of incandescent street lighting has prevailed against the experts' attempt to bathe Toronto in the sodium-vapour orange glow that illuminates most other big cities. The arts in Toronto are generously supported out of the property tax. And the vast new Pickering International Airport, with its prospect of horrendous cost and land use disaster for the whole Toronto region, the stopping of which was my particular preoccupation as a member of city executive, remains but a mad gleam in the eyes of those Department of Transport planners who are still resolved to add this crowning glory to their lesser monument at Mirabel.

Those who say that the civic reform movement of the early '70s is dead often cite the lethargy of ratepayers' groups and the disappearance of such noisy community organizers as CO 72. But they draw the wrong conclusion. Such groups, like Toronto itself, have always been profoundly conservative and conservationist in character. When urban traditions are not threatened, protest groups and urban guerrillas are unnecessary. No one in his right mind wants to spend all his time outsmarting demolition crews and defying bulldozers.

On the negative side of the balance, Toronto's state of well-being is still precarious. The next mushroom growth of office space downtown could require enough new commuter roads and transit lines to destroy the residential inner city; the low-density sprawl of the suburbs is horribly expensive to service; pollution still befouls our beaches and rivers; Toronto's latent racism has been repressed but not exterminated; most newcomers must still work at dead-end, menial jobs and occupy the lower depths of the vertical mosaic; the gospel of heritage and preservation has not been accepted by many business and labour executives—they prefer to demolish and rebuild rather than adapt and restore.

But at least such difficulties can be faced with the same mind and spirit that confronted the problems of the '70s. As the twenty-first century dawns, if the world's cities are standing at all, there is every reason to believe that Toronto will still be the city that works, the city of hope, true to the meaning of its name in the Indian tongue, the name that means "abundance," an abundance for all its people to share.

A LAST WORD

To understand history, one must stand outside history, not just to avoid bias, but to be able to perceive distinctness and relations. Any simple stand to the Left or the Right is still a movement on the same political plane. But above the American Left and Right is Canada, a place free of the American Dream and the European Nightmare. No longer a colony, not yet an independent national power, Canada, like Switzerland, is *The Peaceable Kingdom* to which those weary of conflict go to escape the burden of a national identity. As the Canadian historian John Conway has remarked: "America is Faustian and Dionysian; Canada is not." In the opposition between Apollonian Canada and Dionysian America, one can see that once again the unique excellence of both countries is also their tragic flaw.

Los Angeles is one very obvious example of an edge, but Toronto is also a city at the edge of American history. With its draft dodgers, deserters and émigré academics, it is almost Tolkien's Rivendell, safe from the ragings of the archaic darkness of Sauron and the Ring wraiths. Whether one can live permanently in Rivendell is a question I ask myself daily, but at the moment Toronto seems the perfect retreat in which to look from one end of history to the other.

WILLIAM IRWIN THOMPSON, At the Edge of History *(1971)*

William and Elizabeth Kilbourn at home in Rosedale, 1966, with (from left to right) Michael, Pippa, Nicholas, Hilary and Timothy. Photo by Gerald Campbell.

ACKNOWLEDGEMENTS

For permission to reprint copyright material, the author and the publisher offer grateful thanks to the following publishers, authors and agents: University of Toronto Press for "Shadows on the Street: Toronto During the French Régime" from *Toronto During the French Régime, 1615–1793*, by Percy B. Robinson, by permission of the University of Toronto Press. © University of Toronto Press 1965. Dennis Lee for "WLM/1838" in *Nicholas Knock and Other People*, Macmillan, 1975; "When I Went Up to Rosedale," permission of the author. Jack Ludwig for "Sunday Morning Silence." Copyright by Jack Ludwig, revised 1975. Ron Haggart for "Situation Comedy in City Hall" from *Maclean's*, Vol. 81, November 1968, revised 1975. Norman Hartley for "Toronto Italian: A New Language" from *The Globe and Mail*, December 31, 1971. Raymond Souster for "Separate Inscriptions for the Graves of Lount and Matthews, Necropolis Cemetery, Toronto," from *Change-Up*, Oberon Press, 1974; "The South African War Memorial, University Avenue" from *Double-Header*, Oberon Press, 1975; "The Immigrant" from *The Years*, Oberon Press, 1972; "Flood-Time, Humber River" from *Rain-Check*, Oberon Press, 1975. Reprinted by permission of Oberon Press. Pierre Berton for "'A Feeling, An Echo...' The Life of Union Station" from *The Open Gate: Toronto Union Station*, Peter Martin Associates, 1972. University of Toronto Press for "New City Hall" reprinted from *Toronto, No Mean City*, by Eric Arthur, by permission of University of Toronto Press. © University of Toronto Press, 1974. William Kurelek for "The CN Tower" from Letters to the Editor in *The Globe and Mail*, March 27, 1975. Desmond Morton for "The Righteous Reformers" from *Mayor Howland, the Citizens' Candidate*, Hakkert, 1973. James Lorimer for "The Incredible World of City Politicians" from *The Real World of City Politics*, James Lewis and Samuel Publishers, 1970. Alexander Ross for "Yowling Babies, Jelly Sandwiches, Holy Trinity: The Eaton Centre Debate." Reprinted with permission from *The Toronto Star*, October 16, 1972. Marshall McLuhan for "Hijacking a City," from Letters to the Editor of *The Toronto Star*, April, 1971. Waclaw Iwaniuk for four poems from *Dark Times* and *Evenings on Lake*

Ontario, Hounslow Press, 1981. Pier Giorgio di Cicco for "Sherbourne Morning" and "Nostalgia." George Jonas and House of Anansi for "Landmarks." George Faludy and Robin Skelton (translator) for "Sonnet 89." Michael Bliss for " 'Better and Purer': The Peterborough Methodist Mafia and the Renaissance of Toronto." Gwendolyn MacEwen for "The Elmwood." Harry Rasky for "St. Clair West" from *Nobody Swings on Sundays*. Henry Beissel and the estate of Walter Bauer for "Emigrant." Philip Marchand and *Toronto Life* for "Chinese Toronto." Marq de Villiers and *Toronto Life* for "Farewell to Little Italy." Robert Zend and John Robert Colombo (translator) for "Toronto-Budapest: Fused Personality" from *Beyond Labels*, Hounslow Press. Bharati Mukherjee for "An Invisible Woman" from *Saturday Night*. Maggie Siggins and *Toronto Life* for "To this Cold Place." Josef Škvorecký for "A City after My Own Heart."

I should particularly like to thank McClelland and Stewart for permission to use four of my essays from *Toronto in Pictures and Words* (Photographer: Rudi Christl), Sesquicentennial Edition, 1983; John Robert Colombo for drawing to my attention the work of several of the poets whose work appears here, and for sharing with me his treasure trove of quotations about Toronto; Carl Morey for showing me the Victorian songs which he and his colleagues have been reviving; Maurice Careless and James Lemon for allowing me to read in manuscript their respective volumes on the history of Toronto (to be published by James Lorimer), which no student of the subject will wish to be without; Richard Howard and David Frum for their assistance with the essay on Upper Canada College; Jane Jacobs and John Sewell for reading and making useful suggestions about the essay on city politics; Mr. and Mrs. William Tennison for sharing their magnificent collection of the art of Nicholas Hornyansky and Mrs. Winnifred Hornyansky for permission to reproduce four of these works; Edith Firth and Mary Allodi for their helpful advice on several crucial points; Barrie Hale for selecting and gathering a number of the pictures; and Brenna and Jeremy Brown, Newcastle Publishing, Don Obe and Lynn Cunningham, editors, and Imants Abolins, designer, for their long and invaluable labours in the shaping of this book.

I wish also to thank the many other friends and colleagues who have assisted me with the book at different stages of its making, and to record my profound debt to my parents, Kenneth and Mary, and my wife Elizabeth and my daughter Hilary for their criticism and support.

INDEX

ILLUSTRATION AND PHOTO CREDITS